Other titles by
Eleanor Heartney:

Critical Condition:
American Culture at the Crossroads

Movements in Modern Art: Postmodernism

Postmodern Heretics:
The Catholic Imagination in Contemporary Art

Defending Complexity:
Art, Politics and the New World Order

Art and Today

Kenneth Snelson: Forces Made Visible

Roxy Paine

Renee Radell: Webs of Circumstance

Co-authored books:

After the Revolution:
Women who Transformed Contemporary Art

The Reckoning:
Women Artists in the New Millennium

Eleanor Heartney's *Doomsday Dreams* is a fascinating and thorough examination of the millennia old theme of the Apocalypse, the last days, as it is seen now in contemporary art. A highly original study of the history of such terrifying images throughout history, her focus is how and why the Apocalypse signifying the end of the world is a widespread theme today. Heartney's deep research studies the many versions of the earth's last days as it was pictured and imagined throughout global history. It is a fascinating story revealing the origins and historical background of the Apocalypse from ancient times until the present in many different cultures and religions throughout the world.

– Barbara Rose, art historian,
filmmaker and curator

Once again Eleanor Heartney has fruitfully brought cultural history to bear on the explication of key works of contemporary art. She illuminates the transition of the religious trope of the Apocalypse to a resilient presence in modern secular culture as well, often involving the goal of a violent, cleansing ending that will be followed by an absolutely new era. Her insightful perception of the apocalyptic art focuses the entire genre in a new way.
This is a timely book.

– Charlene Spretnak, author of
The Spiritual Dynamic in Modern Art

Cover: David Wojnarowicz, *Untitled (Burning Boy Installation)*, 1985
Courtesy of the Estate of David Wojnarowicz and PPOW, New York

Heartney explores how many contemporary artists are engaging our fascination with and addiction to things Apocalyptic as a form of protest, as a means of revealing its dark and dangerous side, its potential to disempower and numb. And while she succeeds in demonstrating the important role that theology and religion have (and always have had) in contemporary artistic practice, she also makes a powerful argument for the capacity of art to offer something truly radical and subversive, something that is in very short supply in this cynical world in which we live: hope and belief. Hope that things can be otherwise, that there is a future worth hoping for. And belief, belief in this world, right now, belief that we can change and realize our hope.

– Daniel A. Siedell, Ph.D., Senior Fellow,
The King's College, New York City

"It's the end of the world and I feel fine" REM sang in 1987. Now it's 2019, and it's pretty hard to feel sanguine about where things are headed, whether politically, environmentally, or religiously. Heartney adroitly reads the tea leaves of modern and contemporary art as she identifies varying approaches to the end times, from salivating anticipation to incredulity. Engagingly written, and interlaced with references to popular culture and current events, Heartney proves equally at home deciphering assemblages by visionary outsiders as installations by stars of the contemporary art world."

– Dr. Aaron Rosen, Director of the
Henry Luce III Center for the Arts & Religion,
Wesley Theological Seminary, Washington, DC

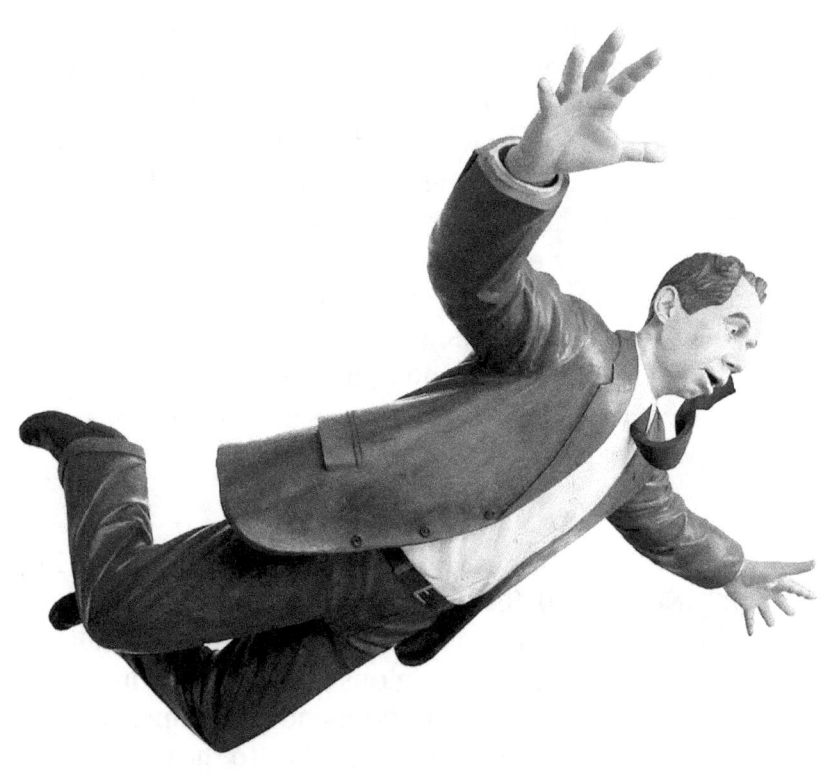

Bob Trotman, *Vertigo*, 2010, wood, tempera,
collection of North Carolina Museum of Art

DOOMSDAY DREAMS

The Apocalyptic Imagination in Contemporary Art

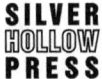

SILVER
HOLLOW
PRESS

DEDICATION

To all those who hold onto hope
in a darkening world.

CONTENTS

FOREWORD

The Apocalypse is coming: we don't know where and we don't know when but it is all around us. Apocalypse permeates our movies, our art, our politics, our science, our social arrangements and our sense of self. How do we know this? We know it because the Apocalypse is hardwired into our heads. It is always just around the corner inflaming our imaginations with the seductive dread of total annihilation.

Doomsday Dreams is an exploration of the ways that contemporary art has helped us understand the obsessive hold of the Apocalypse on nearly every aspect of life today. Artists have approached this subject from many perspectives – as true believers, confirmed skeptics, spiritual wanderers, dispassionate observers and social justice warriors. In doing so, they illuminate the psychological, sociological and philosophical conditions that lure us so powerfully toward a vision of the End.

Doomsday Dreams is the product of my longtime interest in the intermingling of art, religion and politics. As an art critic, I have been following this complicated story for over thirty years. It has taken me through the Culture Wars of the nineties, the late 20th century rise of "post-secular" culture, the post-911 preoccupation with the Clash of Civilizations and the paradoxical emergence of Donald Trump, the irreligious champion of the religious right.

Doomsday Dreams is an outgrowth of my previous book, *Postmodern Heretics: The Catholic Imagination in Contemporary Art*. Published in 2004 and recently updated for the Trump era, *Postmodern Heretics* explores the Catholic roots of controversial artists and the impact of Catholicism on the 1990s Culture Wars. The book grew out of my own immersion in Catholicism as a child and my recognition of its impact on my adult consciousness. As I explored the religious roots of numerous contemporary artists, I found myself moving beyond my initial focus on Catholicism. Instead, my work on *Postmodern Heretics* sparked a larger exploration of religion's profound influence on our individual and collective thinking.

This exploration led me to the Apocalypse. That idea, rooted in religion, is deeply embedded in almost every aspect of Western culture. Our progress narrative, our sense of time, our divisive politics, our cultural myths and our yearning for individual and social perfection are all deeply indebted to a vision of history that originated with the Zoroastrian *Avesta* in Persia three millennia ago. The Catholic Imagination I examined in *Postmodern Heretics* gives rise to an aesthetic of sensuality and sexuality that artists have exploited to create works celebrating the inseparability of body and soul. The Apocalyptic Imagination I investigate in *Doomsday Dreams* is at once more pervasive and more insidious. In fact, political philosopher John Gray suggests it actually forms the bedrock upon which western civilization has been built.[1]

Apocalypse presents a vision of history in which our ultimate salvation will arrive in the wake of enormous upheavals, massive conflict and a cleansing destruction of the world as we know it. Apocalypse has been used to justify genocide, nuclear holocaust, ethnic cleansing and total war. These horrors are twisted into necessary preludes for the purified and harmonious new social order that will arrive after the end of time. To reprise Dr. Martin Luther King Jr.'s famous quote, the arc of Apocalypse may bend toward justice, but it comes only at huge cost to the great majority of mankind.

Once I chose it as a subject, I began to see Apocalypse everywhere. It appears in our spiraling environmental crises, our unending Middle East wars, the escalating violence at home and abroad and the threats to human consciousness and freedom posed by our embrace of Artificial Intelligence. In this darkening moment, there is a sense, reflected in both our political debates and our popular culture, that time is running out. We appear to be slipping over the tipping point into a frightening and inescapable future.

Exacerbating this situation is the ascendance of Donald Trump. Having ridden to power on a wave of apocalyptic foreboding, he encourages his followers to pursue the vision of a world full of evil and rife with enemies. His America is a place that, absent his anti-democratic maneuvers, teeters on the brink of collapse. Nor is he alone. Trump is simply the most self-promoting of a new breed of authoritarian leaders who have come to power throughout this young but benighted century. Why are we so susceptible to apocalyptic thinking? And where is it taking us? These are the questions that run through *Doomsday Dreams*. The artists who explore these issues come from a range of religious backgrounds and exhibit varying degrees of religious faith. What unites them is their ability to expose some of the key consequences of apocalyptic thinking. I have written about most of these artists here in other contexts. *Doomsday Dreams* offers me the opportunity to bring them together so that their ideas can bounce off each other to create a portrait of our collective psyche.

Doomsday Dreams is organized by themes that reflect some of the most powerful tropes found in the apocalyptic narrative. While I reference a variety of apocalyptic texts, including the Zoroastrian *Avesta* in which the idea of apocalypse was first formulated; Daniel, Ezekiel and Isaiah, the prophetic books of the Hebrew Bible; and the apocalyptic strains in the Qur'an, the most fully developed and most historically influential apocalyptic text remains the New Testament's *Book of Revelation*. As we shall see, *Revelation* continually comes into play in the art presented here and serves as a vital interpretive tool for understanding our ongoing preoccupation with Endtimes.

Doomsday Dreams opens with a survey of the historical versions of the idea of the apocalypse as each era reformulates an apocalypse to explain its own anxieties. Chapter 2 presents artists who explore America's special relationship to apocalyptic thinking as embedded in the *Book of Revelation*. Chapters

3 and 4 examine one of the central themes of all apocalyptic narratives, namely the Grand Battle between Good and Evil. In Chapter 3, artists suggest some of the ways that our supposedly objective conceptions of history and political realities are conditioned by this ancient myth. Chapter 4 offers the obverse of this idea, as artists use the myth and metaphor of the Grand Battle to construct imaginary worlds that expose the hidden forces shaping our reality. Chapter 5 takes on the figure of the Antichrist. He is considered here as the specter of false faith whose manifestations include institutional religions that betray their spiritual premises and secular ideologies that assume the trappings of religious faith. Chapter 6 brings us the enduring trope of the Four Horsemen of the Apocalypse. Originally envisioned as the harbingers of war, famine, pestilence and death, they here reappear as the outcome of our ecological disasters and nuclear power plays. Chapter 7 is a reminder that the apocalyptic destruction of the world will be followed by a new order of peace and harmony for the just and virtuous. Artists take on the twin ideas of paradise and utopia, casting an often equivocal eye on the promises of a more perfect world. *Doomsday Dreams* concludes with a brief coda which points to some possible alternatives to Endtimes thinking.

Running as an undercurrent through this book is a sense that it may not be enough simply to understand the influence of the apocalyptic imagination. We need to know, as well, how to break its fatal attraction. We find the instruments for this in the imaginations of contemporary artists.

—Eleanor Heartney,
November 2018

Chapter 1

A SHORT HISTORY OF THE END

Apocalypse, Armageddon, Doomsday, Judgment Day, Endtimes: these words, with varying religious connotations, all point to the End of the World. They originate in the philosophy of eschatology – the study of Last Things – that is as old as the Zoroastrian religion and as contemporary as the Islamic State. The notion that we are inevitably rushing towards a glorious - or horrifying - final moment has long shaped human history and continues to encourage a search for signs that will indicate that the Day of Reckoning is nigh.

Today Apocalypse is the favored term for this anticipated denouement. In political, popular and literary discourse, it serves as shorthand for every kind of natural, political social, economic and personal disaster. But its original meaning is less pessimistic. The word Apocalypse comes from the Greek term for *revelation* or *lifting of the veil*. As laid out in the New Testament's *Book of Revelation*, Apocalypse is an answer to the question of evil. It explains how a world created by a God who is all-good and all-powerful could be so rife with iniquity, pain and suffering. The Apocalyptic narrative makes sense of the apparent chaos of history, seeing it all as the necessary unfolding of a divine plan whose end is prefigured in its beginning. The Evil that entered the world from Satan's rebellion against God and instigated man's fall from grace in the Garden of Eden is finally vanquished in the Endtimes, leading to a restoration of moral order and the elevation of the Just for the rest of eternity.

In a world of woe, the Apocalypse provides both solace and warning. Historically, it has been taken up both by those who wish to preserve the status quo and those who long for the overthrow of the current hierarchy. For those seeking change, an imminent end of the world is much to be desired because out of the ashes will rise a new and perfected world order wiped clean of unbelievers. Speaking to the hunger of the oppressed minority for justice and change, the Apocalypse can be marshaled toward a progressive social and political message. From its earliest days, the belief that the Messiah will return in glory and establish a reign of peace and justice has sustained the powerless and offered hope that their grievances will ultimately be addressed. Read in tandem with the social gospel of Christianity, the *Book of Revelation* and other apocalyptic texts have often provided reinforcement for revolutionary social and political goals.

But Apocalypse has also been a tool of the powerful against believers who might want to stray from the fold. In this role it delineates the Chosen from the Damned, encouraging stark divisions between insiders and outsiders and demonizing those who belong to "deviant" groups. Both of these conceptions of the Apocalypse belong to what Norman Cohn labeled "revolutionary millenarianism"[1]. Cohn links this tradition, not only to various specifically Christian sects of the last two thousand years, but also to modern, apparently irreligious phenomena like Nazism, Fascism and Marxism. Despite their differences, all of these movements shared a collective mentality inspired by the possibility of cataclysmic transformations that would give birth to a new world order.

The meaning of the eschatological narrative also depends on whether it is seen as a beginning or an ending. Ideologies as otherwise apparently different as National Socialism, Radical Islam, Evangelical Christianity and American Puritanism feed hopes for a fresh start in a world cleansed of evil and injustice. But the inevitability of doom also opens the door to unredeemable pessimism, especially for those without faith in the post apocalyptic future. Today, when we use the word Apocalypse, it is generally in this darker, more nihilistic sense, in which the End is bereft of any promise that something better will follow the destruction of the world as we know it.

These contradictions were present in even the earliest eschatological narratives, and have only become more pronounced as the notion of Endtimes has worked itself through human history over the last three millennia. Thus to trace the history of the Apocalypse is to follow a set of shifting meanings as it provides inspiration for hope or pessimism, submission or rebellion, new beginnings or horrifying endings. Every age finds its own Apocalypse as the eschatological narrative is recast to address contemporary conditions.

One can trace the contemporary obsession with Endtimes back to the beliefs of the Zoroastrians of ancient Persia who anticipated a final battle between the forces of order and chaos, ending with the defeat of Evil and the restoration of purified sinners to a state of perfect harmony and happiness. Zoroastrian eschatology became the basis for the better-known apocalyptic traditions of the Abrahamic religions of Judaism, Christianity and Islam. Though Zoroastrianism today claims only a tiny number of adherents, its fingerprints are all over Western thought. Notions of the coming end of the world, belief in a personified evil power and the resurrection of the dead following a final Judgment Day originated in the *Avesta*, the sacred scripture of Zoroastrianism. They can also be found in texts as varied as the Hebrew Books of *Daniel, Ezekiel* and *Isaiah*, the story in *Genesis* of Noah's flood, and the *Qur'an*. In the West, the most influential apocalyptic text has been the *Book of Revelation*. One can trace its continuing hold on the Western imagination through nearly every political and social upheaval of the last 2000 years.

The *Book of Revelation*, which was the last text to be accepted into the Biblical canon, has sometimes been attributed to John the Apostle. However now most scholars agree that it was originally written around 90 CE by another John, a Jewish follower of Christ who was exiled to the small Turkish island of Patmos following the brutal suppression of the Jewish uprising against Rome (66-70 CE). After storming Jerusalem, Roman soldiers burned the temple to the ground, an event prophesized by Jesus in the Gospel of Mark and seen by believers as the prelude to the final coming of Christ. The *Book of Revelation* provides a graphic blueprint for the cosmic upheavals that will accompany that event.

In her sweeping study of the *Book of Revelation*, Early Christian scholar Elaine Pagels outlines the text's debt to Old Testament stories of Noah's Flood, the prophecies of Ezekiel and Isaiah, and *Book of Daniel*. She then traces the book's changing reception during its first three centuries when it went from being a heretical text to the final book of the canonical Christian Bible.[2] While current interpretations tend to frame *Revelation* as a broadside against the Roman enemies of the early Christian Church, Pagels maintains that *Revelation* was also directed against devotees of Christ who failed to follow Jewish law. John of Patmos, she argues, did not see himself as a Christian, but rather as a Jew who had found the Messiah. In *Revelation*, John uses images drawn from apocalyptic prophesies in the Hebrew Scriptures by figures like Isaiah, Jeremiah, Ezekiel and Daniel as coded references to the Roman oppressors of the Jewish minority. Pagels argues that his disapprobation extended as well to "those who say they are Jews and are not,"[3] (in other words, the Gentiles converted to Christ by Paul and other missionaries.)

John's narrower vision of the new religion did not prevail, and by the year 160, presumably long after his death, his visionary book became an inspirational text for a group that now identified itself as 'Christian'. Facing persecution and martyrdom by Roman authorities, they embraced the text that appeared to predict both the tribulations of the faithful and Christ's ultimate victory over their oppressors. It was at this time that Christian leaders like Irenaeus, Bishop of Lugdunum in Gaul, began to use *Revelation* as a cudgel. He turned it not only against Roman persecutors, but also against heretical 'false brethren', those self proclaimed Christians who made accommodations to Rome.[4]

In 312, the persecution of Christians ended when Constantine became Roman Emperor following his conversion to Christianity. From being embattled outsiders, Christians were now the privileged majority. While this might seem to negate the *Book of Revelation's* narrative of the battle of powerless believers against false authority, the text was reinterpreted to support the new Christian orthodoxy. Instead of representing the conflict between Christians and Pagans, it now became the story of the blessed and the damned within the Christian community. Under the watchful eye of religious authorities, once acceptable interpretations of Christianity and readings of the Bible became suspect and their adherents were condemned as enemies of the faith. In 367, ongoing battles over the legitimacy of various prophetic books ended. The *Book of Revelation* was added to the official list of texts making up the Christian scriptures and all other books of revelation were declared heretical. Church fathers reframed the text to direct its litany of torments toward those who challenged the official doctrines of the Catholic Church.

In the early 5th century, Augustine of Hippo challenged prevailing interpretations of the *Book of Revelation* as a map for the imminent End to the World. Instead, in his influential book, *The City of God*, he read the Apocalyptic narrative as an allegory of the spiritual struggle of the individual soul. His views, taken up as official Church doctrine, discouraged precise predictions about the onset of Judgment Day. The faithful were reminded of Christ's injunction in Matthew 25:13, to "Watch therefore, for ye know neither the day nor the hour wherein the Son of Man cometh."

Nevertheless, the *Book of Revelation's* allure as a work of literal prophecy remained powerful, and many Christians continued to search in it for intimations of the End. One of the most influential interpretations of *Revelation* along these lines was formulated by Joachim of Fiore, a 12th century Cistercian monk who used the text as the basis for a vision of history based on the Holy Trinity. According to Joachim, there are three great ages of human history, each a thousand years in duration. (This is the origin of the notion of millenarianism). The first age, presided over by God the Father, is described in the Old Testament. The second, guided by the Son, is depicted in the New Testament and covers the first millennium after the death of Christ. The last, directed by the Holy Spirit, is imminent (or so Joachim thought in the 12th century). He promoted the practice, still pervasive among Evangelicals today, of connecting the signs and symbols in the *Book of Revelation* to contemporary events. Throughout history thinkers as diverse as Dante, Christopher Columbus and Adolf Hitler have used versions of Joachim's scheme to support their conceptions of history.

The religious status of the *Book of Revelation* has waxed and waned over the centuries. It was rejected altogether by the Eastern Church, and greatly de-emphasized both by the present day Catholic Church and the mainstream Protestant denominations. Historically, it has often had its greatest influence outside the sphere of official religious institutions among break-away sects and revolutionary movements. And yet, even when downplayed by representatives of mainstream religions, it has never lost its powerful literary and artistic appeal. Throughout the last two millennia, artists and writers have continually drawn on the *Book of Revelation* during times of political, social and natural turmoil.

In the Muslim world, apocalyptic literature has served similar purposes. The *Qur'an* accepts many elements from Judeo Christian eschatology, including belief in a final Day of Judgment, the resurrection of the dead, and the meting out of everlasting punishments and rewards. The end of the world will be preceded by the arrival of a one-eyed figure, Dajjal, who resembles the Antichrist. He will bring chaos and destruction before being slain by Jesus, who is regarded by Muslims as a prophet. Also central to Islamic belief is the idea of jihad. This term, which literally means struggle, refers in some versions of Islam to an internal striving toward self-perfection. However, it has also been interpreted by some radical groups, including Al Qaeda and the Islamic State, to mandate a militant defense of the faith and a forced conversion of infidels to Islam. Here the *Book of Revelation's* grand battle between the forces of good and evil finds its counterpart in the Islamic crusade against those who threaten the tenets of the faith

As the foregoing suggests, the literature of apocalypse has figured powerfully in the political upheavals of East and West. Historically, however, the influence of visual representations of the apocalypse has been less universal. One finds apocalyptic beliefs expressed strongly in the art of the Western Christian tradition, where Endtimes, Judgment Day and the battle between the forces of good and evil have been continual sources of inspiration. By contrast, the visual representation of apocalyptic themes is less pronounced in religious traditions that otherwise share Christianity's eschatological orientation. In part, this may stem from a tradition of iconoclasm that originated in Zoroastrianism and burrowed into Judaism, Islam and eastern Christianity. In all these beliefs systems, there is a resistance to "idol worship" as a substitute for veneration of the Divinity itself. Tracing this tendency, Zoroastrian scholar Mary Boyce quotes an observation by Herodotus in the mid 5th century BC that Persians did not set up statues, altars and temples. Instead, their icon was sacred fire, instituted to replace the cult statues favored by other religious groups.[5] While the interdiction on figural imagery was never absolute throughout the long histories of Islam, Judaism and Eastern Orthodox Christianity, it has come to the fore again recently in the furious response of radical Islamists to Western representations of the Prophet, in the destruction of the Buddhas of Bamiyan by the Taliban in 2001 and the smashing of ancient artifacts by members of the Islamic State.

By contrast, for much of Western art history, artists worked under the patronage of the Church, creating art that reinforced Christian dogma. In their hands, the *Book of Revelation* provided an inexhaustible source of imagery and inspiration. Throughout the medieval period, officially sanctioned renditions of the Endtimes provided the faithful with terrifying images of the fate awaiting those who defied God's will (and by extension the will of the secular and religious leaders who were his agents on earth). Numerous Apocalypse cycles were commissioned by powerful and wealthy patrons in the thirteenth and fourteenth centuries. Those that have come down to us emphasize the Last Judgment, with its division of mankind into the elect and the damned. They often pay almost gleeful attention to the torments of the latter, in order to stress the role of obedience and personal responsibility in the achievement of salvation. However, the Apocalypse could also be used in the service of more private ends. Dante's *Inferno* (published in 1317) was written while its author was in political exile from his native Florence. While the text doesn't explicitly follow the *Book of Revelation*, Dante borrows from and elaborates on its notion of hell as the place of retribution for sinners. The circles of hell, in which the damned (many of them Dante's personal enemies) are subjected to torture commensurate with their crimes, are his own invention, but reflect *Revelation's* promise that divine justice will rectify the injustices of earthly powers. Dante's vision of hell provides one of the most resilient reworkings of the theme of Last Judgment and has continued to inspire artists and writers down through the ages.

In the mid 14th century, the four horsemen, with their fearsome cargo of pestilence, famine, war and death, were seen as heralds of such catastrophes as the Hundred Years War and the Black Death that killed a third of Europe's population. Now the imagery of the *Book of Revelation* served as a reminder of the fragility of life, the inescapability of death and the leveling of social hierarchies in the face of disaster. (This was the context of Boccaccio's *The Decameron*, which frames the telling of one hundred satirical stories as an entertainment devised by a group

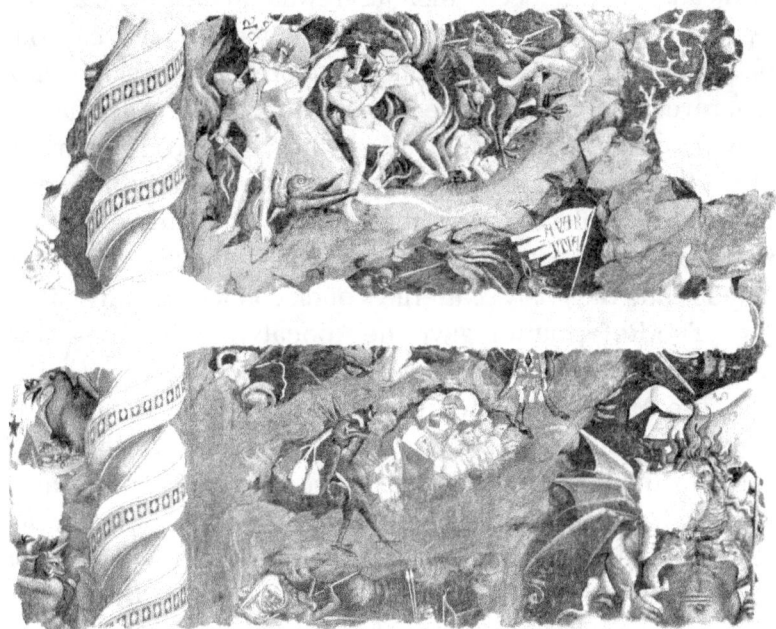

fig. 1 Andrea Orcagna, *Hell* (fragment), c 1350, fresco,
Santa Croce, Florence

of young people who have fled to a deserted country villa to escape the plague.) In art, popular embrace of tropes like the Dance of Death underscored these realities and were reflected in paintings by artists like Francesco Traini and Andrea Orcagna who depicted Death as a fearsome figure personified in the now familiar guise of the black cloaked skeleton carrying a scythe as he comes for rich and poor alike. *(fig. 1)*

The loosening of artists' ties with the Church during the Renaissance produced a more secular and worldly approach even to scenes with religious subjects. Nevertheless the Last Judgment, which had served in medieval paintings and sculptures as a warning to sinners and heretics, remained a popular subject for art. Artists like Giotto, Bosch, Fra Angelico, Luca Signorelli, and Jan van Eyck all took it up, following a template based on descriptions of Christ enthroned in the *Book of Revelation*. Paintings of the Last Judgment are generally divided into two realms. The upper section represents heaven, where the dead are judged and the Blessed take their place alongside Jesus and the angels. The lower section presents the resurrection of the dead, who will receive their just reward in their original bodies, and the disposition of the sinners who have been cast out of heaven. Artists vied to create ever more fantastical tableaux that reveled in the spectacle of the torments of the damned as they were cast into the literal maw of hell, devoured by demons or thrown into a cauldron of fire. The new realism of the Renaissance is reflected in an almost cinematic attention to the agonized expressions of the damned, the mutant bodies of the demons and the grisly scatterings of disconnected body parts.

The Reformation gave the Apocalyptic narrative new life as both sides put the imagery of the *Book of Revelation* to good use. Martin Luther was cast as the Antichrist by defenders of Catholicism, while Lutherans re-envisioned the Church of Rome as the Whore of Babylon. Artists inevitably were drawn into the fray. Though he lived to see and sympathize with the Reformation, Albrecht Durer's famous series of woodcuts of the Apocalypse were created in 1498, nineteen years prior to Martin Luther's break from the Catholic Church. They reflected an unsettled atmosphere as the half millennium approached and such "signs" as the encroachment of the Ottomans on Europe, the visibility of various meteorological wonders and the doomsday predictions of self styled prophets like Savonarola lead some to predict that the millennium would arrive in the year 1500. Durer's twelve illustrations provide representations of some of the most mystical events in *Revelation*, piling detail on detail to create hypnotic visions, conflating certain events for dramatic effect and including contemporary dress and settings.

Luther's condemnation of religious pageantry, idolatry and church decoration did not extend to such popular illustrations of biblical texts, which he understood were essential to the faith of the general populace. Inspired by Luther's writings, Lucas Cranach published a pamphlet in 1521 that paired events from the life of Christ and the legend of the Antichrist, here clearly a stand in for the Pope. In 1541, he also reworked Durer's *Revelation* woodcuts as illustrations for Luther's new German translation of the Bible. Cranach's versions contain more overt criticisms of the Catholic Church, making such alterations as the addition of a papal tiara on the head of the Whore of Babylon, and the transformation of a generic clergyman being devoured by the mouth of hell into a clear representation of a Catholic priest.[6] *(fig. 2)*

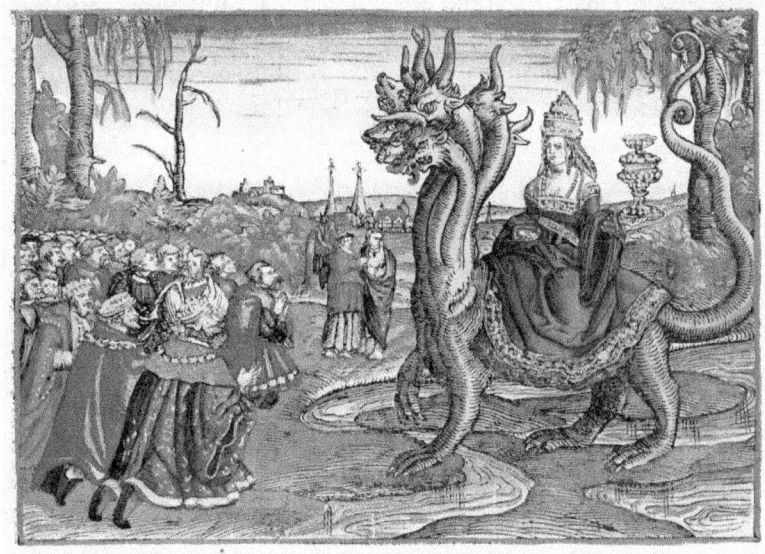

fig. 2 Workshop of Lucas Cranach, 1534, *Whore of Babylon*,
illustration from Martin Luther's translation of the Bible

On the other side of the religious war, Catholic writer Johannes Cochlaeus, who was later to publish a highly polemical biography of Luther in 1549, distributed an anti-Luther pamphlet in 1529. It was accompanied by an illustration depicting Luther as the many headed beast of *Revelation*. Each head is identified with a different aspect of Luther's persona, symbolized in turn by a doctor's cap, a monk's hood, a turban, (a reference to the ongoing threat of invasion by the Ottoman Turks,) a preacher's robe, a wild eyed fanatic whose unkempt hair is buzzing with wasps, a Church "Visitator" usurping the Pope, and finally a bearded figure identified as Barabbas, the robber released in Christ's stead by Pontius Pilate.[7]

Meanwhile, Michelangelo's *Last Judgment* (1536-41) presented a Counter-Reformation vision of Apocalypse drawn from the *Gospel of Matthew* and the *Book of Revelation*, as well as vignettes from Dante's *Inferno*. Located in the Sistine Chapel (the Pope's private chapel), the work provided a powerful affirmation of papal power and authority. This was a particularly pressing need in light of the recent Sack of Rome by mutinous troops of Charles V, the Holy Roman Emperor, which had left the building damaged. The prominent position of Peter, the first Pope, serves as a reminder that the faithful must pass through the Church to attain salvation. However, despite the sanctions given art as a means of religious education by the Council of Trent (1545-63) Michelangelo found himself embroiled in controversy over such non-orthodoxies as the inclusion of the pagan figures of Charon, the ferryman who brought souls across the Styx river to the underworld and Minos, one of the three judges of hell, painted to resemble a Vatican official who had criticized the *Last Judgment*. Even more offensive was the glorious nudity of the figures, now seen as an offense to Counter-Reformation sensibilities. This, despite the fact that only forty years earlier before the schism that lead to the Reformation, Luca Signorelli's monumental frescos of the events of *Revelation* (1499-1502) spread out over the walls of the chapel of S. Brizio in Orvieto, Italy, were equally rife with buff naked bodies.[8]

The *Book of Revelation* continued to be pressed into service during the religious wars of the 17th century and the revolutionary movements of the 18th. During the English Civil War, each side cast its adversary as the servant of Satan. Milton's *Paradise Lost*, published in 1667, is often seen as a political allegory in which the war between Heaven and Hell is a proxy for the battle between the defenders of the monarchy of Charles I and the Republican forces led by Oliver Cromwell. Though God, the King's surrogate, wins (as did the forces of Restoration in 1660), subsequent interpreters have tended to agree with William Blake that Milton was "of the Devil's party."

The late 18th century American Revolution was envisioned by many of its supporters in similar terms. In fact, the breakaway colony owed its birth in part to the Apocalyptic imagination. In a letter written towards the end of his life in 1500, Christopher Columbus maintained, "God made me the messenger of the new heaven and the new earth of which he spoke in the Apocalypse of St. John after having spoke of it through the mouth of Isaiah, and he showed me the spot where to find it."[9] Puritan settlers, many of them religious refugees from England, embraced this interpretation of America as the New Jerusalem. John Winthrop used the phrase "The City upon the Hill" in a 1630 address to the Massachusetts Bay colonists to suggest America's special destiny. (The phrase reappeared in the 20th century in speeches by John F. Kennedy and Ronald Reagan, both proponents of the philosophy of American Exceptionalism). Taken from Jesus' Sermon on the Mount, the phrase also looked back to the description of The New Jerusalem in the *Book of Revelation:* "I saw a holy city, new Jerusalem, coming down out of heaven from God, made ready like a bride adorned for her husband. I heard a loud voice proclaiming from the throne: "Now at last God has his dwelling among men!" (Rev. 21:2) A century later American theologian Jonathan Edwards declared that the millennium would begin in America. He kept a notebook which he called *Notes on the Apocalypse* that attempted to link the prophesies in *Revelation* with current events.

Reflecting these notions of America's privileged status, some colonists interpreted the American Revolution in Biblical terms, viewing King George as the Antichrist and connecting the British imposed Stamp Act with the Mark of the Beast.

Such rumblings reached England where in 1775 on the eve of the American Revolution, John Hamilton Mortimer painted a now lost depiction of *Death on a Pale Horse*. Now known only through engravings, this proto Romantic work presented a crowned skeleton astride a steed that is trampling a group of unfortunates underfoot as the legions of hell follow close behind. **(pl. 1)** Inspired by Durer's depiction of the same subject, the work illustrates Rev. 6:8 "I looked, and there before me was a pale horse! Its rider was named Death, and Hades was following close behind him." Reproductions of Mortimer's painting traveled widely, and served as an inspiration for Benjamin West, an American born British émigré, who in 1796 took up the same subject as part of an aborted *Revealed Religion* cycle for Windsor Castle. West's version, titled *The Opening of the Four Seals (Death on a Pale Horse)* represents four horseman charging through a body-littered battlefield in the vanguard of a horde of fearsome demons. **(pl. 2)** While the scene is Biblically based, it was read as a reference to such contemporaneous events as the end of the American War of Independence and the French Revolution. Responding to its implied democratic sympathies, King George III denounced the work as a "Bedlamite scene from *Revelations*"[10] and withdrew support from the Windsor commission.

Following close behind the American war for Independence was the French Revolution. It was initially seen by radicals inside and outside France as the fulfillment of apocalyptic prophecies. However, as the revolutionaries descended into terror and chaos, they began to seem less exemplars of righteous justice and more the agents of the false messiah. Eventually, the ascendance of Napoleon III restored an authoritarian order and put an end, for the time being, of hopes for an apocalyptic reordering of society. In French art of this time, references to the *Book of Revelation* tended to be more sublimated, as one of the tenets of the French Revolution was the overthrow of the tyranny of religion. Nevertheless, works like Jean-Pierre Houël's anarchic 1789 *Storming of the Bastille* and later, Théodore Gericault's 1819 *Raft of the Medusa* retain an apocalyptic undercurrent that harks back to *Revelation*.

Disillusionment with radical politics following the excesses of the French Revolution gave the apocalyptic imagination a more inward turn. William Blake borrowed directly from the *Book of Revelation* in works that expressed the Romantic era's spirit of individualism and subjectivity. In both poems and images, he expressed his antagonism to the institutions of Church and State through a vision of apocalypse as a state of personal enlightenment. Writing about his watercolor, *The Last Judgment*, he noted, "whenever any Individual Rejects Error and Embraces Truth a Last Judgment passes upon that Individual."[11] During the last decade of the 18th century and the first decades of the 19th, he returned frequently to the theme of *Revelation* in watercolors. His images reject the literalism of Benjamin West's apocalyptic representations. Instead, his characters – the Great Red Dragon, The Woman Clothed in the Sun, The Beast from the Sea - are ethereal and dreamlike, and float like visions above the tiny human figures below. Blake's late illustrated narrative, *Jerusalem: the Emanation of the Giant Albion* (1804-20) weaves together a variety of private and traditional myths centering on a Holy City that is at once Jerusalem during the Golden Age and the decadent Babylon of modern London. The images and poetry reflect Blake's abhorrence of the false religion of rationalist modernity. In creating such narratives, Blake placed himself in the prophetic tradition, as a latter-day embodiment of John of Patmos.

By the mid 19th century, Blake's subjective vision of Apocalypse was eclipsed by the theatrical paintings of John Martin who was for a time the most popular artist in England. His illustrations of various scenes from the *Book of Revelation* were largely shorn of political or philosophical content, offering instead dramatic tableaux that played on the spectacular nature of the narrative. A trio of Apocalyptic works completed in 1853 (*The Last Judgment, The Great Day of His Wrath*, and *The Plains of Heaven*) went on world tour for 25 years and later served as an inspiration for the grand visions of D.W. Griffith and Cecil B. DeMille.[12] **(pl. 3)**

The clunky naturalism of Martin's paintings are in stark contrast to the late, near abstractions of J. M. W. Turner, whose renderings of scenes from the *Book of Revelation* have fared far better critically. Like Blake, Turner employed *Revelation* allegorically to suggest the supremacy of the artistic spirit over the mundane world. Among his works is *Death on a Pale Horse* (1825-30). It departs from conventional representations of the theme by erasing all actors but the shadowy horse and skeletal rider who lies draped over his steed like a casualty himself. The whole painting is enveloped in a fiery mist that suggests the obliteration, not just of the damned, but of all reality. **(pl. 4)** Another *Revelation* based work by Turner is the golden *Angel Standing in the Sun* (1846) in which a winged herald emerges from a vortex of light to the consternation of the tiny demate-rialized figures below. Turner accompanied this work with an inscription from *Revelation* (Rev 17, 18) as well as a bit of verse from Samuel 'The morning march that flashes to the sun; The feast of vultures when the day is done.") suggesting an End that is anything but glorious.

The pessimism of Turner's apocalypse finds echoes in the writings and artwork of the Decadents, an offshoot of the Romanticism, a movement that emerged in Western Europe in the second half of the 19th century. The Decadents stripped any vestige of hope or redemption from the Apocalyptic narra-tive, focusing instead on the inevitable and imminent decline of mankind. Charles Baudelaire, one of the movement's most prominent members, made explicit reference to the *Book of Revelation* in a poem inspired by John Hamilton Mortimer's *Death on a Pale Horse*. Published in 1857 in *Les Fleurs de Mal*, his poem *Une Gravure Fantastique (A Fantastic Engraving)* drew on the motif of the horsemen of *Revelation* to express his sense of the exhaustion of civilization. The poem presents a fevered read on Mortimer's painting (which Baudelaire knew only through a graphic reproduction) as a description of the final disposition of "History's great sepulchered masses". Other visual artists associated with the Decadents went directly to the textual sources, yielding such masterpieces as Gustave Doré's 1861 illustrations for the *Inferno (fig. 3)* and Odilon Redon's 1899 lithographs for *The Apocalypse of Saint John. (fig. 4)*

In America, apocalyptic rhetoric drove both sides of the

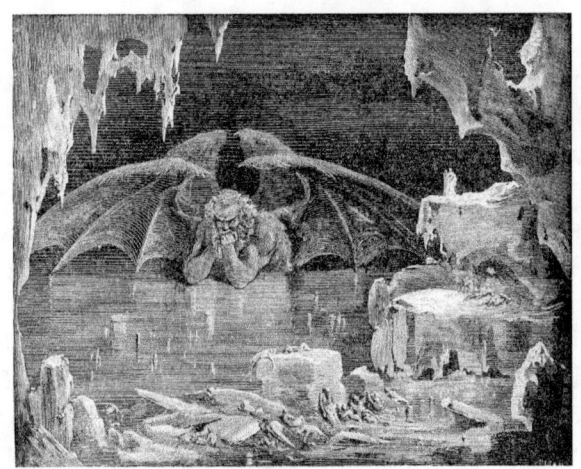

fig. 3 Gustave Doré, illustration of Dante's *Inferno*
1861–1868, Canto XXXIV: *Lucifer, King of Hell*

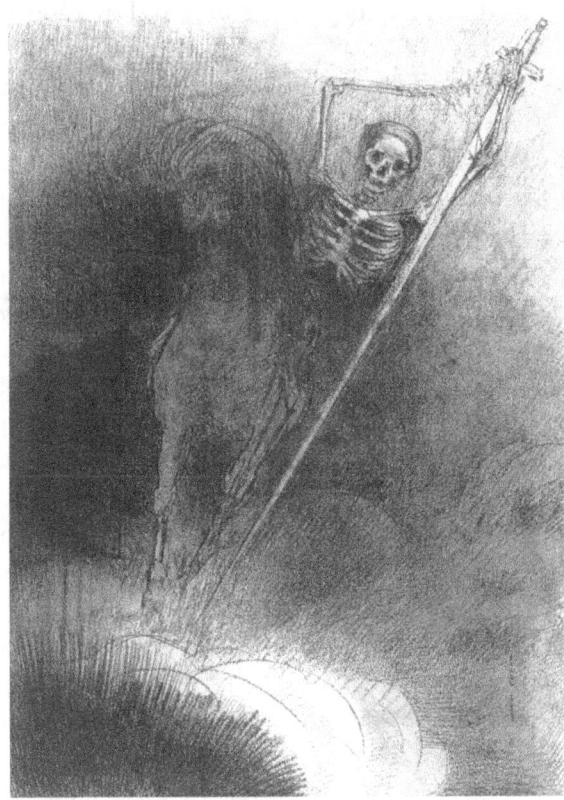

fig. 4 Odilon Redon, *And His Name That Sat on Him Was Death*,
1899, Lithograph with chine collé from a portfolio of 13 lithographs

Civil War. Harriet Beecher Stowe ended *Uncle Tom's Cabin,* her 1851 battle cry against slavery, with the words, "Read the signs of the times . . . Who may abide the day of His appearing? For that day shall burn like an oven." At the onset of the Civil War ten years later, Julia Ward Hall drew on the *Book of Revelation* for her stirring Battle Hymn of the Republic whose first stanza reads: "Mine eyes have seen the glory of the coming of the Lord; He is trampling out the vintage where the grapes of wrath are stored; He hath loosed the fateful lightning of his terrible swift sword; His truth is marching on." Meanwhile the Confederacy denounced the Yankees as allies of the Devil and posed the fight against them as "a religious duty."[13]

The advent of the twentieth century brought renewed interest in apocalyptic scenarios ranging from the hopeful, future oriented visions of the utopian movements of the first half of century to the dark nightmares inspired by their fearsome failures. On the eve of the First World War, apocalyptic imagery provided expressionist painters with a language for their anxieties about the coming catastrophe. These works stressed the tragic nature of an end that held out no possibility of redemption. Franz Marc, who was later to die in the War, created a work titled the *Fate of the Animals* in 1913 that presents a scattered group of forest animals caught in the knifepoint of a matrix of light shafts. *(fig. 5)* Oskar Kokoschka's 1914 *The Tempest* depicts himself and his lover Alma Mahler sheltered within a cockleshell against a raging storm. A set of *Apocalyptic Landscapes* by Ludwig Meidner painted in 1912 and 1913 are composed of images of people fleeing and buildings toppling beneath fiery skies dotted with comets and cannon fire. **(pl. 5)** However the most direct borrowing from the *Book of Revelation* appears in the *Improvisation* series of Wassily Kandinsky. Created between 1910 and 1914, these works draw directly from biblical sources. For instance, in *Improvisation 20* (1911), Kandinsky adapts the motif of the Rider, originally inspired by Russian folk art, into a reference to the Four Horsemen of the Apocalypse. Other works in this series contain abstracted images of Paradise set off against turbulent shapes and lines suggesting deluge, fire, serpents and other figures familiar from *Revelation.*

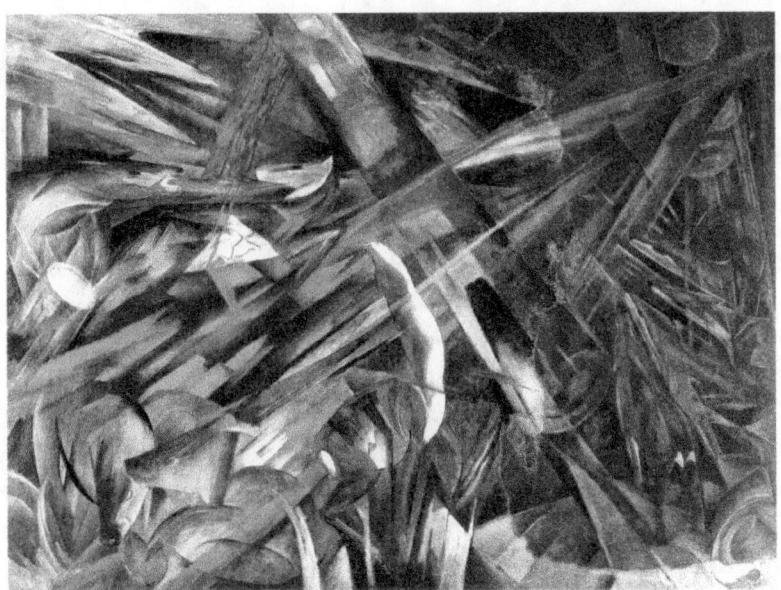

fig. 5 Franz Marc, 1913, oil on canvas, *Fate of the Animals*,
Kunstmuseum Basel

The huge waste of the First World War culminated in the triumph of the apocalyptically tinged Marxism of the Russian Revolution. Elsewhere, the war's aftermath produced a deep disillusionment with both traditional religion and the 20th century's faith in progress. The Death of God, which had been proclaimed by Nietzsche in 1884, led not to the triumph of reason and the apotheosis of man, but to chaos and pointless destruction. In the period between the wars, artists, writers and philosophers explored the psychological impact of that fact. The images of apocalypse from *Revelation* served now as allegories of a human-wrought catastrophe. William Butler Yeats' 1919 *The Second Coming* provides a resonant description of the postwar world: "Things fall apart; the centre cannot hold," ending the poem with an invocation of modern civilization as the ravaging Beast of *Revelation*:

> *And what rough beast, its hour come round at last,*
> *Slouches towards Bethlehem to be born?*

A few years later, T. S. Eliot authored an apocalyptic poem that has become equally iconic. His 1925 *The Hollow Men* describes the modern world's state of spiritual death and closes with the proclamation:

This is the way the world ends
This is the way the world ends
This is the way the world ends
Not with a bang but a whimper.

This idea was resurrected in the 1979 film *Apocalypse Now*, when Frances Ford Coppola paid tribute to the power of this dark vision by having Colonel Kurtz read those exact lines to the accompaniment of the Doors' apocalyptic anthem *The End*. As the Second World War loomed, the darkness continued to gather. Responding to the rise of Nazism in a text written just months before his suicide on the Spanish border with France, Walter Benjamin used the figure of the Angel of History to expose the fallacy of theories of human improvement. Once again, the avenging angels of *Revelation* loom behind this image, though here they are rendered powerless by the relentless flow of history. Benjamin writes: "A Klee drawing named 'Angelus Novus' shows an angel looking as though he is about to move away from something he is fixedly contemplating. His eyes are staring, his mouth is open, his wings are spread. This is how one pictures the angel of history. His face is turned toward the past. Where we perceive a chain of events, he sees one single catastrophe that keeps piling ruin upon ruin and hurls it in front of his feet. The angel would like to stay, awaken the dead, and make whole what has been smashed. But a storm is blowing from Paradise; it has got caught in his wings with such violence that the angel can no longer close them. The storm irresistibly propels him into the future to which his back is turned, while the pile of debris before him grows skyward. This storm is what we call progress." [14] *(fig. 6)*

In the art of this period, apocalyptic undercurrents took many forms. Artists who had directly experienced combat created horrific mixtures of reality and allegory, using images that echoed the searing imagery of the *Book of Revelation*. Otto Dix, who had served in the front in Russia and France, based his

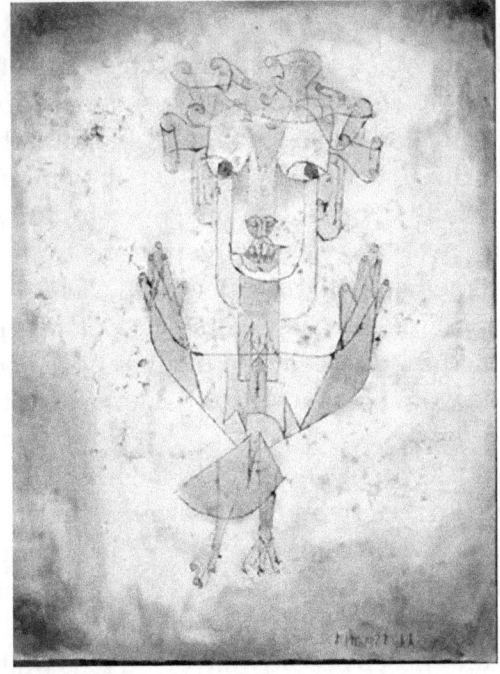

fig. 6 Paul Klee, *Angelus Novus*, 1920, oil and watercolor
on paper, The Israel Museum, Jerusalem

1924 *War* series on the carnage in the trenches of the Great War. Often compared to Goya's *Disasters of War*, it is full of dark and hallucinogenic images of smoldering ruins, worm-ridden skulls, ghostly figures in gas masks and uniformed skeletons. Max Pechstein published a set of prints in 1919 that included an image of a German soldier grappling with a many-headed mythical monster that seems inspired by *Revelation*'s Beast from the Sea. Adolf Uzarski's 1916 lithographs *Der Totentanz (The Dance of Death)* depict skeletons looming over battlefields. In 1917 George Grosz, having just been released from a military mental asylum following his breakdown during military service, painted *Explosion*, a spiraling vortex of collapsing buildings, shattered windows, body parts, smoke and shadowy faces suggesting the fiery destruction of the prewar urban order. **(pl. 6)** A never finished painting by Max Beckmann, begun in 1918, is titled *Auferstehung (Resurrection)* and depicts the scene as a contemporary Judgment Day, crowded with wounded bodies surrounding a central corpse lying abandoned in a ruined landscape.[15]

The social and economic chaos that followed Germany's defeat provoked yet further expressions of despair. During the interwar period German Expressionists borrowed heavily from Biblical themes, using tropes like the mocking of Christ, the Crucifixion, the Last Judgment and the martyrdom of Saint Sebastian as allegories for the suffering of the German people. A set of illustrations to the *Book of Revelation* created in 1940-41 by Beckman was peopled with theatrical and bourgeois characters who portray the pagan idols and misled followers in the manner of a modern day Antichrist. The work presents the artist himself as the figure of St. John of Patmos.

Even as such works were being condemned by the Nazis as "degenerate art," German fascists were usurping the language of apocalypse for their own ends. They identified with the eschatological vision of history as a struggle that would end, after violent conflict, with the vanquishing of evil by good. For the Nazis the chosen people were the Aryans while the evil powers that threatened their utopian future were personified by the Jews. The total destruction of this enemy would ensure the triumph of history. Interestingly, though they rejected explicit ties to Christianity, the Nazis took the name for their future utopia from the Christian apocalyptic tradition. The notion of a thousand year Third Reich is a borrowing from Joachim of Flore, referring to his third millennium of The Spirit, in which universal brotherhood would reign until the last coming of Christ.

Italian fascism was similarly millennial in conception. Mussolini conceived of Fascism as part of a historical continuum that stretched back to the ancient Roman Empire, on which it modeled itself, and forward to a coming technological future. Fascism took its name from the ancient Roman fasces, the bundle of wooden rods bound around an axe that symbolized the power of the Roman magistrates. In its early days Fascism was closely associated with Futurism, the art movement that emerged in Italy in 1909 through the efforts of its maestro Filippo Tommaso Marinetti. Futurism aimed to establish a new order through the violent destruction of the past. The Age of Futurism was to be created by harnessing machines, steam and electricity. Marinetti wanted to remake everything from art and architecture to language and food (his platform included the banning of pasta, Italy's signature dish.) Futurists expressed their philosophy through paintings and sculptures that transformed the cubist fracturing of space into an expression of the dynamic movement of time. They combined this revolution in art with a call for revolution in society. In a phrase that echoes the radical cleansing that precedes the establishment of the *Book of Revelation*'s Christian utopia, Marinetti, founder of Futurism titled his 1911-15 manifesto, *War, the World's Only Hygiene.*

While Mussolini remained attached to the symbols and historical glories of ancient Rome, his regime was marked by an abhorrence of the traces of the past that followed it. Excavating Roman ruins that lay beneath the structures of subsequent centuries, he remade Rome along what he believed were classical lines. He also remade Italian society with himself as the absolute dictator presiding over a society devoted to militarism and state control of the economy. In an entry on Fascism that he co-wrote for the 1932 Italian Encyclopedia, he echoed Marinetti's manifesto: "Fascism . . . believes neither in the possibility nor the utility of perpetual peace. . . War alone brings up to its highest tension all human energy and puts the stamp of nobility upon the peoples who have courage to meet it. All other trials are substitutes."[16]

Soviet communism, though overtly atheistic, also grew out of millennial roots. Marx's vision of history expressed itself in tropes that derived from the Christian apocalyptic narrative. Transplanted to Russia, these provided the framework for a radically new social order. As George Steiner writes, "Nothing is more religious, nothing is closer to the ecstatic rage for justice in the prophets, than the socialist vision of the destruction of the bourgeois Gomorrah and the creation of a new, clean city for man."[17]

Thus, despite their apparent differences and disavowals of established religion, the totalitarian movements of the 20th century shared visions of history that were deeply indebted to

Christian eschatology. The tenets of Christian faith were simply reconfigured to serve apparently secular ends. John Gray describes the common thread uniting these philosophies: "It was no longer God that would bring about the salvation of the world. 'Humanity' - or a privileged section of it, thought to be especially progressive or racially superior - would initiate the miraculous transformation. While the content of belief had been modified with secularization, the structure of thought had not changed. History was still seen in apocalyptic terms as a struggle between good and evil, which would end - though only after the most violent conflicts - with the victory of good." [18]

In the immediate Postwar era, the apocalypse was shorn of its hopeful aspects, assuming instead its now familiar secular pessimism. Even in America, once the bastion of millenarian optimism, a sense of the tragic nature of history took hold. Apocalyptic fears coalesced around such markers as the Holocaust, whose full extent was not made public until the opening of the camps; the dropping of the Atomic Bomb and the possibility it posed of a human-caused annihilation of the planet; and the onset of the Cold War, which was framed on both sides as a contest between the powers of good and evil. (This notion was articulated on the Western side in 1983 with Ronald Reagan's designation of Soviet Russia as "the Evil Empire.")

Contemporary art historians like Katy Siegel and Irving Sandler have interpreted the emergence of Abstract Expressionism through the lens of the era's apocalyptic fears. They point to statements by artists, poets and critics that tied the search for a radically new art to the sense of impending doom of the nuclear age. In commentaries on the movement, both authors reference Barnett Newman's 1948 remark, "We now know the terror to expect. Hiroshima showed it to us. . .The terror has indeed become as real as life. What we have now is a tragic rather than a terrifying situation. [No] matter how heroic, or innocent, or moral our individual lives may be, this new fate hangs over us."[19] Sandler adds to this an epigram from Frank O'Hara "[The] new painting does have qualities of passion and lyrical desperation, unmasked and uninhibited, not found in other recorded eras; it is not surprising that faced with universal destruction, as we are told, our art should at last speak with unimpeded force and unveiled honesty to a future which may well be non-existent. . .."[20]

While Siegel sees this a particularly American phenomenon, linked to the long standing eschatological bent of American thought and culture, Sandler points out that a similar sense of dread underlay European avant-garde culture in the wake of both the nuclear bomb and the annihilation of Old European order by the Second World War. In America, these anxieties manifested themselves in art that laid waste to the utopian minded geometric abstraction pioneered by artists like Malevich and Mondrian. Instead, the paintings of artists like Jackson Pollock, Mark Rothko, Willem de Kooning and Clyfford Still were coarse, apparently unfinished, and infused with dark brooding colors and inchoate form. They spoke of a state between the destruction of one world and the uncertain future that would follow. The "tragic sense" has become part of the mythology of postwar Art, in particular with reference to Abstract Expressionism. A certain dark romanticism remains part of the continuing appeal of work from this era. However, even at the time, critic Harold Rosenberg warned about the potential for existential struggles to devolve into formula. He decried the domestication of genuinely revolutionary impulses into a species of, in his piquant term, "apocalyptic wall paper."[21]

In Europe, the postwar era's sense of impending doom took the form of a literal assault on the picture plane. This tendency was the subject of a fascinating exhibition organized by the LA MoCA in 2012. *Destroy the Picture Painting the Void 1949-1962* explored the international dimensions of the destructive impulse in work by artists from France, Japan, England, Italy, Spain, Austria and the United States. The creative destruction pursued by European artists like Luca Fontana, Alberto Burri, *(fig. 7)* Yves Klein and Otto Muehl, American artists Robert Rauschenberg and Lee Bontecou and Japanese artists Kazuo Shiraga, and Shozo Shimamoto is often framed in terms of the tendency toward formalist reduction or private metaphysical speculations. Here their torn, burned, slashed and bullet-ridden canvases were seen as manifestations of the

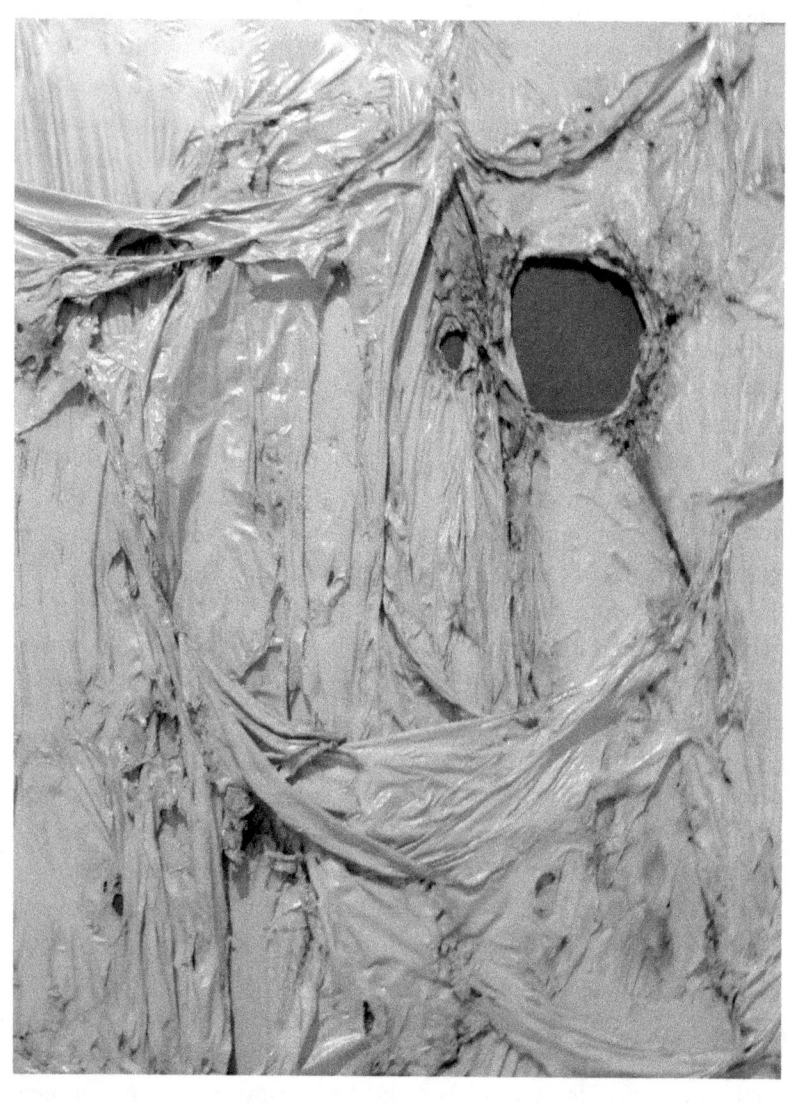

fig. 7 Alberto Burri, *Grande Rosso*, 1964, Plastic (PVC),
acrylic, and combustion, National Modern Art Gallery of
Rome

psychic scars left by the cataclysms of World War II. Corroborating the apocalyptic intent of such work is a statement by Muehl in a 1961 letter in which he declares, "I destroy the surface, its glorious whiteness, and at the same stroke the old order, the world. I drive it toward its ruin, although you might as well say towards its perfection. Everything is striving towards new and ever newer states of being until in the end everything explodes. Is this not the purpose of the world?"[22]

In the immediate postwar years, a sense of dread also infected popular culture. The secular apocalypse became a stock scenario in Hollywood movies, popular novels and television shows. Fears of a nuclear holocaust brought on by the standoff between the United States and the Soviet Union found expression in the 1950s and 60s in films like *On the Beach* (1959), *Fail Safe* (1964), and *Dr. Strangelove* (1964). In Japan, which had experienced this catastrophe first hand, Godzilla, a mutant monster created by a nuclear disaster, became an iconic figure, subject of dozens of films between 1954 and the present.

During this period, the religious message of *Revelation* appeared to have largely disappeared from view. In both high and low culture, it remained visible only in skeletal form as a metaphor for the kinds of tribulations that would come as the result of nuclear firestorm or post apocalyptic struggles for survival. But the demise of Christian eschatology proved remarkably short. Philosopher Mark C. Taylor maintains that "Since the early 1970s we have been in the midst of what might be called the Fourth Great Awakening, which was unanticipated by all the most sophisticated cultural critics."[23] (The reference here is to the three other earlier waves of religious enthusiasm that swept through the United States during the eighteenth and nineteenth centuries.) Taylor is pointing to the rise of Christian fundamentalism in the United States over the last four decades, as evidenced by the mainstreaming of Christian ministries, widespread embrace of literal interpretations of the Bible, and ever growing influence of religion on American politics.

With this reawakening has come renewed interest in the *Book of Revelation*. One early sign of this was the unprecedented success of Hal Lindsay's *Late Great Planet Earth*. This book, first published in 1970s, has sold tens of millions of copies, and has been translated into fifty languages. It offers a compendium of signs that link contemporary events and personalities to the prophecies in *Revelation*. As historian Paul Boyer points out, for Lindsey the Bible becomes a manual of atomic age combat in which *Revelation*'s fire and brimstone are reinterpreted as tactical nuclear weapons. Its falling stars are warheads fired from space platforms and its incinerating heat are the effects of radiation. The scenarios leading to Armageddon in *Revelation*, among them the rebuilding of the temple, world government and the rise of the Antichrist are reconfigured into such modern events as the founding of the State of Israel and its victory in the 1967 Six Day War, the formation of the United Nations, NATO and the European Union, and the emergence of an Arab alliance opposing Israel. [24]

The Turner Diaries, written in 1978, might be seen almost as the "evil twin" of Lindsey's apocalyptic prophecies. This text was created by William Luther Pierce, a former leader of a white nationalist organization named the National Alliance. Writing under the pseudonym "Andrew Macdonald," he produced a white supremacist fantasy that describes a violent revolution fought by white "Patriots" against an evil federal government permeated by Jews, blacks and gays. Pages from this tract on the fictional bombing of FBI headquarters were found in the car driven by Timothy McVeigh, perpetrator of the Oklahoma City Bombing.

The widespread popular appeal of books like these underscores the enormous impact of apocalyptic thinking on the postwar American imagination. As Paul Boyer remarks, "In unraveling the details of pre-millennial eschatology, then, we must keep the larger picture in view: from the end of World War II to the closing years of the twentieth century, scores of prophecy writers, in books selling millions of copies, as well as TV and radio preachers reaching more millions of individuals, taught that Russia's destruction is explicitly foretold in a sacred text most Americans revere as divinely inspired. We cannot fully understand Cold War politics and culture without close attention to this religious component."[25]

The peaceful end of the Cold War and the demise of the Soviet Union would seem to refute Lindsey's predictions. In fact however, in more recent writings he and other seers have simply pivoted away from a vision of Russia as the seat of the Antichrist, locating it instead in the Muslim world. In this formulation, both the first and second Gulf Wars are portents of the end. Saddam Hussein's massive release of oil in Persian Gulf in 1991 appeared to validate *Revelation*'s prophecies of a sea turned to blood, while the Shock and Awe aerial bombardment of Baghdad that opened the 2003 Iraq war took place, as many pointed out, at the spot over the Euphrates River where *Revelation*'s angel pours the cup of God's wrath.

Related to this is the *Left Behind* phenomenon. Since 1995, this American series of best selling novels, film adaptations and video games has presented *Revelation* based narratives set in contemporary times. The common plot point involves the chaotic struggles of those "left behind" to deal with the Great Tribulations after believers are literally raptured out of homes, cars and airplanes. According to the series coauthor Tim LaHaye, "*Left Behind* is the first fictional portrayal of events that are true to the literal interpretation of Bible prophecy." He adds, "The novels are written to wake people up to the fact that Jesus is coming again, and they need to be prepared."[26]

Outside the United States, once adamantly secular states in Europe, the Middle East and the Russian continent have experienced equally powerful religious revivals. As a result, it has now become quite fashionable in academic circles to refer to ours as a "post-secular" age. One proponent of this deliberately awkward phrase, Jürgen Habermas, uses it to maintain that secularism is no longer a necessary condition of modern society. Instead, he argues, the reason-based Enlightenment model of society has been superseded by faith-based ideologies that are simultaneously traditional and modern. The effects, he warns, can be combustible. "Often smouldering conflicts that are profane in origin are first ignited once coded in religious terms. This is true of the 'desecularisation' of the Middle East conflict, of the politics of Hindu nationalism and the enduring conflict between India and Pakistan and of the mobilisation of the religious right in the United States before and during the invasion of Iraq."[27]

In a post-secular age, it becomes hard to separate secular and religious visions of the future. Anticipation of an approaching Endtimes, influenced covertly or overtly by religious metaphors and assumptions, seeps into all kinds of discourses. In February, 1981 Ronald Reagan's Secretary of the Interior James Watt remarked in testimony before the House Interior Committee, "I do not know how many future generations we can count on before the Lord returns. Whatever it is, we have to manage with a skill to leave the resources needed for future generations." Following the dismantling of the Berlin wall, Francis Fukuyama's influential 1989 article, "The End of History and the Last Man" (later expanded into a best selling book) offered a paean to the triumphant arrival of the final stage of human society. "What we may be witnessing is not just the end of the cold war, or the passing of a particular period of postwar history, but the end of history as such: that is, the end point of mankind's ideological evolution and the universalization of Western liberal democracy as the final form of human government."[28] Though Fukuyama has subsequently distanced himself from some of his more extreme implications of this view, versions of this triumphalism have remained staples of political rhetoric by neo-conservatives and neo-liberals alike.

Indeed, since the 1970s, an ever multiplying set of signs and wonders have been interpreted through the Endtimes narrative. Portents of the End have been seen in the AIDS epidemic, the Y2K virus that was supposed to paralyze the world's computer networks in 2000, the attacks of September 11, 2001, the Afghan and Iraq Wars, the 2008 global economic crisis, the escalating series of natural disasters, including Hurricanes Katrina, Irene and Sandy and the Fukushima nuclear disaster, which may bring on the end of the world through disastrous climate change.

In pop culture as well, eschatology provides a default mode for thinking about the future. Since the demise of the Cold War, films like *Independence Day, The Day After Tomorrow, Waterworld* and the *Matrix* and *Terminator* series have implicated myriad other agents in wholesale annihilation, including aliens, environmental disasters, technology and global corporatism. Meanwhile the ever popular zombie genre seems to have gained new traction in recent years, so much so that in 2011 the U.S. Center for Disease Control and Prevention issued a graphic novel titled *Preparedness 101: Zombie Apocalypse* as a tongue in cheek vehicle for promoting emergency preparedness in the face of natural disasters.

The religious structures of the apocalypse – the grand battle between good and evil, the emergence of evil agents cloaked with a false raiment of virtue or righteousness, the imminence of a period of catastrophe and tribulation, the promise (or threat) that the world as we know it is rapidly coming to an end – remain powerful even for those who are not overtly religious. What follows in this book is an exploration of the apocalyptic imagination as it manifests itself in the works of a diverse group of contemporary artists. Avant-garde art has long been considered a powerful bastion of secularity, holding strong against the creeping return of religion in contemporary culture. But in fact the works discussed in the following pages testify to the degree to which the religiously based myth and metaphor of the apocalypse remains an inescapable undercurrent in the work of a surprising number of contemporary artists. The continuing potency of the Endtimes narrative underscores the point made by philosopher Mark C. Taylor: "Religion doesn't return," he notes, "because it never goes away. To the contrary, religion haunts society, self, culture even – perhaps especially – when it seems to be absent."[29]

Chapter 2

REVELATION AS INSPIRATION: THE AMERICAN APOCALYPSE

"The American finds God in herself or himself,
but only after finding the freedom to know
God by experiencing a total inward solitude."
– Harold Bloom[1]

In *The American Religion*,[2] a quirky and highly personal meditation on faith first published in 1992, literary critic Harold Bloom surveys a vast swath of homegrown American religious cults and sects. He takes up, among others, Mormons, Southern Baptists, Pentecostals, Seventh day Adventists, Jehovah's Witnesses, and Christian Scientists. All these American inventions, he believes, have a common thread, making them simply different forms of what he calls "the American religion". According to Bloom, this religion is always millennial, motivating its followers with the vivid visions of the Last Judgment and promises of the coming Kingdom of God. It is intensely nationalistic, proposing that we regard America as the fulfillment of prophecies about the New Jerusalem that will be established following the Second Coming of Christ. It is also, Bloom suggests, essentially *Orphic* – by which he means radically individualistic, focused on the believer's personal relationship with God and convinced of "the potential divinity of the elitist self."[3] Exploring the particular histories, heroes, and tenets of each of these belief systems, Bloom regards them all as manifestations of the American longing for personal transcendence. However, he concludes: "American ecstasy is solitary, even when it requires the presence of others for an audience for the self's glory." This, he warns, has unfortunate consequences: "A religion of the self is not likely to be a religion of peace, since the American self tends to define itself through its war against otherness."[4]

As the preceding chapter suggests, the *Book of Revelation*

is only one among a crowded field of apocalyptic texts that can trace their lineage back to Zoroaster. However, perhaps because of its compatibility with a peculiarly American vision of morality, the *Book of Revelation* holds a special place in the American eschatological imagination. Rich with striking tableaux and unforgettable characters, *Revelation* reinforces the sectarian, literalist and often Manichean beliefs that are shared by America's myriad religious sects. And thanks to its striking imagery and compelling narrative, it has provided metaphors that have burrowed deeply into American high and popular culture, as well as its political discourse. Its influence can be felt among both believers and secularists, among those for whom the events described in the book are fact, to be passively or actively awaited, and those who adopt its tropes as free-floating signifiers that coalesce around any number of contemporary anxieties. More than any other apocalyptic text, the *Book of Revelation* has served as an inspiration for American writers, filmmakers, musicians and visual artists.

Why has this ancient text retained its authority for nearly two millennia? Historians believe that the *Book of Revelation* was originally addressed to the embattled early Christian community suffering the persecutions of the Roman Emperor Nero. It describes a series of dramatic visions. These include the unleashing of four horsemen signifying war, famine, pestilence and death; the destruction of the city of Babylon, believed to be a stand-in for Rome and figured here as a harlot on a scarlet steed; and the emergence of a great beast from the sea, who has become known as the Antichrist and who rallies the force of evil against the faithful. The narrative culminates in a grand battle between the Angels of God and Satan who is depicted as a great red dragon with seven heads and ten horns. With God's triumph, Satan is cast into a bottomless pit for a thousand years, after which he is released for one last onslaught before his final imprisonment and the reign of The Just for the rest of eternity.

The language is hypnotic and hallucinogenic. Consider a few passages that have provided grist for artists throughout the ages:

And I looked, and behold a pale horse: and his name that sat on him was Death, and Hell followed with him. And power was given unto them over the fourth part of the earth, to kill with sword, and with hunger, and with death, and with the beasts of the earth. [Rev 6:8]

Lo, there was a great earthquake; and the sun became black as sackcloth of hair, and the moon became as blood . . . [Rev 6:12]

And I stood upon the sand of the sea, and saw a beast rise up out of the sea, having seven heads and ten horns, and upon his horns ten crowns, and upon his heads the name of blasphemy. [Rev 13:1]

. . . and I saw a woman sit upon a scarlet coloured beast, full of names of blasphemy, having seven heads and ten horns. And the woman was arrayed in purple and scarlet colour, and decked with gold and precious stones and pearls, having a golden cup in her hand full of abominations and filthiness of her fornication: And upon her forehead was a name written, MYSTERY, BABYLON THE GREAT, THE MOTHER OF HARLOTS AND ABOMINATIONS OF THE EARTH. [Rev 17: 3, 4, 5]

Whatever the theological interpretations of these symbols – and there are many - their offspring are everywhere today. We speak blithely of the "Four Horseman of the Apocalypse," humorously or not so humorously, categorize adversaries as "the Antichrist," and dub any dreaded outcome "Armageddon." Apocalyptic tropes like the battle between Good and Evil, the inevitability of Judgment Day and the horrors of the post-apocalyptic world are no longer strictly tied to religious belief.

Instead, such images become grist for high and low art, serving as metaphors for reflection on issues as diverse as climate change, AIDS, racism, war, greed and materialism.

Despite the important psychic role that he attributes to this text, Harold Bloom is no fan of the *Book of Revelation*. But even as he characterizes it as "a nightmare of a book: without wisdom, goodness, kindness or affection of any kind,"[5] he acknowledges its power. In a coda to *The American Religion* written at the height of the Bush era, he remarks, "The influence of *Revelation* always has been out of all proportion to its literary strength or spiritual value. Though it has affected the strongest poets, from Dante and Spenser through Milton on to Blake and Shelley, it also has enthralled the quacks and cranks of all ages down to the present moment in America."[6]

These latter manifestations are one of the great subjects of artist Jim Shaw. As part of a multi-faceted career, Shaw has compiled a remarkable archive of the myriad products of America's esoteric mythologies and beliefs. Under the umbrella title *The Hidden World* (which suggests their invisibility in mainstream culture), he has exhibited his collection of posters, pamphlets, videos, banners, comic books and other ephemera that promote fringe religions, crackpot science, conspiracy theories, not so secret societies and paranormal research. His finds include the books of Zecharia Sitchin, a Russian author who maintained that human life on earth was the product of an alien invasion; the Universal World Church, a show biz mega church, that, during the 1950s was situated under a perpetually hovering "glory cloud" that would emit a pillar of smoke by day and fire by night; and publications by Jack Chick, evangelical comic book artist who espoused the belief that the Catholic Church is behind Islam, Jehovah's Witnesses, communism and the Holocaust.

Shaw locates America's soul at the intersection of popular culture, commercial kitsch and eccentric spiritualities, drawing a line between Hollywood (whose purpose, he noted in an interview, is "to mythologize rebellion"[7]) and the proliferation of American messianic sects and cults. The connection comes easily to him, as a former special effects designer for such off-beat Hollywood films as *Earth Girls Are Easy*, *Nightmare on Elm Street part 4* and *The Abyss*. Like the artifacts from *The Hidden World*, such productions valorize paranoia, retribution, and a Manichean sense of good and evil.

Recoiling from a conventional Episcopalian upbringing in the small town of Midland, Michigan, Shaw fell in with a group of what he calls "rebellious Catholics,"[8] most notably the artist Mike Kelley, with whom he founded the cult band *Destroy all Monsters*, and with whom he later enrolled in art school at Cal Arts. Kelley went on to achieve art world notoriety with a vast body of work that explored the dark side of childhood innocence and conventional morality while flouting all standards of good taste. While Shaw's equally massive oeuvre is more restrained and introspective, it draws on similarly discordant elements of American pop culture and commercialized spirituality.

Shaw's artwork is deeply indebted to his collection of objects, and shares with them a deliberately eclectic sensibility. He works in series that have the appearance of compendiums of diverse materials from multiple sources. One of his most epic works, *My Mirage*, which he worked on from 1986-1991, is a lightly autobiographical narrative that tells the story of Billy, a young Midwesterner whose search for meaning leads him through the turbulent currents of the 1960s and 70s. He careens between various lifestyles and belief systems, throwing himself into sex, drugs, rock and roll, and finally, evangelical Christianity. The story unfolds through "chapters" composed of mashups of text and imagery incorporating drawn, photocopied, silkscreened and collaged material from myriad sources. Each section uses elements appropriate to the phase of Billy's life, so that, for instance early montages are heavy on comic book imagery, while during Billy's hippie era, the images draw on psychedelic posters and rock album covers.

My Mirage is the story of the coming of age of an American Everyman. It shares the spirit of Puritan morality tales like John Bunyan's 1678 allegory *The Pilgrim's Progress*, and like that work presents a journey through the temptations and hazards of life as its hero works his way toward ultimate redemption. However, Shaw is more equivocal than Bunyan about the final stage of his hero's life as Billy reinvents himself as a televangelist hawking a patently dubious version of Evangelical Christianity.

Shaw's affinity with Bloom's *The American Religion* reappears in a series of works inspired by the bestselling Christian *Left Behind* novels written by Tim LaHaye and Jerry B. Jenkins. Shaw's *Left Behind* paintings present allegorical paintings designed to capitalize on the associative link between fundamentalist Rapture and the American working class. Writing of this series from 2004, Shaw describes his motivation in terms that have eerie resonances with analyses surrounding the aftermath of the 2016 election. He says, "The title *Left Behind* refers both to the bestselling series of books in history, right wing Christian fantasies about the rapture and coming apocalypse, and the American worker, left behind by globalism, with a weak labor movement and little support from the Democrats. Many have turned to born-again Christianity in lieu of any other hope for the future, which in turn has been exploited heavily by the right wing."[9]

The works are painted over monumental theatrical backdrops that Shaw acquired in Los Angeles. The backdrops offer bland suburban and urban landscapes which Shaw alters with comic overlays of images from pop culture, politics, and 50s era advertising. In a book about the work, he provides a detailed key to the iconography, revealing, for instance, that in a painting titled *Dream Object: (I dreamt of an image of a yellow walled city with a yellow kid sticking his finger in the outer wall*, the yellow maze floating over a backdrop of an urban downtown circa 1950 is based on *Revelation's* description of the New Jerusalem. Caught within its tunnels are contemporary versions of the Horsemen of the Apocalypse in the personages of Tom DeLay, Pat Robertson, Ayn Rand and Ronald Reagan. The role of the Whore of Babylon goes to Britney Spears and the Beast with Seven Heads displays the visages of the leaders of the G7 countries. In another work in this series, the Jolly Green Giant represents the angel of *Revelation*, while a vacuum cleaner with multiple attachments becomes Kali, Hinduism's multi-armed goddess of Death.[10] He has also created many stand-alone images inspired by Revelation, for instance, *Whore of Babylon + Robber Barons* from 2015, in which a psychedelic poster provided the inspiration for a representation of the scarlet woman conveyed over a sea of political conventioneers by a motley crew of 19th century capitalists. **(pl. 7)**

Eventually, Shaw carried his homage to the American Religion to its logical conclusion with the creation of his own religion which he calls Oism. Oism contains echoes of Mormonism, Scientology, Christian Science and the American utopian tradition as embodied in communal experiments like New Jerusalem, the Shakers, and the Amana Colony. Shaw presents Oism as a goddess centered religion founded in upstate New York in the mid 1800s by a prophet named Annie O'Wooten. A feminist allegory, Shaw's religion centers on a virgin who gave birth to herself at the dawn of history. According to the mythology of the religion, she brought writing and agriculture to society, but was eventually toppled by the "I" – a stand-in for patriarchy/ego. Oism is an ongoing project expressed in music, video, installation, performance, comic books, drawings, photographs, and paintings.

Shaw's references to the myths surrounding American patriotism, capitalism and religion go to the heart of the nation's current pathologies. They offer a vivid realization of what Richard Hofstadter referred to in a now classic essay as "The Paranoid Style in American Politics." Writing in 1964 following Senator Barry Goldwater's selection as the Republican nominee for President, Hofstadter examines the peculiarly American romance with conspiracy theories. He unearths the paranoid underpinnings of political and social currents ranging from the anti Masonic, anti-immigrant and anti Catholic movements of the 19th century, the John Birch Society, the Ku Klux Klan and the Cold War embrace of McCarthyism. Hofstadter sees a continuity of world view among these groups which he characterizes thus: "America has been largely taken away from them and their kind, though they are determined to repossess it and to prevent the final destructive act of subversion. The old American virtues have already been eaten away by cosmopolitans and intellectuals; the old competitive capitalism has been gradually undermined by socialist and communist schemers; the old national security and independence have been undermined by treasonous plots having as their most powerful agents not merely outsiders and foreigners as of old, but major statesmen who are at the very centers of American power."[11]

The essay makes sobering reading in the wake of the election of a conspiracy minded purported populist to the American Presidency. In considering his own work, Shaw underscores the religious basis of such obsessions, noting, "its very hard not to succumb to those Christian based – or maybe Zoroastrian – polarities and points of view . . . It's hard to be an American and side-step the apparently innate moralizing that comes along with it."[12]

Shaw's compendium of eschatological materials and artworks inspired by them point to an intimate tie between American identity, the country's national mythology and visions of apocalypse. This is reflected in the work both of contemporary American artists who are believers and in that of those who are not. There is, of course, a difference between apocalyptically inspired art works created by artists of these different persuasions. The question of evil, so present to modernist artists during the two World Wars, provokes a certain discomfort among many ironic secularists of the present day. As a result, direct borrowings from the *Book of Revelation* by otherwise unreligious artists like Shaw often appear as if surrounded by quotation marks.

For members of religious sects devoted to a literal reading of the Bible, by contrast, the *Book of Revelation* provides a factual blueprint of human history. This has sparked a rich vein of work by self-taught "outsider" artists who translate visions inspired by this text into art. These artists, often Southern, self taught, and sometimes folded into the categories of folk art or visionary art, create outside the established canons of art history. Many are adherents of versions of Evangelical Christianity that stress the authority of the Bible and the life transforming experience of being "born again." Things take an apocalyptic turn when they are premillenarians, which means they adhere to a worldview in which human history is destined, after a series of ever darker collisions with evil and sin, to descend at last into complete chaos and catastrophe. Following the scenario set out by the *Book of Revelation*, this view holds that only after this debacle will Christ reappear for a thousand year reign of peace and justice. The Jews hold a special place in this scenario since premillenarians believe that the return of the Jews to the Holy Land is one of the prerequisites for Christ's second coming. (By contrast, postmillenarianism, a position adhered to by more mainstream Protestant sects, holds that it is the mission of humanity to perfect the world prior to Christ's final return.) Premillenarians thus solve the age-old "problem" of evil by seeing it as an essential part of God's plan. In this scenario, only the spiritually reborn have any hope of avoiding the inevitable suffering of mankind.

This harsh vision of humankind's future is tempered by a sense of God's personal involvement in the lives of the faithful. For "visionary" artists, the *Book of Revelation* serves as an underpinning for dramatic visions of human guilt and divine justice. However, unlike the officially sanctioned religious paintings of earlier Christian eras, works by these believers are rarely embraced by the leaders of fundamentalist churches that share their literal acceptance of the prophecies of the *Book of Revelation*. In keeping with a suspicion of art and artists that goes back to the Reformation and was reinforced by the austerities of the Puritan revolution, premillenarian groups tend to privilege the word over the image and to dismiss visual art as a manifestation of "Popery." As a result, so called "outsider artists" inspired directly by the *Book of Revelation* tend to be outsiders not just from mainstream art world, but also from the religious communities from which they spring.

Art historian Carol Crown maintains that representations of hellfire and retribution by self taught artists are expressions of a prophetic inclination grounded in the history and religious culture of the South.[13] Southern evangelicalism centers upon the authority of the Bible, whose texts, however contradictory, are believed by the faithful to present the authentic words of God. It has been deeply influenced by the teachings of the 19th century British Evangelist John Nelson Darby, who was the first to articulate such now familiar tenets of Southern faith as the central role of Israel in the events leading up to Armageddon and the promise that the faithful will be raptured up to heaven before the bloody chaos of the final battle between good and evil. Such teachings were appealing to a society still reeling from its loss in the Civil War. For white Evangelicals in the South, Biblical narratives about the power and ultimate triumph of God are haunted by their own sense of political and psychological defeat. For black evangelicals, accounts of the Israelites' delivery from Egypt into the Promised Land are tied up with the legacy of slavery. The *Book of Revelation* speaks to both these groups because it promises the liberation of the just and the ultimate defeat and punishment of God's enemies.

Self-taught religious artists frequently partake of the Southern tradition of the itinerant preacher called to testify by visions or Divine Command. For them, art is the product of a direct communication with God and their works are the instruments of their evangelical mission. The current vogue for "outsider art" among museums and secular art collectors has created a market that somewhat dilutes this purpose, but a very real belief in good and evil remains embedded in the works. Artists like Howard Finster, Myrtice West, William Thomas Thompson and Robert Roberg fit into this mold. Each of them came to painting later in life and turned to a deeper connection with religion in response to traumatic or life altering events. All found answers to their dilemmas in *The Book of Revelation*, as well as other scriptures.

A self-proclaimed man of visions from rural Georgia, Howard Finster received his first revelation when he was three years old as he watched his recently deceased older sister rise up before him and climb a flight of steps to heaven. After four decades of preaching the Gospel as a Baptist minister while supporting his family with odd jobs, Finster found his new calling at age sixty. One day a voice interrupted him while he was repairing, a bicycle and commanded him to "paint sacred art." His most ambitious sacred artwork was *Paradise Garden*, a four acre environment comprising sculptures created from salvaged junk, mosaic walkways, signboards and the World's

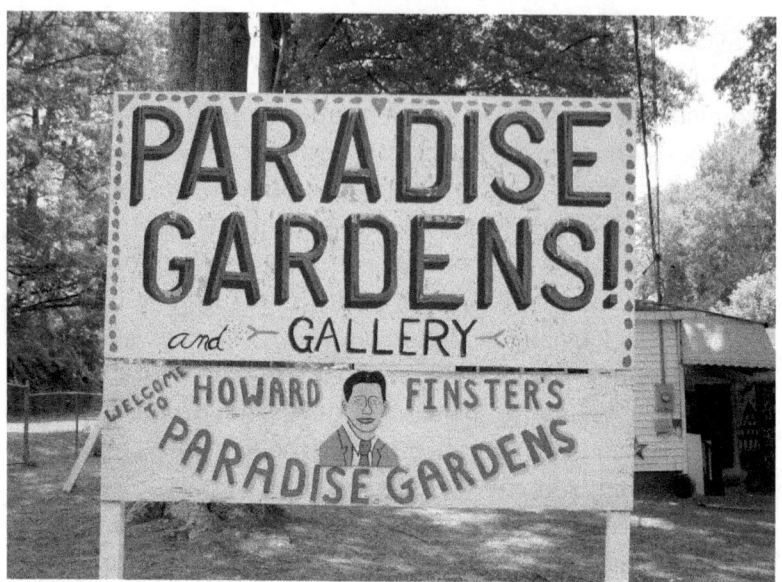

fig. 8 Howard Finster, *Paradise Garden*, 1961- 2001, signboard

Folk Art Church, a chapel with a 16-sided cupola. *(fig. 8)* He continued to elaborate on this work for the rest of his life. He also began to create "sermons in paint," which consisted of paintings of evangelical messages in text and images. These involved both Biblical quotations and Finster's own commentaries on them. Some, addressed to sinners, are meant to be terrifying. Others present reassuring images of paradise and peace. The former category includes *Vision of a Great Gulf on Planet Hell*. This dense work entwines various beasts and demons as described in *Revelations* with blocks of text meant to scare viewers into reforming their ways. "Serpents, Saten (sic) and Devils will be cursed by those they deceived," he advises. "No one likes it here." And pointedly, "If you make it to Hell, you can say Howard told you about it on earth." While such paintings manifest Finster's adherence to Biblical descriptions of the coming End Times, *Paradise Garden* offers a different story. In its celebration of the beauty of nature and the immanence of God in the world, it embodies what Crown calls Finster's theology of amilennialism, the belief that the Judgment Day of *Revelation* has already happened and manifests itself within the hearts of the faithful.

Unlike Finster, whose take on scripture is more personal and idiosyncratic, the paintings of Myrtice West present a literal reading of the events and images from *Revelation*. West was Finster's friend and neighbor. Her vision is tied up the difficulties of her own life. These include several miscarriages, brothers lost in the Second World War, states of depression, and most horrifically, the murder of her beloved daughter by the girl's ex-husband in the presence of their two children. Like Finster, West traces her commitment to art to a vision that descended on her when, in the midst of a church service, she began to speak in tongues. This coincided with a period in which she was turning obsessively to the Bible to deal with the news that her son-in-law was beating her daughter. She created her first paintings of the *Book of Revelation* at this time. Colored, perhaps, by these events, West's focus in this series is on the guilt of sinners and the fury of God. Adhering to *Revelation's* prophecies about the rebuilding of the Temple of Jerusalem, West was obsessed with the role of the Jews as precipitators of the End Times. Softening this a bit is a promise of his mercy toward believers

In her work, text is kept to a minimum. Episodes appear as described in the Biblical narrative, with multiple vignettes arranged on vestigial landscapes without regard to conventional perspective. The more important images - Christ returning on a large steed, the multi-headed beast, or the woman on the moon - are rendered largest, with flocks of angels, marauding demons and other supporting characters scattered behind.

One work from this series is more improvisational, as it was based on a dream inspired by West's immersion in the *Book of Revelation*. In *Satan Takes Over*, a giant head with pointed ears and an open mouth overlays a contemporary landscape. Small figures cower as a flood unleashes snakes, here representing Satan's agents, toward oblivious bystanders. At the upper corners, the scene is flanked by a Church and the U.S. Capitol Building, both infiltrated by agents of the anti-Christ. The End Times are graphically suggested by a representation of the hand of God on a stopwatch, about to switch time off. Evil has invaded the contemporary world, the work tells us, and the end is almost here.

In *The Colorful Apocalypse*,[14] his fascinating study of the Apocalyptic tendencies in outsider art, English professor Greg Bottoms questions West about the respective messages conveyed by herself and her neighbor Finster. West tells him, "If you want to know the difference between me and Howard, it's that Howard was always trying to help the sinner. He wanted to forgive people and help people. There was people around here all the time, laughing and carrying on, lots of them sinners. Howard wanted people to find God and love each other and be happy. I reckon that was the Southern Baptist in him." Bottoms asks her to describe her message. She replies, "My message is that this is the end. I saw Jesus in that Holiness Church. His hands was braided together, held up over his head, like this here and in between his fingers, in the light, was a message about the Jews and the end of the World."[15]

Another take on *Revelation* appears in the work of South Carolina based artist William Thomas Thompson. A fundamentalist Christian since age 13, Thompson is a self-described, self-made millionaire who lost his fortune in the late 1980s when the market for his imported silk flowers dried up. During this difficult period he also contracted Guillain-Barre syndrome, a disorder of the nervous system that left him semi-paralyzed. His transition from businessman to painter occurred in 1989. One Sunday during a church service in Hawaii where he was being treated for his condition, he experienced a vision of the Apocalypse. He took the vision as a call to art, and though he had no artistic training, immediately bought some paints and began to recreate what he had seen. Eventually, he received the divine command to paint the entire *Book of Revelation*.

In some ways, Thompson's handicap has been an asset. Because he has difficulty handling the brushes, he works on the floor and mixes the paint directly on the canvas. This gives his paintings a loose gestural quality that works beautifully with his dramatic imagery. His *Revelation* saga is a three hundred foot long continuous mural pieced together from six square foot pieces. **(pl. 8)** Thompson has also created smaller, stand alone representations of the various characters in the text. His paintings include both images from the *Book of Revelation*, hand written transcriptions of the relevant passages and Thompson's own commentaries. Thus they function like annotated illuminated manuscripts. He makes the most of the hellfire and brimstone aspects of *Revelation*, with giant swells of water and walls of fire created from torrents of brushstrokes that overwhelm the smaller human figures in their wake.

In *The Colorful Apocalypse*, Bottoms describes several weeks he spent with Thompson. He reveals Thompson's own belief system to be an amalgam of the standard fundamentalist teaching on *Revelation* combined with other more idiosyncratic views on the villainy of Catholics, Jews, and Masons, the perfidy of organized religion and Thompson's belief that the real lost tribes of Israel are the Anglo Saxons of Western Europe. Thompson posts these views on his website[16] as part of a daily journal in which he sees signs of the Endtimes in contemporary developments as diverse as the wars in Iraq and Afghanistan, the "socialism" of the Democrats, the earthquake in Haiti and the international banking crises. Bottoms highlights Thompson's marketing savvy, as he downplays his incendiary rhetoric when speaking to collectors, curators and dealers who might be uncomfortable with his views on Muslims and Jews and his decidedly non-ironic vision of Evil.

Robert Roberg's transforming vision occurred in 1977 while he was driving through the night in the California desert with his family sleeping in the back of his Volkswagen van. He reports that he was lifted from his vehicle into a bright light where Jesus told him he had to change. Prior to this, Roberg considered himself a Christian, but was floundering spiritually and economically. Having served in the Peace Corps after college, he was drafted into the Vietnam War. He ran off to Mexico before he was shipped off, eventually doing time in a military prison in Texas for desertion. For a time after that he was employed as a child abuse investigator for the State of Washington, a job that left him emotionally depleted. At the time of his vision he was between jobs and uncertain of his future.

The vision prompted Roberg to join the Mennonite church. Church officials sent him to Nashville to set up new congregation. One day, when attempting to connect with strangers while preaching on the street, he took up some chalk and began to illustrate his sermon with drawings on the sidewalk. Suddenly bystanders who had been ignoring him took an interest in what he was saying. He realized that art was a way to purvey his message. In the years since, he has created hundreds of Scripture-based paintings, including a large number based on the *Book of Revelation*. These brightly colored works incorporate glitter, Dayglo paint and even nail polish. Often they include snippets of floating text and creatures drawn from Scriptures or from his own sermons interpreting those passages. The flat frontal representations and stylized landscapes may owe something to the folk art he observed while serving in the Peace Corps in Peru. The paintings often include topical and even humorous details, as when he depicts the Whore of Babylon as a blond woman in a slinky evening gown riding a hot pink beast. *(fig. 9)*

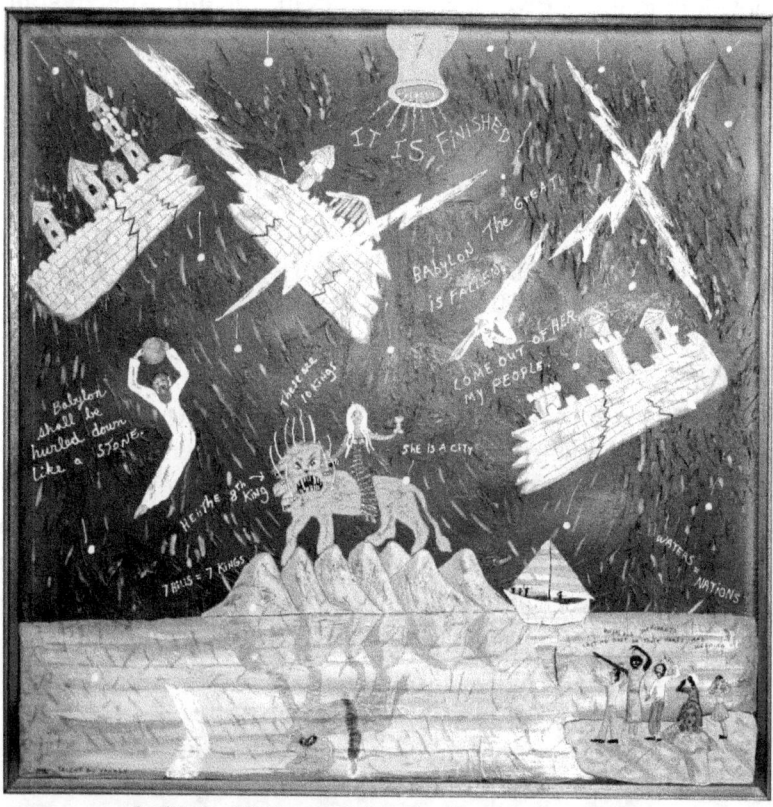

fig. 9 Robert Roberg, *Babylon, the Great, is Fallen*, 1992,
Smithsonian American Art Museum

Unlike some other visionary artists, Roberg sees himself as a pacifist and has criticized the hypocrisy of a "Christian war," noting, "Those who preach militarism in Jesus' name are preaching damnable lies."[17] He adds, "Looking at the whole book [of *Revelation*], God comes off as a peevish, flip-flopping tyrant who wallows in blood. It was then that it hit me that Jesus never taught this and all those other writers had it wrong. The God of Jesus is loving and kind. This put me way out of step with the Amish-Mennonites and I left the church." No longer officially affiliated with any church, he maintains his ministry through painting and teaching.

Not all visionary artists take their mission public. James Hampton, like Henry Darger, who will be discussed in chapter 4, did his work in secret for some presumably future unveiling that never occurred. Details about Hampton's life are sketchy. He was born in 1909 into a community of African-American sharecroppers and tenant farmers in Elloree, South Carolina and was raised a fundamentalist Baptist. His father was a Gospel singer and self-ordained Baptist minister who left the family to pursue his calling. At age 19 Hampton moved to Washington D.C. and worked as a short order cook. He was drafted into the army in 1942, where he served in Saipan and Guam. He was employed in Washington D.C. as a night janitor for the General Services Administration from the War's end until his death in 1964.

Hampton never married and had few close friends. But as with many visionary artists, an apparently impoverished outer existence masked a rich interior life. His magnum opus was *The Throne of the Third Heaven of the Nations Millennium General Assembly*, a massive room size installation created in a rented garage and fashioned from such found and scavenged materials as aluminum and gold foil, discarded furniture, desk blotters, cardboard rolls, jelly glasses, mirror shards and light bulbs. **(pl. 9)** Because this installation was not discovered until after his death, it is not clear when and how Hampton received the calling to devote himself to art. His writings suggest that he experienced a series of visions throughout his life beginning when he was twenty-one.

The Throne, which occupied him from 1950 until his death, consists of 180 objects, including an altar, a throne, offertory tables, pulpits, mercy seats, and other objects. Its debt to the *Book of Revelation* is evident both in scraps of inscribed texts and in the arrangement of the whole, which reflects *Revelation's* separation of saved and damned. Objects referring to the New Testament are placed on the right side of the central throne and to the Old on the left. The throne itself is a realization of verses from *Revelation:* 20 and 21. There is also an accompanying commentary in an invented alphabet that fills a 108 page loose leaf notebook and is titled *St James: The Book of the 7 Dispensations.*

On Hampton's death, his landlord took the installation in lieu of unpaid rent. It is now in the collection of the Smithsonian Institution and has attracted serious commentary. Scholar Robert Farris Thompson links the ornamental style of the work to Kongo -American practice of decorating ritual objects made from cast offs and foil as well as the Haitian practice of inserting tinfoil into a charm to attract the spirits.[18] Scientist Stephen Jay Gould, meanwhile, has been intrigued by the conceptualization of time he perceives in this work. He argues that it offers a reconciliation of the tension inherent in Judeo Christian thought between "time's arrow" – a linear conception of history – and "time's cycle," a vision of time as a set of recurring events. Gould points the mirror image symmetry of the work's Old Testament and New Testament halves. He believes these express a sense of time that is both linear and progressive and faithful to the process by which events in the Old Testament prefigure events in the New. [19] Meanwhile, evidence in Hampton's own writings suggest that he was planning, upon completion of this work, to use it as the basis of a new religion.

For artists like these, painting (or in Hampton's case, sculpting) the Apocalypse is a sacred charge, part of a larger evangelical mission. Artists within the mainstream art world who employ *Revelation*-inspired imagery also tend to come from intensely religious backgrounds. However, having moved on from their childhood faith, these artists transfer the Apocalypse from the realm of fact into that of metaphor. The questions of evil, guilt, judgment and salvation embodied in the Endtimes narrative are personalized and internalized in their work. A veneer of humor or irony often allows them some distance from the still powerful pull of these religious doctrines, and in the gap between faith and disbelief they find other ways to exploit these powerful images.

The work of Howard Finster and other visionary artists greatly influenced Roger Brown, the Chicago Imagist. Brown was raised in Alabama in the Church of Christ, a fundamentalist denomination that embraces a fire and brimstone interpretation of Christianity. In his youth, Brown was steeped in this teaching, to the point of aspiring to be a preacher. However his interest in art eventually won out and he moved to Chicago to study at the School of the Art Institute of Chicago. There he left the Church of Christ behind but biblical imagery, especially relating to apocalypse and rapture, remained a powerful source for his art. Brown's *Beast Rising from the Sea* (1983) follows the biblical description closely. (**pl. 10**) It presents a black silhouette of the Beast's seven heads, leopard body and bear feet emerging from a still lake against the artist's trademark billowing sky. Yet, as artist and writer Jerry Bleem points out, this beast has little authority and no teeth.[20] A more free form version of *Revelation* appears in a work titled *An Actual dream of the Second Coming* (1976) that transports *Revelation's* doomsday vision to a waterfront city not unlike Brown's adopted city Chicago. In the foreground are boxy buildings whose windows serve as stages for figures in different poses of despair. Outside, the edge of the water bursts into flames while above, a progressively redder sky is dotted with angels ascending to heaven. Meanwhile the earth and water open up to expel the skeletal figures of the risen dead.

In these and other works, Brown cultivated a neo-naïve style, born equally of comics, folk art, cinematic posters and surrealism. His paintings employ small highly stylized silhouette figures with bouffant hairdos and dramatic gestures; skyscrapers inscribed with grids of windows which frame backlit figural tableaux; swelling skies whose clouds hang like swags of drapery; and fearsomely flat farmlands dotted with tiny farmhouses. The works are at once dryly comic and quietly moralistic and the horrors they portray are offset by the apparent innocence of the childlike presentation. But whether dealing with religious or secular themes, these paintings are conditioned by Brown's early exposure to a world with strict demarcations between good and evil where human folly ushers in some form of divine or natural wrath.

Brown returned continually to biblical themes, but always with a twist. His *Story of Creation* (1989) offers his version of the expulsion from Paradise, that moment in Genesis that sets in motion the series of events that will lead to the final Judgment. Here three small figures representing Adam, Eve and the angel move to the right, like figures exiting offstage. Above the face of the country singer Kenny Rogers appears in a gold nimbus in the role of God. A round target of red, white and blue stripes contains an outline of north and South America. One senses a reference to the notion of the New World as the Promised Land, and wonders whether it represents a place of exile or redemption. The *Seven Last Plagues* (1988), meanwhile, presents the end of the biblical narrative, with seven discrete vignettes of modern day figures buffeted by drought, famine, plague, pollution, moral decadence warfare and natural disaster.

As a gay man who rejected the repressive teachings of his childhood religion, Brown's work is permeated with his skepticism toward established church teachings on sexuality and sin. At the same time, one senses his continuing attraction to Christianity's message of hope and salvation. This is particularly clear in *The Devils Surprise* (n.d.). Here, it is the churchgoers who are consigned to the flames of hell, while above, on billowing clouds, the 'saved' continue their earthly pursuits of dancing and lovemaking.

One finds a similar mix of spiritual yearning, religious skepticism and refigured Christian imagery in the work of Keith Haring. Like Brown, Haring cultivated a deliberate stylistic naiveté, in his case drawing on popular forms like cartoons, graffiti and also Art Brut, or Raw Art, as practiced by artists like Jean Dubuffet and Pierre Alechinsky. His deceptively simple line drawings are composed of an ever-evolving vocabulary of pictographic images that allowed him to comment on politics, sexuality, religion, literature and art history.

Haring first came to public notice for his guerilla subway drawings dashed off in chalk on black papered boards awaiting advertisements. Because these ephemeral works presented accessible imagery in the service of an apparently sunny world dominated by dancing figures, barking dogs, flying saucers and winged angels, Haring is sometimes dismissed as a lightweight, commercially oriented artist. But in fact, in drawings and paintings for a less public audience (and sometimes in the subway works as well), Haring explored a much darker and more complex reality. Much of this, it turns out, was deeply indebted to his religious upbringing.

Recently this side of Haring's work has come under greater scrutiny. Haring, who was born in 1958, was raised in Kutztown, Pennsylvania in the United Church of God, an evangelical Protestant sect that promises the establishment of an earthly paradise after the Second Coming of Christ. The damned, in this version of the Endtimes, will not be cast into hell but will be utterly destroyed and obliterated. As a young teen, Haring moved away from the harsher elements of this teaching. Instead he was swept up into the Jesus Movement, a countercultural version of Christianity that reached its heights in the late 1960s, and emphasized spiritual fellowship, community action and compassion. The movement also involved a fervent belief in the imminence of Apocalypse. One of the favorite books of these so-called "Jesus Freaks" was Hal Lindsey's *The Late Great Planet Earth*. This wildly popular reworking of the *Book of Revelation* discerned in contemporary events the fulfillment of the eschatological prophecies in the Bible.

Art historian Natalie Phillips has detailed Haring's involvement with the Jesus Movement and argues that this brief involvement, along with his childhood immersion in the United Church of God, left an indelible imprint on his work.[21] Recurring symbols in his work include crosses, haloes, angels, demons, bleeding hearts and of course his signature emblem, the radiant child. This cherubic baby has been interpreted in multiple ways: as a self-portrait; a representation of the Christ Child emanating rays of light; and an irradiated victim of nuclear holocaust. In the paintings and drawings, these and other emblems are arranged in complex tableaux that illustrate Haring's views on good, evil, love, death and sexuality. Many of Haring's compositions reveal a rejection of organized religion, and in particular a sharp anger against religious leaders who saw the AIDS epidemic as divine retribution against homosexuals like himself. But other works suggest the powerful hold that Christian doctrine retained on his view of the world.

Haring's life, like his art, was rife with contradictions that tend to cloud our understanding of his work. On one hand, he was an obsessively drug using, night clubbing hedonist. On the other, he loved and was loved by children and worried that news of his homosexuality might make it difficult to continue to work with them. In certain ways he personified the "radiant child" while at the same time he used his work to plumb the depths of human corruption and depravity. His popular commercial work existed in tandem with works that contained acid social critique. Such contradictions parallel the contradictory meanings of religion in his life. As a gay man who rebelled against the homophobia of his childhood religion, he also embraced its ecstatic visions and powerful images of heaven and hell. And he produced some of the most powerful contemporary visions of the Endtimes.

For instance, an untitled work from 1985 uses images drawn directly from the *Book of Revelation* to suggest the horrors of hell. Set against a fiery red backdrop are all manner of humanoid and animalesque demons. Delineated in Haring's signature black line, they simultaneously devour and sexually assault the unfortunate damned. The center of the composition is claimed by Haring's version of *Revelation's* Whore of Babylon, here a half-figure with an erect penis. His/her torso sprouts writhing serpents and he/she sits astride a multi eyed, many teated beast. *Revelation* returns in a collaboration with William Burroughs. Titled *Apocalypse* (1988), it is a set of prints which pair Burroughs' hallucinogenic texts about a very New York centered apocalypse with visualizations by Haring. These play off rather than directly illustrate the texts. Each combines one or more images taken from art history or advertising with frenzied line drawings that modernize *Revelation*'s most perverse creations in Haring's inimitable style. **(pl. 11)** Haring used many of the same motifs in other works in which mushroom clouds, nuclear molecules and the radiant child carry a double reference to enlightenment and to radioactive fallout.

Haring's final work, finished just two weeks before his death from in 1990, was a bronze and gold triptych for the Cathedral of St. John the Divine in New York City. It is a representation of *The Life Of Christ* and depicts a baby nestled in a pair of arms above a crowd of agitated figures as winged figures ascend toward heaven. This work suggests the other side of religion – the hope for the future embodied in the eschatological narrative.

Raymond Pettibon is Haring's contemporary and like Haring, he was shaped by the post-1960s hangover that descended after the Age of Aquarius disintegrated into the nightmares of Watergate, Charlie Manson, and the Symbionese Liberation Army. While Haring found solace in the Jesus Movement, Pettibon drifted toward Punk. He grew up in the surfing enclave of Hermosa Beach, California, and was raised as a Christian Scientist over the objections of his Catholic father. It is tempting to read that sect's metaphysical idealism as the original target of Pettibon's restless, demolition prone imagination.

After earning an economics degree from UCLA in 1977 and working briefly as a high school mathematics teacher, Pettibon turned to art, gaining his first recognition as the creator of fliers, album covers and gift items for Black Flag, the punk band started by his brother Greg Ginn in 1977. Although his work reflects the anarchic anti-authoritarian outlook of Punk, Pettibon has always distanced himself from identification with that movement. And in fact his dark, skeptical work mocks Punk as much as it does hippies, religious cultists, acid freaks and other countercultural icons.

Pettibon's collage-like drawings and wall works reflect an omnivorous populist spirit. He combines text and images, references to high and low culture, and historical, fictional and contemporary figures. The drawings are composed of reassembled bits of Victorian poetry, rewritten slogans, and partial thoughts scrawled over cartoonish images of surfers, mushroom clouds, iconic superheroes, political figures, baseball players and gruesome crime scenes. In Pettibon's leveling process, Gumby meets Socrates, and Saturday morning cartoons mingle with quotations from Proust, Blake, Beckett, and the Bible. At first glance, the work appears deliberately adolescent, like the tapestry of sketches, scrawls, and fanzine pages one might have once found tacked on a teenage boy's bedroom wall. But in fact Pettibon is grappling with profound issues.

Chief among these are questions about the false promises of politics, religion, art, drugs, sex and rock and roll. There are frequent references to Christianity, as in a 1985 drawing in which the text reads: "One mustn't pray too hard, or God will think you are dissatisfied with life, and scoop you up." The Christian Diety often appears, as curator Ulrich Loock has noted, in humiliating circumstances.[22] In a 1988 drawing an image of Christ is accompanied with the question "Have you cured cancer?" Other works turn spleen upon believers. Pettibon's installation for the 2004 Whitney Biennial provides a veritable inventory of creation, from jellyfish to humans to supernovas, overwritten with the scrawled question: "How can we have projected onto him lights so dim and powers so unsteady?" A 1991 drawing from a series that simply depicts the black front cover of the Bible (a book Pettibon reports he has read twice in its entirety), is given the inscription, "It is idle to look for proportion and design in a book that contains the world?"

Through the 1980s Pettibon turned frequently to the motif of Charles Manson. The notorious murder of actress Sharon Tate and six others by Manson's "family" of misfits occurred in 1969 when Pettibon was twelve. He recalls a neighbor remarking that Manson was the personification of Evil. Reportedly, Manson was inspired by the Biblical apocalypse as reinterpreted through the Beatles song *Helter Skelter*. In Pettibon's hands Manson becomes a figure of the Antichrist, at once a scapegoat, a media distraction from the other evils of the time and the specter of middle America's fears of the era's social and sexual upheavals. One particularly menacing portrait of Manson from

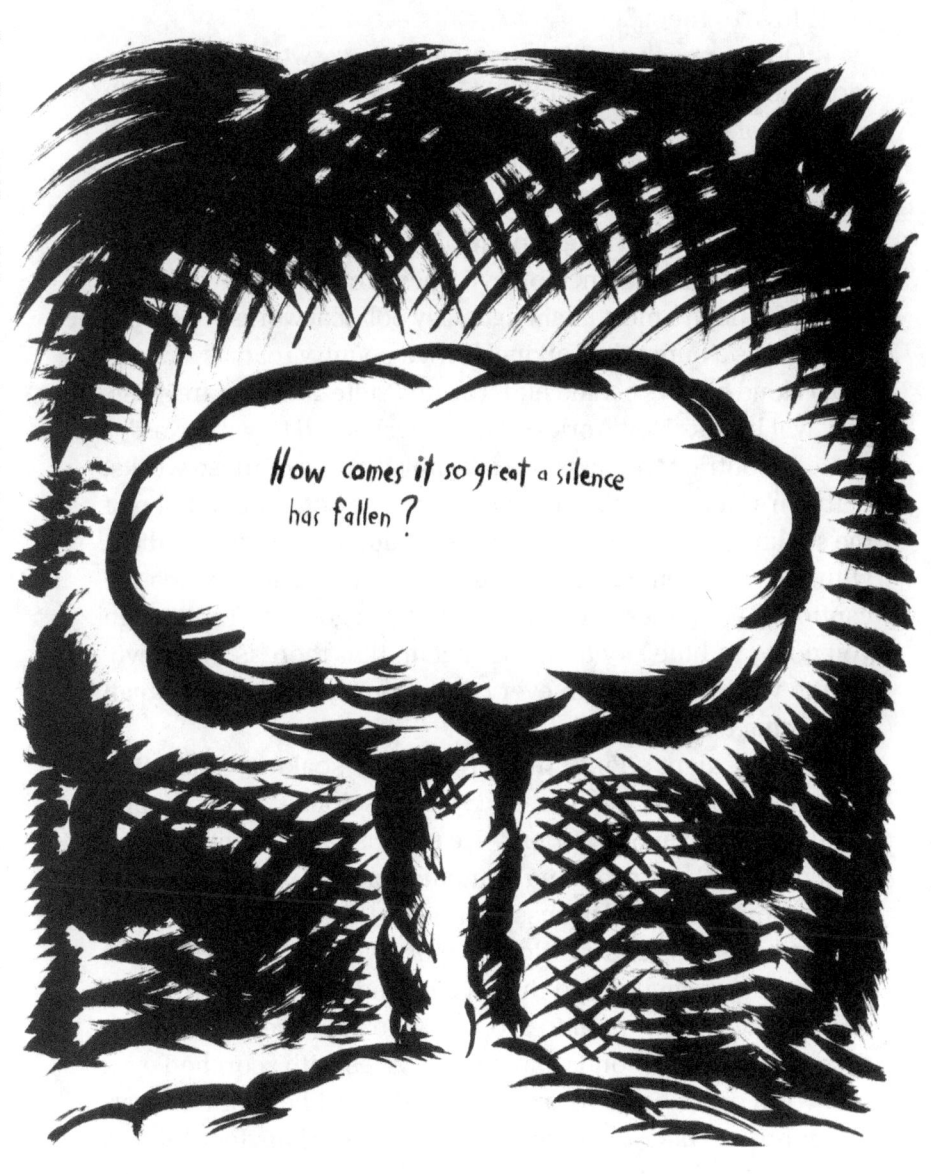

fig. 10 Raymond Pettibon, *No Title (How comes it...)* from *Plots on Loan I*, 2000,
lithograph print on paper, 19 x 14 inches

1987 includes a scrawled epithet that make the connection explicit: "Crucify me – I'm completely innocent" along with the notation, "They would rather I slaughtered their daughters than made love to them."

Other apocalyptic themes include fires, swords and mushroom clouds that later morph into representations of the Shock and Awe of the Iraq War. *(fig. 10)* A 2008 drawing is dominated by a fiery blossom accompanied by texts that read: "The flower of Fallujah opens its every petal . . . They love us, they love us n (sic)." While earlier images of death and destruction are more ambiguous in their stance on evil, these Iraq war drawings are among Pettibon's most unambiguously political works. One from 2010 shows a bumpkin walking down a country road as a mushroom cloud billows behind him. The text states, "If they are smart they will bypass New York and Los Angeles and target Texas."

In contrast to the darkly pessimistic tone of these works, Pettibon's iconic drawings of surfers are, he notes, his version of the sublime. Giant waves dwarf small figures, or surround them with uncertain energy. A 2001 drawing of a surfer carries the caption "That underneath your feet, if you go down far enough you come to blue sky and stars again; that there is no 'down' for the world, but only in every direction 'up' and this is an all embracing truth."

Like a giant sponge indiscriminately soaking up the flotsam of society's conscious and subconscious, Pettibon spits out unexpected juxtapositions. He reflects on humanity's fallen condition with an arresting combination of existential dread and gallows humor. Discussing the anti-theological currents in Pettibon's work, critic Robert Storr writes, " . . . Pettibon's art speaks in tongues and they speak End Times. However we are dealing with a Gnostic prophet who promises no rapture, no salvation, no Second Coming. Who sees with scorched eyes the world described by Hazel Motes, the anti hero of Flannery O'Connor's *Wise Blood*, before he recovered his lost faith, a world where the blind stay blind and dead stay dead, in truth a planet on a death trip which is nearing its destination . . . In his still evolving Book of Revelations, there is no Heaven but there is a Hell – and it is here on earth."[23]

Brown, Haring and Pettibon all were raised under the influence of versions of Bloom's American Religion. Within their evangelical communities references to *Revelation*'s beasts, sinners, false prophets and demons are commonplace and almost second nature, so it is not surprising to see such motifs surfacing in their work. Catholics and mainstream Protestants place much less emphasis on the *Book of Revelation*. The end still looms for them as it does for their fire and brimstone brethren. However, as we shall see in Chapter 7, their view of the Second Coming of Christ differs markedly from that of most evangelical Christians. In place of the evangelical focus on retribution, death and destruction, members of these more mainstream groups envision the final stage of history as a movement toward the perfection of the Christian community. This may explain why artists from these backgrounds tend to picture the End in a more abstract manner.

This is evident in the works of Paul Pfeiffer and Ed Ruscha. Pfeiffer is the child of Methodist missionaries. Born in Hawaii, he was raised in the Philippines and went to high school on a Navaho reservation. His work involves the digital manipulation of both found and newly created film footage, much of the latter consisting of clips from Hollywood movies or archival televised sports footage. His manipulations radically alter the sense of time and space conveyed by the original clips. He frequently takes a very short sequence and runs it as a loop after having digitally removed the most significant details of the action. Thus for instance, in a short clip of Knicks forward Larry Johnson jumping elatedly after a successful shot in a stadium, he erases all details of audience, other players, Johnson's own insignia and even the ball itself. The resulting clip becomes strangely ritualized. We see an isolated figure on an empty court caught in an endlessly repeated facial expression that appears more like existential pain than frenzied triumph. Pfeiffer presents such works on miniature video screens attached to the wall, further estranging them from the pop culture contexts that are their sources.

On the surface, Pfeiffer's oddly mesmerizing videos have little to do with religion. Instead they seem to deal with the experience of spectatorship and perception. But the artist frequently gives his works evocative titles drawn from the Bible, thus suggesting a deeper significance. The work described above, for instance, is titled *Fragment of a Crucifixion, After Francis Bacon* (1999), an acknowledgment of its kinship with Bacon's paintings of screaming Christs on the cross. His *John:13* (2000), meanwhile, presents a video loop of a basketball game from the perspective of the ball. It hovers, slightly vibrating in the center of the screen as hands, basket and details of the court flash by. As the still center of this frenetic world, the ball presents a metaphoric homage to the passage in the Gospel of John referred to in the work's title, a passage that promises believers eternal life.

Another series is named *Four Horsemen of the Apocalypse* (2006), even though, as Pfeiffer admits, there are actually more than four figures involved. An early version of this series involved the erasure of the image of Marilyn Monroe from a found movie clip, leaving behind only a ghostly aura. Later versions involved video clips drawn from the online archive of NBA games. In these works, Pfeiffer removed all context, even at times the focal figure. All that remains is the inexplicable actions of some secondary player jumping on an empty court. In combination with the title, the erasure of most of the details of the world from these works begins to feel apocalyptic, as if we are watching the world as we know it disappear.

Pfeiffer's *Study for Morning After the Deluge* (2001), takes this feeling even further. **(pl. 12)** The title of this work evokes both the flood in Genesis that almost annihilated humankind as well as the luminous, nearly abstract canvas of the same name by J.M.W. Turner. (Turner's title in full is *Light and Color (Goethe's Theory) – The Morning After the Deluge – Moses Writing the Book of Genesis* (1843). Turner's painting is one of his late nearly abstract canvases. A tiny figure of Moses emerges from a circular whorl of blinding light just above a small depiction of the Brazen Serpent that Moses erected in the desert as a cure for the plague. The work is inspired by Goethe's theory of perception and presents a world in which all ordinary coordinates of time and space have disappeared. In Pfeiffer's version we get a repeated loop of the sunrise and sunset, shot in real time. The two halves of the sun are cropped together to make one whole sun, and because the camera is fixed on the sun rather than the horizon, the glowing orb wanders down the frame. Finally it disappears altogether before starting the cycle again. Only an occasional bird flying by ties the image back to our familiar world. As with the Turner painting which it references, one is left with a vision of the fullness of the void in a world nearly bereft of life and human presence.

Absence is also the great subject of California artist Ed Ruscha. An artist associated both with Pop art and the California obsession with light and space, Ruscha is known for works that use words, type faces and rudimentary images in a cinematic way, creating paintings that often resemble the rolling end credits of old style Hollywood Technicolor extravaganzas. There is often a deadpan irony to Ruscha's works – words are presented as graphic demonstrations of the meanings they connote – for instance the word *brews* painted in foamy letters, or *ripe* in what appears to be a gooey mess of juice and pomegranate seeds. Meanwhile, the fields on which they float have an air of unreality. Sometimes they are nothing more than an expanse of saturated color, bringing to mind the suspended rectangles of Mark Rothko. In other works floating words and images are placed within turbulent skies that evoke the noirish atmospherics of the opening sequences of Hitchcock's *Rebecca*. Similarly, the occasional images – a palm tree, a gas station, a galleon in silhouette - are more like markers of a particular kind of scene than they are representations of the things themselves. Indeed, as Ruscha has noted, when he paints say, a mountain, he is really painting "the idea of the idea of the idea of the mountain."[24]

Ruscha is often understood as a commentator on a Hollywood saturated popular culture. However, his works also betray a fascination with mortality and the afterlife that is tied to his Roman Catholic upbringing. Words drawn from catechism (*Sin, Hell, Heaven, Gospel, Devil* and *Angel*) materialize in his paintings, and the dramatic light itself seems as much progeny of Baroque religious art as of Hollywood. In fact, in the mid 1970s he created a set of wordless *Miracle* drawings in which

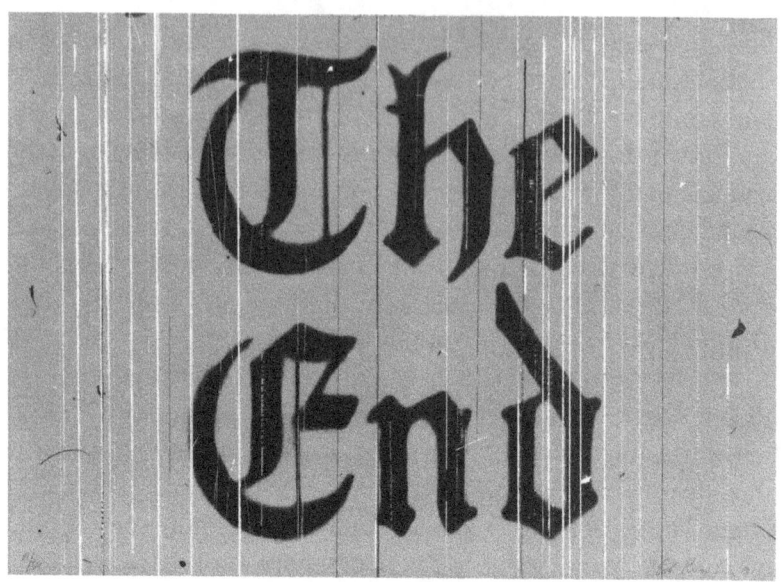

fig. 11 Ed Ruscha, *The End*, 1991, 3-color lithograph,
26 ¼ x 36 5/8 inches, edition of 50

shafts of light burst forth from dark skies. This was reprised in a painting commissioned by the Getty Center in 1998 titled *Picture without Words*. Here light pours into a room from a high window and forms a dazzling white patch on the floor below.

Of particular interest to us are a series of paintings that play with the words *The End*, or simply *End*. On one hand, these mimic the closing screens that used to appear at the end of movies. But set in various typefaces against moody backdrops, they also conjure the idea of Apocalypse. Several form the words *The End* in a Gothic script familiar from old Bibles. *(fig. 11)* Sometimes in these works, the two words rest one on top of the other on a grey striated ground that suggest scratched and spotted celluloid film. In others they are doubled and appear to be slipping off the top and bottom the painting, as if the phrase has been caught between two film frames. In one version, the script is streamlined and the single word *End* (1983) falls across a fiery red and yellow sunset that brings to mind a finish served up with fire and brimstone.

In an interview with art historian Charlene Spretnak, Ruscha discussed his debt to his Catholic upbringing. He remarked, "The [Catholic] Church has, throughout history, presented us with a rich tradition of imagery, and this imagery has had a lasting affect on how I proceed to make an object of art. Icons and their presentations, religious tableaux, incense pendulums, chalices, holy cards, stigmata and rays of light, vestments, the Stations of the Cross, symmetry, and framing all combine to be part of my thinking. These icons and emblems were always more elaborate and deeper in history than the Protestant ones. They enrich my approach to the world and are things I don't want to escape."[25]

Though their approaches are visually quite distinct, Pfeiffer and Ruscha both present a fusion of popular culture and religion under the influence of the Apocalyptic imagination. Less preoccupied with guilt and retribution than visionary artists and their mainstream counterparts Shaw, Brown, Haring and Pettibon, these two instead evoke an emptiness at the core of contemporary experience. In place of Satanic machinations, they evoke the Augustinian notion of evil as the absence of good. In this view, evil is a void in the hearts of men. Pfeiffer and Ruscha suggest that even our most vibrant forms of entertainment - sports and cinema - are shadowed by a sense of dread and unwelcome finality. They offer a vision of the End that manifests itself, in T.S. Eliot's memorable phrase, "not with a bang, but a whimper."

Chapter 3

THE GRAND BATTLE: POLITICS AS METAPHOR

"Fictions, notably the fiction of apocalypse,
turn easily into myths; people will live by
that which was designated only to know by."
– Frank Kermode[1]

Endtimes narratives share certain habits of thought. First and foremost is a preoccupation with evil as an active force in the world. As we noted in the last chapter, this is a departure from the more reassuring vision promulgated by St. Augustine and assumed by more mainstream versions of Christianity, in which evil is simply the absence of good. In this latter formulation, evil is an interior state, the manifestation of human failures of compassion, empathy and love. By contrast, apocalyptic literature views evil as a thing that exists in its own right. This sets up a grand battle between good and evil. Mankind is caught between two supernatural forces whose engagement will inevitably result in the catastrophic end to human endeavors and the ultimate triumph of righteousness, justice and truth. According to this schema, only those who align themselves with the right side will be saved, while those who make the wrong choice deserve their destruction. Such thinking is at its most distilled among adherents of various fundamentalist sects of Christianity, Judaism and Islam, many of whom are waiting, actively or passively, for a sign that the final conflict has begun.

By the second half of the 20th century, it was possible to believe such thinking to be on the wane. As recently as 1995 Humanities scholar Andrew Delbanco could argue that our sense of evil had all but dissipated. In the face of moral relativism, the psychologization of deviance, and the spread of postmodern irony, even Hitler might be seen as a victim of circumstance. In a thoughtful book titled *The Death of Satan*, Delbanco noted, ". . . the triumph of irony has never been as complete as it is today." This, however, is not something Delbanco considered a good thing. He continues, "We have reached a point where it is not only specific objects of belief that have been discredited but the very capacity to believe."[2] Elaborating, he says, "... our culture is now in crisis because evil remains an inescapable experience for all of us, while we no longer have a symbolic language for describing it."[3]

Yet from the perspective of the early 21st century it seems clear that belief in evil, and with it, apocalyptic thinking, have returned with a vengeance. Their influence is striking, whether one looks at popular culture, political discourse, art or literature. Polls consistently suggest that a quarter of the American population believes we are living in the Endtimes. Millennial anxieties lay behind the Y2K, or Year Two Thousand scare, which predicted a worldwide computer shutdown at the turn from the 20th to the 21st century. A year later, the attacks of September 11 provided new grist for Endtimes thinking. A "War on Terror" was declared by a President devoted to a Manichean vision of reality and envisioned by many of his political supporters as a battle that pitted a beneficent democratic West against the evil of "Islamofascism." For many evangelical Christians (and perhaps even the President himself) this conflict was the beginning of the one predicted in the *Book of Revelation*. They believed that it would end in a worldwide reign of peace, in this case, based on the model of American democracy. Such beliefs were encouraged by the fact that the infamous Shock and Awe campaign that opened the war and rained bombs down on Baghdad took place at the geographical location where, according to the *Book of Revelation*, the Sixth Angel is to pour down the wrath of God.

In the region-wide destabilization that followed the Iraq War, old alliances were shaken and long standing leaders challenged during the reform movements known as Arab Spring.

However the initial euphoria soon faded. Non-violent demonstrations and protests were violently suppressed, leading to outbreaks of civil war in Syria, Egypt, Yemen and Libya. Out of this chaos came ISIS (The Islamic State of Iraq and Syria), a virulent version of Islamic apocalypticism that recruited young jihadists with the vision of the utter annihilation of the infidel under the triumphal rule of a world-wide caliphate. While Osama bin Laden had dabbled in apocalyptic rhetoric, the new group maintained that the arrival of the Messiah, the Day of Judgment and the Final Battle are imminent. Its promise of Holy War proved remarkably effective in encouraging disaffected young Muslims throughout the world to flock to the Middle East to join the Islamic State's army or to take the battle to their home countries through suicide missions and terrorist bombings.

In the U.S., doomsday rhetoric seemed to subside after the fizzle of Y2K, the departure of the Bush Administration and the failure of the 2012 Mayan apocalypse to materialize. But in 2016, it returned with a vengeance. During the Presidential campaign, Hillary Clinton continually warned her supporters, "I am the last thing standing between you and the Apocalypse" while veteran Clinton critic Dick Morris's titled his prescient election strategy primer: *Armageddon: How Trump Can Beat Hillary*. These references to *Revelation* may have been metaphorical, but for many evangelical Christians, Trump's election was a sign of the imminence of Apocalypse. Despite the real estate mogul's obvious departure from their prescribed codes of conduct, evangelical Christians formed one of Trump's most important voting blocks. Playing to them he ramped up his anti-Muslim rhetoric, reframing the nation's security concerns as a battle against "radical Islamic terrorism." Closer to home, he referred to his opponent Hillary Clinton as "the devil" and encouraged the view of immigrants and non-whites as aliens stealing the birthright of God's "chosen" people. Disagreement raged in evangelical circles on whether Trump was the Antichrist - the Beast who rises from the sea - or the righteous instrument of a vengeful God. But as one-post election blog put it, "Even if Donald Trump is Satan's chosen one, it is by the <u>Will of God</u> that he should win the election for the purpose of setting the stage for the Second Coming of Jesus Christ, the Messiah." [4]

As these developments demonstrate, politics often exacerbates the more insidious aspects of Endtimes thinking. The apocalyptic mindset provided powerful support for the *us* versus *them* thinking put in place by two World Wars and decades of a battle against 'godless communism,' aka the Evil Empire. The persistence of Endtimes thinking suggests why it has been so easy to conceive of today's political upheavals as simply a reconfiguration of Cold War terror in which communist ideology is replaced by Islamic culture as the source of discord. As developed by political scientists like Samuel Huntington and Bernard Lewis, this tension has been reinterpreted as the "clash of civilizations," shorthand for the belief that the values of the Western and Muslim worlds cannot be reconciled and must inevitably lead to social and military conflict.

Artists with a historical bent help us complicate this apparently simple scenario. Drawing on actual events, they reveal the degree to which "true stories" and "realpolitik" are an amalgam of myth, fantasy, ideology and desire. Take, for instance, the loaded history of the city of Jerusalem. In all three monotheistic traditions, Jerusalem holds a special place, historically and spiritually. It is both the religious capital of Israel and the spiritual homeland of the Jewish people. For Christians, it is the sacred site of Christ's death and resurrection. For Muslims, it is the place where Mohammad ascended to heaven and brought back one of his revelations. Thus, as art historian Abby Kornfeld notes, "Although the city's significance and symbolism vary widely in Jewish, Christian and Islamic traditions, there is a consensus that Jerusalem functions as the meeting place of God and man, the gateway to heaven, the terrestrial threshold of the eternal world."[5] In Jewish, Christian and Islamic literature it serves as the prototype of the Kingdom of Heaven, which is referred to as the New Jerusalem.

Because of its status as a Holy City, the control of Jerusalem has always been an imperative that exceeds nationalistic and strategic concerns. It has changed hands more than twenty times since its establishment by King David as the united capital of the twelve tribes of Israel in 1000 BCE. Sacked by the Babylonians in 597 BCE, it was subsequently ruled by the Persians, Greeks, Romans and eventually various Islamic dynasties before the onslaught of the Crusaders in 1099. They occupied the city, only to lose it to Saladin in 1187. More jostling between various Muslim and non-Muslim tribes followed until the Ottomans took control for four centuries, only losing the Holy City, and in fact their entire empire in the wake of their defeat in the First World War. The British governed an increasingly fractious city until the end of the Second World War and the establishment of the modern state of Israel. Today Jerusalem is a key locale in the ongoing Israeli-Palestinian conflict and the struggle to find a negotiated settlement. Surveying this contentious narrative, historian Hunt Janin remarks that "it is possible that more blood has been shed for Jerusalem than for any other city on the face of the earth."[6]

Central to Jerusalem's turmoil are the prophecies surrounding the Temple of Jerusalem. These provide the background for Israeli artist Yael Bartana's cinematically spectacular video, *Inferno*. The Temple plays a key role in the apocalyptic narratives of Judaism, Christianity and Islam. A symbol of the unity of the Jewish people, it was originally built in 957 BCE by King Solomon and destroyed in 587 BCE when the Babylonians sacked the city of Jerusalem. The Temple was rebuilt in 538 BCE after the fall of the Babylonian empire, and remained the center of Jewish worship for centuries. It appears in the New Testament as the place where Jesus was christened and where he later banished the money lenders. At the moment of his death, the evangelist Matthew reports that the veil separating the Holy of Holies from the rest of the Temple spontaneously ripped. Hebrew history, meanwhile, describes how the Temple was expanded by Herod in 20 BCE, and then destroyed in 70 AD by the Romans during Emperor Titus' siege of Jerusalem.

As we noted in Chapter 1, this second destruction inspired John of Patmos to write the *Book of Revelation*. The rebuilding of the Temple is foretold both in that text and in its predecessor, the Hebrew Bible's Book of Ezekial. It is a dream cherished both by Zionist groups who see it as a symbol of Jewish nationalism and Christian fundamentalists who regard it as a necessary prelude to the onset of the Endtimes. However, the situation is greatly complicated by the presence of an Islamic shrine, the Dome of the Rock, which was constructed on the site of the former Temple following the Muslim conquest of Jerusalem in the seventh century. Most recently, the Trump Administration's transfer of the American Embassy to Jerusalem threatens to upend a tenuous power balance. No wonder this small piece of land is one of the central sites of the Clash of Civilizations.

With her 2013 video *Inferno*, Bartana plunges into this stew of competing claims. **(pl. 13)** The work came about when she was invited to do a project in Brazil and discovered that an evangelical Christian group was rebuilding the prophesied Third Temple of Jerusalem in the city Sao Paulo. Bartana used the plans for this new Temple as a template for her own version. In the video, Bartana's Temple provides the destination for a videotaped procession comprised of Brazilians garbed in white and sporting Carmen Miranda style headgear. Once there, we see the performers celebrate the inauguration of the New Temple. The ceremony is presided over by a high priest played by Marcia Pantera, a famous Sao Paulo drag queen. The joy of the faithful is short-lived, however, as the Temple is beset by fire and earthquake. It crumbles around the participants in a conflagration worthy of Hollywood. The film ends at the Wailing Wall, a rebuilt remnant of the Second Temple in Jerusalem that serves now as a Jewish pilgrimage site. In Bartana's video, various characters from the Sao Paolo celebration, including a Christ-like figure in ancient garb, wander among the present day tourists and worshipers.

The mix of history and fiction in *Inferno* is in keeping with Bartana's best-known project *And Europe Will Be Stunned*, (2011). That three part video work chronicles a fictional movement to establish a Jewish homeland in Poland following the near destruction of that country's Jewish population in the Holocaust. Similarly playing with historically inspired hopes and fears, *Inferno* acknowledges the Temple's multilayered symbolism. The participants' mix of races reflects both Brazil's ethnic diversity and the hope for universal salvation embodied by the local Christians who are somewhat absurdly rebuilding the Temple in Sao Paolo. The apocalyptic denouement of the video drew very different responses when the work was shown to various audiences. In Brazil, blogs denounced the "gay movie about destroying Solomon's Temple in Brazil," a reference to the presence of Marcia Pantera. Germans saw the video as a reference to Kristallnacht. Jews in the United States saw it as a statement about the impossibility of rebuilding the Temple. In Israel, the main reaction seems to have been confusion, re- flecting perhaps the similarly confused debate over the present and future disposition of the Temple Mount itself.[7] Playing with fact, fiction and myth, Bartana reveals how the same history gives credence to religious "truths" that directly contradict each other.

Jerusalem reappears as a contested site in a three part vid- eo epic by Egyptian artist Wael Shawky. His *Cabaret Crusades* (2010-2012) takes as a point of departure Amim Maaalouf's 1984 revisionist history *The Crusades through Arab Eyes*. Like the book, Shawky's elaborate series of videos offers an alternative version of the Clash of Civilizations. As seen here, the focus shifts from the Christian narrative of the Crusades as a war to reclaim Jerusalem from the Muslims to a much more confusing history marked by a complicated series of shifting political and religious alliances and conflicts.

The three films, each of which was commissioned by a different presenter, all employ puppets moving through elabo- rate sets to a voiceover script in classic Arabic. Each has a very distinctive aesthetic. The first installment, *The Horror Show File*, uses refurbished 200-year-old wooden marionettes from the famous Lupi collection in Turin. It chronicles the bloody years of the first crusade, beginning with a prequel that depicts the plague that devastated the Byzantine Empire in the years 541-543. This disaster weakened the empire and provided an opening for the Muslims who, by the start of the main action in 1096, had become a powerful force in the region. The puppets are outfitted in clothes that indicate their roles as crusaders, Christian or Muslim leaders and warriors. They reenact the battles resulting from the alliance between the Roman Pope and Byzantine emperor to expel the Seljuk Turks and retake the

Holy Land. The film recounts the skirmishes and historically accurate atrocities performed on both sides, including a vignette of cannibalism by the Frankish crusaders. The film ends with Jerusalem in flames as the Crusaders take over the city in an orgy of destruction.

As the series progresses, the puppets and the settings become more abstract. The second film, *The Path to Cairo*, recounts the tumultuous events in the half-century between First and Second Crusade. **(pl. 14)** In this installment, Shawky worked with master ceramists in Aubagne, France. Together they designed puppets that suggest human/animal hybrids complete with expressive eyes that open and close. Again the puppets were clothed in evocative costumes that indicated their status and allegiance. In contrast to the more or less realistic sets of the first film, this time characters move through flat painted paper backdrops based on Ottoman miniature paintings. This time the action begins in the still smoldering Jerusalem and shifts between cities still very much in the news, among them Baghdad, Antioch, Aleppo and Damascus, as the Muslim leaders vie for power among themselves and against the Franks. The film ends with the Muslim conquest of the Christian city of Edessa, an event that triggered the Second Crusade.

Film three is called *The Secrets of Karbala*, and covers an even wider swath of history, from 1144 to 1204. This period saw the Second, Third and Fourth Crusades; Saladin's reconquest of most of the lands seized by the Christians; and the destruction of Constantinople by Venetian crusaders who turned aside from their mission against the Muslims to plunder the capital of their fellow Byzantine Christians. This installment also contains a flashback to the 7th century Battle of Karbala, a clash that took place in what is now Iraq and instigated the continuing schism between the Sunni and Shia Muslims. This vignette has been inserted to explain the willingness of Muslim factions to intrigue and turn against each other. For this film, Shawky commissioned glass blowers in Murano, Italy to create luminous, highly abstracted puppet characters whose fragility offers a contrast to the brutal actions they portray. Much of the action takes place on a revolving stage that was inspired by medieval images of the zodiac.

By focusing on the actual history of the Crusades, these three films complicate the narrative of good and evil as told by both Christians and Muslims. Far from documenting a unified offensive against the enemies of the faith, it reveals individual leaders making dubious alliances in an effort to advantage themselves. The narrative offers moments when Shias and Sunnis fight each other and others where they make alliances with the Franks. It also shows Christians turning on each other. In the end *Cabaret Crusades* suggest that betrayal is the common currency. Questions of faith appear as pretexts for otherwise inexcusable actions. In the midst of bloodshed and atrocities that seem to echo current conflicts, the worst and best of human nature are on display. Saladin, Sultan of Egypt and Syria, provides a model of religious tolerance toward the Christians, while the Doge of Venice is a symbol of expediency as he makes multiple promises that he can't possibly keep. Enacting these events with puppets allows Shawky to suggest a world in which people are subject to forces beyond their control. These are forces, he suggests, that continue to reverberate down to our own time.

Both these projects suggest how inextricably mythology is entwined with history and how the former often drives the latter. In *The Sense of An Ending*, his brilliant adaptation of eschatology to literary theory, critic Frank Kermode maintains, "...a myth, uncritically accepted, tends like prophecy to shape a future to confirm it."[8] Jerusalem here ceases to be an actual city and becomes the mythic prize and proof of competing religious belief systems. These in turn seal its fate in a cycle of never ending conflict. Today the myths that inspire war may still originate in holy books, but they are likely to be expressed in more popular formats. During his presidency, Ronald Reagan tended to see the world through a Hollywood lens, even to the extent of recalling as real events various plots and characters that in fact he had seen in movies. It has been argued that his vision of the Soviet Union as the "Evil Empire" and his quest to create a ballistic missile defense system (not coincidentally dubbed Star Wars) were deeply indebted to the world view expressed in films like the George Lucas epic that debuted at the same time.[9] Nor was Reagan alone in filtering foreign policy through this blockbuster movie. The swift U.S. victory in the 1991 Iraq War is attributed to the tactics of a group of five officers who dubbed themselves the Jedi Knights and who sliced through the Iraqi army's westward flank in a maneuver that was reportedly based on the actions of the warrior knights in Star Wars.[10]

Meanwhile, Michael Rakowitz, an American artist of Iraqi parentage, has explored the Star Wars influence on Saddam Hussein. Rakowitz frequently draws on his Iraqi heritage in works that deal with the cultural consequences of the 2002 invasion of Iraq and the needs of the Iraqi diaspora community. In his 2009 installation, *The worst condition is to pass under a sword which is not one's own* he uses a variety of materials, including sculptural installations, found objects and a graphic novel, to examine the ways adolescent fantasy is woven into the pursuit of modern warfare. His graphic novel is titled *Strike the Empire Back. (fig. 12)* It combines handwritten text with line

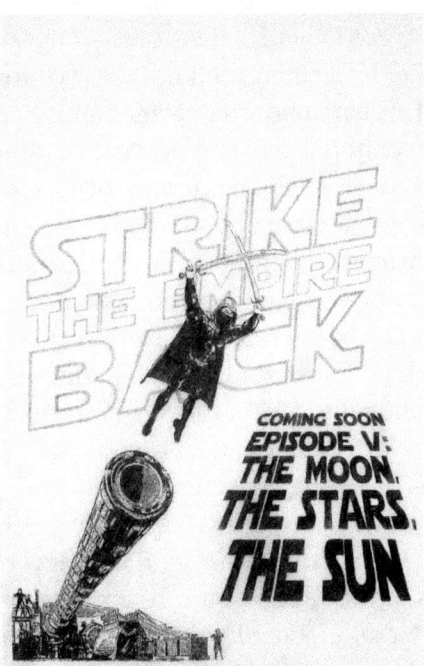

fig. 12 Michael Rakowitz, *Coming Soon- The Moon, The Stars and The Sun (Strike the Empire Back Series), 2009, pencil on vellum*

drawings to recount historical convergences between fantasy and fact. For instance, Rakowitz narrates the history of the hot air balloon. Deployed by the French military during the Revolutionary War as a means for spying on the enemy, the hot air balloon later inspired Jule's Verne's *From the Earth to the Moon*. Another narrative involves the tale of Gerald Bull, who heard Orson Welles' 1938 radio broadcast of *The War of the Worlds* when he was a child. Sci fi took on a new dimensions when, as an adult, he worked on the creation of a never realized American missile defense shield. This project was originally disguised as a space travel experiment and, when unveiled, came to be known as Star Wars.

But these appropriations of popular culture pale beside Saddam Hussein's use of the *Star Wars* mythology in the years leading up to the first Iraq war. Again using hand drawn graphic panels, Rakowitz reveals that Hussein's son Uday based the design of the uniform worn by members of Fedayeen Saddam, Hussein's fearsome paramilitary group, on costumes in the *Star Wars* films. They were attired in black shirts, ski masks and helmet that were exact replicas of the one worn by Darth Vader. Meanwhile, Iraq celebrated its 1988 "victory" over Iran with a triumphal arch composed of giant hands holding crossed swords. These echoed a famous poster for Spielberg's *The Empire Strikes Back*. At the beginning of the 1991 Gulf War, Iraqi soldiers participated in a televised performance in which they marched through this arch to the movie's theme music. Rakowitz underscores the adolescent fantasies embodied in this military gesture by recreating a sculptural version of this arch **(pl. 15)**. His version replaces the original swords with red and green light-sabers from the *Star Wars* films. These are surrounded with Darth Vader helmets composed of clear plastic molded over bits of GI Joe figurines.

There are other interesting convergences between fact and fiction here. In the graphic novel, Rakowitz conjectures on possible echoes of the father son relationship between Spielberg's Darth Vader and Luke Skywalker in the equally peculiar ties between Saddam and his brutal son Uday. The installation also includes a copy of the aforementioned *Star Wars* poster, later discovered in Saddam Hussein's personal quarters, as well as a pulp fiction paperback bearing a cover illustration appropriated from the poster's artist. A wall text in Rakowitz' installation reveals that this is a "turgid romance novel" reportedly authored by Saddam Hussein himself.

Why Star Wars? Theologian John Caputo maintains that the Star Wars epic is essentially a theological narrative that simply transcribes classical religious figures and narratives into a high tech world. He notes that, "In George Lucas's intergalactic version of Luke's nativity story, there is a high tech-holy family, a "virgin birth" and blessed mother, a child with a human mother and fathered by a heavenly power, all of which is part of a piece of popular science fiction that is laced with religious import and trades on religious structures."[11] He adds that the greeting "The Force be with you" is a transcription of the Christian *dominus vobiscum*, "The Lord be with you". In an echo of the eschatological narrative, the war at the center of the epic looks ahead to a messianic age. This will be a time of peace as the opposition between science and religion are reconciled within the harmonious flow of the Force.

The influence of Star Wars on the architects of our current Middle East turmoil poses the question: would war be possible without the psychological assistance provided by cultural myths? And would our myths be possible without real life war to provide a model? It becomes hard to separate the two, because, as Roland Barthes points out, the relationship between myth and truth is not so much a matter of fiction versus fact as it is a layering of one interpretation atop another. As Barthes notes, "Myth hides nothing and flaunts nothing: it distorts; myth is neither a lie nor a confession: it is an inflection."[12] The history of Jerusalem is inseparable from the interpretations laid over its successive invasions and capitulations, while the architecture of the Star wars epic is at once an echo of the reported histories of ancient wars and a prototype for future conflicts.

Which leads to a third question: Where does religion fit into all this? To what extent do religious beliefs create the myths that shape our most basic cultural assumptions? It is the contention of this book that religious narratives surrounding the apocalypse have permeated almost all aspects of contemporary life, influencing believers and unbelievers alike. But if these narratives seep into even the most apparently secular notions about morality, truth and responsibility, to what extent is religion to blame for our unraveling world? In a series of works that reflect on the political and psychological upheavals of our new century, artist Paul Chan implicates religion in our contemporary pathologies.

Chan is known both for multi-referential animations and videos and more direct political activities. He has on occasion called for the separation of art and politics, though in his own work the distinctions are often quite blurred. Chan reports that the aftermath of the attacks of September 11, 2011 brought religion back into his focus in a new way. As he noted to one interviewer, "We want answers. We want to guarantee things. And this is of course why institutional religion has taken center stage again, and this is why I took a certain religious turn." Pressed to elaborate, he added, "I mean that after 2001, after the Afghanistan and Iraq invasions, my antennas were more tuned to certain theological precepts and ideas. I would never have thought that in the twenty-first century I would have to think about religion anew. But once you do, you realize how the religious infects everything. Even that supposedly secular field called contemporary art."[13]

In his political work, this has involved recognizing the role played by religion in the lives of Iraqi citizens in the run-up to and aftermath of the American occupation and in the thinking of Americans back home in the so-called Bible Belt. (Hong Kong born Chan focuses in particular on Nebraska, where he was raised). Both these groups have been subjects of Chan's quasi-documentary videos as he explores the impact of their beliefs on their visions of the world. By contrast to this more straightforward presentation, Chan's artistic works offer densely layered mixes of allusions to post-structural theory, literary figures like Beckett, William Blake and the Marquis de Sade, "outsider" art, old masters like Goya and Caravaggio and contemporary hip hop. These works are frequently peppered with religious references and symbols, but it is really at the level of structure and theme that they most deeply connect with the idea of apocalypse. Undercurrents of disaster and destruction mingle with fantasies of utopia and redemption, while the reliance on looping videos provides a paradoxical sense of endlessly recurring finality.

Chan's first major video animation, for instance, draws on the epic battle narrative of "outsider artist" Henry Darger, whose work will be discussed in more detail in the next chapter. Titled *Happiness (Finally) After 35,000 Years of Civilization – After Henry Darger and Charles Fourier* (1999–2003), the work represents Chan's rather eccentric vision of Darger as a political philosopher along the lines of Charles Fourier, 19th century French socialist. Playing on both sides of a long horizontal screen, scenes reminiscent of Darger's superficially naive tableaux present sexually ambiguous prepubescent little girls frolicking in bucolic landscapes, engaging in group sex, and being slaughtered and brutalized by ferocious male armies. The work becomes a kind of *Paradise Lost*, suggesting the inevitable intrusion of death and destruction into even the most utopian of social fantasies.

Chan's next video, *My Birds...Trash... the Future*, 2004 is even bleaker. **(pl. 16)** This is also an animation projected on two sides of a long horizontal screen. Unlike *Happiness*, however, the two sides are not identical. Each offers the back view of the other, so that as one moves from one side to the other, one seems to be looking across the same scene toward the position that one has just vacated. This time the setting is a post apocalyptic landscape dominated by a single dead tree. A variety of different characters move through this panorama. They include vultures, hunters, backpack wearing suicide bombers and camera snapping tourists. Also making an appearance are two of Chan's real life heroes – filmmaker Pier Paolo Pasolini and hip hop star Biggie Smalls - both of whom were murdered by unknown assailants. In the animation, smoke billows, a haze moves through the landscape, and a gust of wind blows reams of paper, actually a discontinued Microsoft Windows screen graphic, through the air like the leaves in Hiroshige's famous woodcut. At one point the tree is hung with naked corpses in a deliberate reference the most notorious image from Goya's *Disasters of War*. A soundtrack fills the air with the sounds of modern life sampled from the internet. It is a symphony of bird songs, car alarms and mobile phones playing snippets of contemporary pop songs. Visuals and sound effects are realized in a style reminiscent of low-tech video games and provide an odd distance from the mayhem depicted.

This work was followed in 2005-07 by *The 7 ~~Lights~~*, a set of computer-generated projections of shadows that fall or rise as if beyond a window frame. *(fig. 13)* Chan told an interviewer that the strikethrough refers to the fact that shadows are light that has been struck out. Unlike the two previous animations that are realized in the crude color of animated cartoons, the projected shadows are black against a mostly white backdrop. They offer silhouettes of figures and quotidian objects of the contemporary world. These images slide across the gallery floor, and in one case fall as if thrown from a nonexistent window. (The format of the light cast from a window is oddly reminiscent of Ruscha's *Picture Without Words*, discussed in Chapter 2.) The objects include flocks of birds and other animals, cars, bikes, cel phones, ipods and finally humans, who descend, fall-

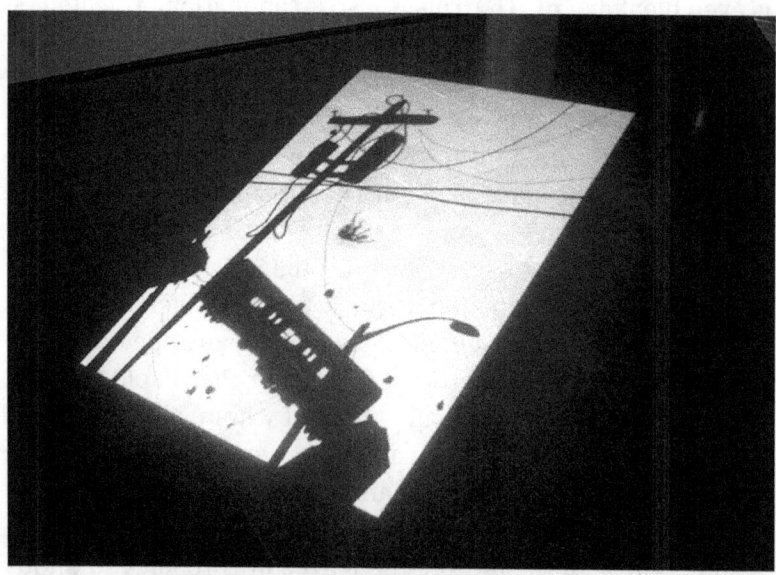

fig. 13 Paul Chan, *1st ~~Light~~*, 2005, digital video projection, 14 minutes, installation view, Serpentine Gallery, London, 2007

ing counter to the ascending objects. In the initial video, *First Light*, the scene is anchored by a telephone pole that New Museum curator Massimiliano Gioni likens to a crucifix.

The *7 Lights* have been interpreted as an allusion to the play of reality and illusion in Plato's Cave; the events of September 11, 2001 when bodies did literally fall from the burning Trade Towers; and traditional representations of the Last Judgment. However, as one reviewer notes, "The structure of *The 7 Lights* can be seen as a reversal of the Rapture Theory. The symbols of consumerism ascend into heaven, but human beings literally fall from grace."[14] The apocalyptic connotations were underscored by the appearance, in the weeks leading up to the presentation of an installation of *The 7 Lights* at the New Museum in New York, of anonymous posters in the museum vicinity that bore the message:

> You ~~think~~
> ~~things~~ will ~~end~~:
> ~~And that will be~~ the
> opening.
>
> ~~I want you to know~~
> ~~things don't think~~ to
> end.
> ~~And that is~~
> the promise and the
> threat.

Composed by Chan, the text can be read with or without the strikeouts, in a way that mimics the alternation of shadow and light in the installations themselves.

Not all critics agree on the work's religious overtones. Giving *The 7 Lights* a more secular spin, critic William McManus argues "Rather than referring vaguely to Biblical events, or pointedly and repetitively to the trauma of 9/11, perhaps *The 7 Lights* articulate the more specific but widespread disintegration of modern civil society. Perhaps *this* is the disaster moving through Chan's work. Perhaps as well, it was felt more acutely in the Middle East and elsewhere long before it re-registered in the capitals of Western society."[15]

Though Chan has repeatedly stressed his desire to keep his political and artistic lives separate, in 2007 he became involved in a project that brought the two together. In two of the neighborhoods most hit by Hurricane Katrina, Chan staged performances of Samuel Beckett's *Waiting for Godot*. The bare tree that Chan borrowed from Beckett and Goya in *My Birds* returned here. Here it was the primary prop in a production performed in the Ninth Ward in front of a house that survived Katrina. In this context, the bleakly funny, existential drama tapped into a widespread perception of post-Katrina New Orleans as a post-apocalyptic landscape, struggling in the aftermath of a flood of biblical proportions. Not content merely to stage an artistic project in this devastated neighborhood, Chan also engaged in several months of teaching in public schools and universities before and after the production as well as fundraising for local grass roots organizations.

Running through all Chan's work is a resistance to religion's rhetoric of healing and hope. But at the same time, he is also suspicious of secular utopianism. Events like the Iraq War, which he viewed up close, and the man made apocalypse of Hurricane Katrina, have revealed for him the fallacies of modernity's claims to progress and rationality. Instead, he argues, "Secularization has not separated and freed us from divine authority, but has instead retooled it. It left its authority intact and simply moved it from one place to another, displacing a heavenly hierarchy onto an earthly one. So grace becomes re-described as progress and sacrifice is elevated to a divine right. In our modern transfiguration, every exchange is an unwitting prayer for the continuance of the economic miracle."[16]

Caught between two untenable philosophies, Chan creates works that posit disaster as a basic condition of contemporary life. But all is not lost. Read in personal terms, the notion of change inherent in *the Book of Revelation* can also be read as a metaphor for imaginative possibility. In a somewhat more hopeful mood, Chan reflected in one interview on what this might mean. He remarked, "The philosopher Alain Badiou just wrote a book on Saint Paul, trying to re-describe Christianity as a radical and secular philosophical project that commits itself to an event that changes you, an event that you can neither control nor predict. And the idea of truth is how faithful you are to this initial event."[17]

Pakistani artist Saira Wasim explores similar questions in a series of paintings that reveal both the continuing toll of conflicts between western and Muslim powers and within Islam itself. Wasim is a member of the Ahmadi, a minority Muslim group that does not believe that Mohammed was the last prophet. Instead they follow the teachings of Mirza Ghulam Ahmad of Qaadiyaan (1889-1965) who claimed to be the promised Messiah and argued against jihad and for the peaceful propagation of Islam. Since the Pakastani constitution was amended in 1974 to declare the Amhadis non-Muslims, they have suffered periodic persecution.

Wasim was born in Lahore in 1975. To escape harassment, she was sent to a convent school where she absorbed western influences while being schooled in her faith at home. Her work is imbued with the multiple perspectives inculcated by this upbringing. Her métier is miniature painting, a genre that was all but wiped out during the colonial era. Since the 1990s it has begun to enjoy a revival as an expression of Pakistani identity. Noting that in its original form, miniature painting served as a form of political propaganda for the Mughal emperors, Wasim chooses to employ this technique to express political sentiments. Her first mature series critiqued the government of Nawaz Sharif, the conservative Prime Minister who was removed from office by a military coup in 1999 and imprisoned following a military trial for corruption and terrorism. Later she set her sights on Pervez Musharraf who presided over Pakistan during the early years of the Iraq War. Other works dealt with incendiary subjects like honor killings, military dictatorship and nuclearism. Seeking a more congenial environment for her art, she applied for residencies in the United States, and found herself moving there in 2003, a few days before the American invasion of Iraq.

Wasim's background gave her a privileged position from which to observe the unfolding of that conflict. Using the stylized imagery of the miniature and combining traditional and personal symbols, she transforms the Clash of Civilizations into a theatrical tableau teaming with mythological, historical and contemporary characters. There is often a comic tone, as in *Regime Change*, a painting based on the famous, and later discredited media image of the toppling of the statue of Saddam Hussein in the center of Baghdad. In Wasim's version, the toppling statue is replaced by a white marble sculpture of George Bush in the form of the Roman Emperor Augustus Caesar. Lying in a jumble below are various Muslim leaders as well as a clown whose figure is repeated in the form of a marionette manipulated by Bush. *Clash of Civilizations* presents a pair of elephants locked in battle beneath a huge American Flag which as been unfurled by the fearsome Old Testament God of Michelangelo's creation. **(pl. 17)**

Wasim employs satire and unexpected analogies to undermine the credibility of the political myths that sustain both sides of the Middle East conflict. She explains her approach thus: "With Mughal allegorical symbolism, we miniaturists have created our own visual semiotics and metaphors. For example, the extremist mullahs who have hijacked Islam for their own political agendas and manipulate Muslim youth in the name of Jihad are allegorized by Greek-satyrs; Muslim leaders are depicted as string puppets in the hands of President Bush; Pakistani army generals wearing Hawaiian sandals indicate the irony that this nation is the world's seventh nuclear state and is spending on a defense budget of over $3.5 billion a year in spite of a national debt of over $40 billion; the Shia-Sunni clash in Iraq is a bullfight and the bogeyman media is a monkey with a camera."[18]

Like the other artists discussed above, Wasim reveals how the blurring of real events with religious myth can make otherwise horrific impulses laudable. Myth inflected history can be used to justify sectarian conflict as an inevitable consequence of the eternal clash between good and evil. Beliefs grounded in theological narratives assure combatants of the righteousness of their cause and of the ultimate triumph of their version of justice and retribution. Through these devices, the unbearable is made, not only palatable, but absolutely necessary.

Apocalyptically tinged history is permeated with ideological myth, suffusing it with interpretations of the past that validate contemporary political and social arrangements. Here metaphor invades politics and transforms it from a transactional relationship between various groups into a divinely ordained order. But the apocalyptic narrative also interacts with politics in a less pernicious manner. Some of the greatest works of apocalyptic literature meld myth and reality in an imaginative exercise that draws out its larger humanistic lessons. Many artists and writers have adapted the Grand Battle as it appears in *Revelation* and similar texts to suggest alternatives to humanity's apparent death drive. In doing so they emphasize the redemptive aspect of the apocalyptic narrative. Turning from the destructive impulses that drive apocalyptically oriented ideologues, these creators instead celebrate what artist Matthew Ritchie deems "world building." It is to such works that we turn next.

Chapter 4

THE GRAND BATTLE: METAPHOR AS POLITICS

Truly there are two primal spirits, twins,
renowned to be in conflict. In thought and word
and act, they are two, the good and the bad. . .
– Zoroaster,[1]

The literary canon has been greatly enriched by complex sagas that mirror the breadth and symbolic import of the narratives found in ancient apocalyptic texts. The sweeping historical arc which draws humankind inexorably from creation to the ultimate battle between good and evil has inspired creators as diverse as John Milton, William Blake, J.R.R. Tolkien, and Kurt Vonnegut. It is also, as we have noted in the last chapter, a feature of cinematic narratives like the Star Wars saga, which, theologian John Caputo argues, simply transcribes classical religious figures and narratives into a high tech world.

One even finds the Apocalypse working its way into children's literature. C.S. Lewis's *Narnia* books create a parallel world in which the Christian narrative from creation to Last Judgment is retold through the adventures of four English school children who find themselves in a world of talking beasts. Written as a riposte to the Christian subtext of *Narnia*, Phillip Pullman's popular children's trilogy, *His Dark Materials*, is in part a reworking of Milton's apocalyptic saga *Paradise Lost*. Like that text, it culminates in a battle between the armies of good and evil presided over by God. However, Pullman employs the Endtimes myth in an unconventional way. He reverses the hierarchy of good and evil to suggest the hypocrisy of the religious institutions that declare their righteousness while serving the forces of evil. Small wonder that his books have been savaged by the religious right, and the film version gutted and ultimately jettisoned in face of religious opposition. And of course Harry Potter presents another version of the Christ-like figure born to battle and triumph over the forces of evil. (This despite the fact that certain Christian groups have condemned and even burned copies of the book in accordance with *Revelation* 21:8 a verse that promises death to those who practice "magic arts.")[2]

Such controversies turn on a failure to properly separate myth from fiction. Here again we turn to Frank Kermode who has tellingly provided the distinction: myth claims to be true, while fiction is a sense making operation that we acknowledge is not. He explains: "Fictions can degenerate into myths whenever they are not consciously held to be fictive. In this sense anti-Semitism is a degenerative fiction and *Lear* is a fiction. Myth operates within the diagrams of ritual, which presupposes total and adequate explanations of things as they are and were; it is a sequence of radically unchangeable gestures. Fictions are for finding things out, and they change as the needs of sense-making change. Myths are the agents of stability, fictions are the agents of change."[3]

Contemporary visual artists also create eschatological fictions to grapple with the problem of evil, the alien nature of the "Other" and the inexorability of history. In creating elaborate alternative worlds shaped by the conflict between opposing moral forces, some artists reference specific literary works while others simply borrow their ambience and narrative arcs. Such works are necessarily multi-disciplinary. To create stories that unfold over time, apocalyptically inclined artists must look outside the mainstream art world to other story telling traditions, among them "high brow" genres like literature and poetry and "low brow" ones like graphic novels, movies and video games. Drawing on such sources, visual artists have created full blown sagas that take characters through long, complex and often ongoing stories and reveal the moral choices demanded by the clash between good and evil.

One of the most remarkable of such novelistic art narratives was the creation of a reclusive, unschooled janitor named Henry Darger (1892-1973). This work revealed Darger to be one of the world's master storytellers. It was discovered just before his death, when his landlord went to clean up his apartment during his final illness. Darger's epic consists of a twelve volume, 1,900 page narrative of a war between the forces of good and evil on an unnamed planet. It is illustrated by hundreds of watercolor paintings in which the images of his legions are created by combining collage elements cut from magazines with tracings from children's book illustrations and comic books. Darger titled his narrative *The Story of the Vivian Girls, in What is known as the Realms of the Unreal, of the Glandeco-Angelinnian War Storm, Caused by the Child Slave Rebellion.* **(pl. 18)** It draws on an enormous trove of historical and cultural references, among them the American Civil War, Robert Louis Stevenson's *Kidnapped*, the novels of Harriett Beecher Stowe, the multi volume Oz saga by Frank Baum, Johanna Spyri's Heidi chronicles and, of course, the *Book of Revelation.*

While Darger is generally classed as an "outsider" artist, it is important to bear in mind curator Brooke Davis Anderson's caveat that self-taught artists are not so much outsiders as "our culture-bearers, revealing ideas and concepts about our society."[4] Unknown in his lifetime, Darger has practically become an industry since his death. Films, scholarly books, exhibitions, graphic novels, video games, popular songs and even a book length poem by John Ashbery have been inspired by his art. Younger artists continually cite the influence of his work, a tendency that Davis Anderson has dubbed *Dargerism.*[5] Klaus Biesenbach, author of a monograph on Darger, asks, "Why is Darger so relevant today?" He answers himself, "Perhaps it is because his focus on war and violence, belief and despair, and the heaven and hell of human interaction seem all too contemporary and speak to the deepest anxieties of our media driven society."[6]

The Realms, (as it will be called here) follows the travails of a tribe of seven princesses known as the Vivian Girls who represent the forces of good and innocence. They are daughters of the emperor of Abbieannia, one of the four great Catholic nations engaged in an epic war against the Glandelinians, an evil empire that practices child slavery. The action centers on the Vivian Girls' efforts to free the kidnapped children. In the course of Darger's narrative, the Vivian girls are enslaved, tortured, thrown into ferocious battles and beset by dragons and demons and other natural and supernatural phenomena. There are scenes of epic violence, with girl soldiers disemboweled and garroted amid dreadful carnage. There are also scenes of pastoral bliss, in which our heroines frolic with human sized butterflies in bucolic landscapes. Throughout the sixty years Darger labored over his saga, he engaged in his own struggles with God, whom he blamed for the loss of a newspaper photograph that he was using as source material for a key character. When he failed to retrieve the photograph, he assailed God, threatening to throw the battle to the Glandelinians. In the end, he was apparently unable to resolve this crisis and offered two alternative endings, one in which Christianity and the Vivian girls ultimately triumph over their enemies and one in which they are vanquished.

If Darger's characters are grandly heroic, his own life was full of quiet pathos. Darger was born into a working class Catholic family in Chicago. His mother died in childbirth when he was four and the sister born of that tragedy was given away for adoption. He lived with his father, a tailor, until Darger père became lame and was unable to work. At this point young Henry was placed in a Catholic Boy's home. At age twelve Darger was sent to the Asylum for Feeble Minded Children in Lincoln, Illinois. After five years and several escape attempts, he succeeded in catching a train to Decatur Illinois, and, according to the autobiography also found among his effects, walked the 175 miles back to Chicago. His father was now dead. Aside from a short stint in the U.S. Army, Darger spent the rest of his life employed at menial jobs in Chicago Catholic Hospitals. He lived alone, had only one documented friend, and showed no one his great creation during his lifetime.

What makes the world created by this recluse so compelling? One answer is the range of aesthetic invention exhibited by the paintings. Because Darger lacked confidence in his own drawing skills, he created his characters and settings by tracing images collected from newspapers, advertisements, children's books and especially coloring books. He added his own details – among them the butterfly wings, serpent bodies and ram's horns that adorn various guardian figures and of course, the curious male genitals found in the nude representations of his female heroines. (It has been suggested that this was due to his own lack of familiarity with female anatomy, though Michael Moon also sees a connection to the sexual ambiguity of characters in the Frank Baum books that Darger used as inspiration.)[7] The adult soldiers are portrayed in Civil War uniforms, underscoring the notion that *The Realms* is a war narrative greatly influenced by accounts Darger read of the fight to abolish slavery during the American Civil War. The settings include tidy farmhouses adapted from children's books, dark forests, arid battlegrounds and profuse fields of flowers. Darger's method led him to repeat various images with slight variations, lending a pleasing decorative abstraction to many of the tableaux.

But the other source of Darger's continuing interest derives from the ambiguity of his moral universe. A lifelong Catholic who was known to attend Mass several times a day, Darger incorporated many aspects of Catholic ritual and belief into his work. His characters are starkly divided between the virtuous and the fully evil, and with his Vivian Girls assuming the role of virgin martyrs and their tormentors the unbelieving enemies of faith. In his writings, Darger reveals that he saw himself as a "protector of children," a response, his various biographers have suggested, to his own troubled childhood. Yet, as an author, he was willing to subject them to horrific tortures, and even to contemplate allowing the forces of evil to triumph over them. And at one point a character named Captain Henry Darger goes over to the dark side.

The visual naiveté of Darger's source images, so integral to the charm of the drawings, allow him to purvey images of extreme violence in a spirit of guileless innocence. Some of the most graphic scenes present tableaux in which girls dangle from trees with nooses around their necks or are scattered, dismembered and bloody over the ground. In his narrative he recounts various instances in which girls are "raped," though in the absence of any actual knowledge of the mechanics of sexual intercourse, he apparently conceived of that as a form of disembowelment. The striking contrast between perversity and innocence in *The Realms* led one of his biographers to ask whether Darger was in fact a latent serial killer.[8]

In fact, such contradictions reflect the complexity of Darger's moral vision. Good and evil are sharply delineated, but Darger's own place within them is less clear. At times he takes on the Creator's role in his universe, even to the extent of bargaining with God as to the outcome of the story. At other times he acknowledges his impotence against forces larger than himself. Not least of these were the forces of psychology. The narrative contains numerous instances where Darger comments on his own role in a way that suggests he was very conscious of his own peculiarities. For instance, speaking in third person of his obsession with the Vivian Girls, he notes, "Probably he had them to use as company, as he was childless.... He must have been a very odd man." Discussing his anger at God over the lost photograph, he says, "The man must be a nut for how cold [sic] the loss of a picture be responsible for the disaster?"[9]

His writings also reveal an ongoing battle with God over the path of his internal and external lives. At one point he rages, "God is too hard to me. I will not bear it any longer . . . I'm my own man!"[10] In Darger's writings and paintings, the weather becomes a metaphor for the arbitrary nature of God's will. The Vivian Girls and their allies are pursued, not just by Glandelinian soldiers, but also by typhoons, firestorms, lightning storms and hurricanes. This may explain the fact that, after completing *The Realms*, Darger spent ten years meticulously chronicling the weather in a journal that takes the weatherman to task for his errors. His autobiography gives an account of his outward life, but curiously never mentions the creation of his magnum opus. It includes a long narrative about a horrific tornado named Sweetie Pie that wreaks a kind of apocalyptic havoc not unlike that visited upon the Vivian Girls. Darger asks, "Why did the Good God allow the most greatest tornado catastrophe, the most destructive the world has ever seen?"[11]

It is a rhetorical question that might serve as well as the theme of his entire opus. The nominal simplicity of Darger's visual and writerly style mask a complex meditation on the nature of evil; the culpability of a God who allows such things to happen; and his own responsibility in the horrors of the world. These are questions his saga shares with other apocalyptic narratives and help explain the genre's enduring appeal.

Like "outsider art," underground comics are considered outside the mainstream culture. But they also are places where some of our deepest cultural anxieties and desires are processed. Nowhere is this clearer than in the work of Gary Panter, a cartoonist, painter, album cover artist, Emmy award winner (for the set design of the television series Peewee's Playhouse) and all around cult hero of the Los Angeles post punk scene. Panter was raised in Texas in the fundamentalist Church of Christ. Many of his dark tales appear as updates of *Revelation*'s apocalyptic scenarios and in fact two of his graphic novels, *Jimbo's Inferno* (1996) and *Jimbo in Purgatory* (2004) are deliberate reworkings of Dante's *Inferno* and *Purgatorio*. In Panter's versions, the Poet Dante, renamed Jimbo, a freckle faced all-American boy, ascends the Mount of Purgatory and descends into the seven circles of hell where the dead do penance for their sins on earth.

Panter's apocalyptic landscape is rife with profligate cultural borrowings, mutant creatures and scatological references rendered in expressionistic lines and hallucinogenic imagery. His Dante based works are part of an ongoing exploration of a post-apocalyptic world he has dubbed Dal Tokyo and which he describes as "a vast Martian colony a few hundred years from now where Japanese, American and European cultures have collided."[12] Dal Tokyo, first conceived in 1983, has remained the setting for Panter's subsequent comic narratives. It allows him to mingle fact and fantasy in a manner quite reminiscent of Dante's own combination of literature, politics, science, poetry and theology. Panter notes that *Jimbo in Purgatory* and *Jimbo's Inferno* are deeply indebted to his evangelical background. As he remarked to an interviewer "The Church of Christ was such a formative thing to rebel against. I don't know what I'd be without it."[13]

Panter was born in Oklahoma, but grew up in Texas where his religious father ran a five and dime store. Though he now expresses a deeply ambivalent relation to religion, he has remarked: "As a kid, though, I was certainly religious. I preached Wednesday nights, not that I was very good at it. I couldn't memorize anything. But I was a good Bible student, and I got sent to Ireland to do missionary work. I didn't have a choice; I was really brainwashed. But I was deeply conflicted about it on another level, questioning everything and going crazy and getting ulcers. My grandparents had this very old Doré bible, and the engraved illustrations really fascinated me, like when Ezekiel (or whoever) calls the flesh back on the skeletons, and the images of the witches of Ensor. I really liked Adam and Eve: naked people with snakes. I liked angels with flaming swords. The earth swallowing people up was always good too. I had these crazy distant relatives who'd write their own interpretations and revelations and handprint pamphlets. That was great."[14]

These fascinations were to reappear decades later in *Jimbo in Purgatory* and *Jimbo's Inferno*. Panter notes that these works came about after he created a comic in 1988 titled *Jimbo: Adventures in Paradise* and realized he was referencing Dante without having read him. To remedy this deficit, he plunged into a reading, not only of *The Divine Comedy*, but also related works indebted to Dante, among them Boccaccio's *Decameron* and Chaucer's *Canterbury Tales*. The result is a pair of graphic narratives that adopt the frame of Dante's *Inferno* and *Purgatorio* while reimagining their characters as modern day figures from Panter's own music saturated, post punk late twentieth century world.

An allegory of the soul's journey towards God, *The Divine Comedy* is divided into three separate poems detailing Dante's travels through Hell, Purgatory, and Heaven. *Jimbo's Inferno* transforms Dante's Hell into Focky Bocky, a giant subterranean mall. *(fig. 14)* Dante is supplanted by Jimbo, the artist's alter ego, while his guide Virgil becomes Valise, a boxy robot

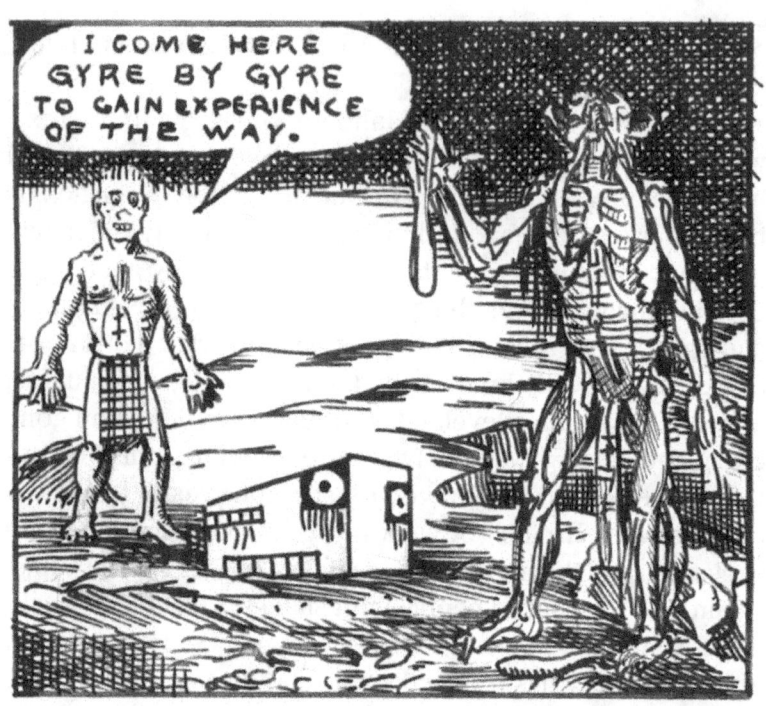

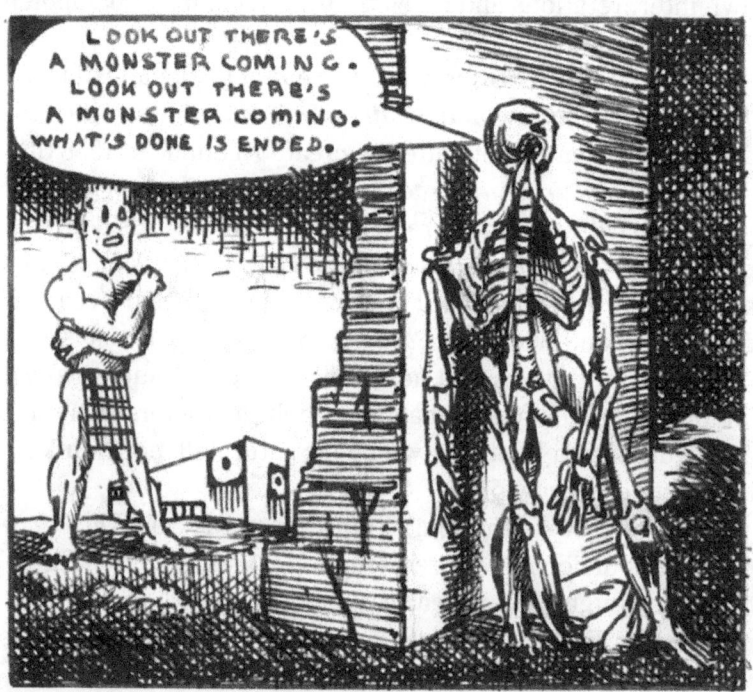

fig. 14 Gary Panter, *Jimbo's Inferno*, 2006, page from graphic novel

suitcase who is Jimbo's parole officer. As in Dante's *Inferno*, the pair meet up with figures undergoing torments tailored to their sins, which here seem to revolve mostly around drugs, sex and rock and roll. Realized in a rough *MAD Magazine* style, Jimbo's adventures include an encounter with a giant mother obsessed minotaur, coke sniffing punkettes, a fleet of Japanese Manga beasts, a warlord turned pacifist tractor, UFOs and ever fornicating mutants. Dialogue ranges from obscure to cheeky, as when Jimbo poses the eternal question, "Why do so many recreational activities involve smoke and heat?" At the pit of hell he whirls through a bat inspired amusement ride before finally escaping Focky Bocky. In the final panel he comes upon a giant screw-shaped tower surrounded by figures from the astrological constellations beckoning him toward the next step in his journey to heaven.

Jimbo's Inferno seems straightforward compared to *Jimbo in Purgatory*, which has been called Panter's masterpiece. This graphic narrative offers a complex visual and textual interweaving of historical, literary, theological and contemporary references. In format, it draws on medieval illuminated manuscripts, with each page surrounded by intricate illustrated borders full of patterns and decorative motifs that have occasional connection to the action inside the panels. Again, Panter has followed Dante's cast of characters and narrative, replacing Dante's contemporaries with twentieth century music and pop culture characters like John and Yoko, Tiny Tim, Alice Cooper, Yul Brynner in Westworld, Frank Zappa, and Bruce Lee. The text is an intricate, footnoted pastiche of quotes from both medieval and contemporary sources. In a hand lettered prologue to the work, Panter notes that his reimagining of the original *Purgatorio* derives from his rather idiosyncratic readings of the classics in which he draws a line from Dante to Boccaccio to Chaucer to Joyce.

Dante's *Purgatorio* draws on the Catholic understanding of Purgatory as the realm between heaven and hell where sinners are purged of their sin so that they may be eligible for salvation. The work chronicles Dante's climb up the Mount of Purgatory. It is divided into a bottom ante-purgatory section, seven levels of suffering and spiritual growth, each linked to one of the seven deadly sins, and finally at the top, the Earthly Paradise, where the saintly Beatrice takes over from Virgil as Dante's guide.

In Panter's version, the Mount of Purgatory is transformed into a vast infotainment testing center. It occupies a ringed tower, each tier of which corresponds to one of Dante's levels. While Dante's characters seek purification and redemption, Panter notes in his introduction that his figures are caught up in the quest for university degrees in literature. This explains the knowing exchange of quotations that make up the somewhat bewildering dialogue of the narrative.

Visually and textually, *Jimbo in Purgatory* is full of pop culture allusions and substitutions: The Roman politician Cato the Elder who meets Dante and Virgil at the foot of the mountain becomes Kato, the character played by Bruce Lee in the TV series *The Green Hornet*. Dante's angel descending from the mountain becomes the robot woman from Fritz Lang's 1927 film classic *Metropolis*. Where Dante observes a set of sculptural reliefs relating tales from classical mythology, Jimbo finds himself walking over a floor made up of posters from Japanese monster movies. Similarly, Dante's discussion of art and creativity becomes a duel of dirty limericks. And in the end, Beatrice is transformed into the 60s supermodel Twiggy. She is represented here wearing a crown of thorns with her face spread across nine panel cels to fill an entire page of the book.

Panter notes that the specific references in his narrative were influenced by contemporary events. "One thing that was happening was the bombing of Serbia, and when Jimbo is on the mountain with all the dead bodies - that was Serbia. And I have the death of Princess Di, the crashed car, in the place of Violent Death, along with John Lennon. I have Frank Zappa in the Valley of Negligent Kings. I was looking for specific traits in many of the pop-culture figures, much in the way that Ben Johnson derives the humor of his characters from giving each of them a distinct character trait. I for example place Boy George amongst the slovenly, who are too lazy to seek out their own salvation, preferring to loaf around and wait for it to come to them."[15]

Dante's theme throughout *The Divine Comedy* is the redemption of humanity. Panter's is the same, though in his version, the struggle of the soul against sin is reimagined as a struggle with contemporary evils of consumerism, drug addiction, celebrity worship, hedonism and escapism. Like Dante, Jimbo must transcend these in order to gain admission to Paradise. In the end, Panter argues, the two visions are perfectly compatible. He points out: "The same important messages that used to be conveyed by mythology are today conveyed by popular culture and that's not to excuse popular culture - most of it is mind numbing - but it definitely reflects important things about us and our time." [16]

Painter Trenton Doyle Hancock has acknowledged the influence of both Panter and Darger on his own complexly imagined eschatological narrative. From its first appearance in 2000 to its completion in 2012, his saga recounted the battle between the peaceable Mounds, who combine characteristics of trees, animals and humans and represent nature and sensuality, and the more humanoid evil Vegans, who live underground, and are vegetarian, puritanical, color blind and bent on world domination. *(fig. 15)* The saga has numerous chapters, in which the antagonists clash, Vegans almost wipe out the Mounds, and then are themselves transformed by a Mound friendly Vegan minister. But in the end, the redemption of the Vegans is undermined by a Judas character.

Among the heroes of this saga are Homerbuctus the progenitor of both the Mounds and the Vegans, who created the latter by promiscuously spilling his seed on a verdant field; the Vegan minister, Sesom (Moses spelled backward) who, like his namesake, offers the possibility of salvation to his unruly and war-like people; and Painter, the spirit of color and art. Throughout, Hancock's references to religion are often quite overt. For instance, he dubs of the place where Sesom gathers the Vegans to regain their humanity the Blestian Room, which he describes as a combination of the words "blessed" and "Christian." In fact, he notes this is a "place where good things are supposed to happen, but it's slowly going towards something that is very wrong."[17]

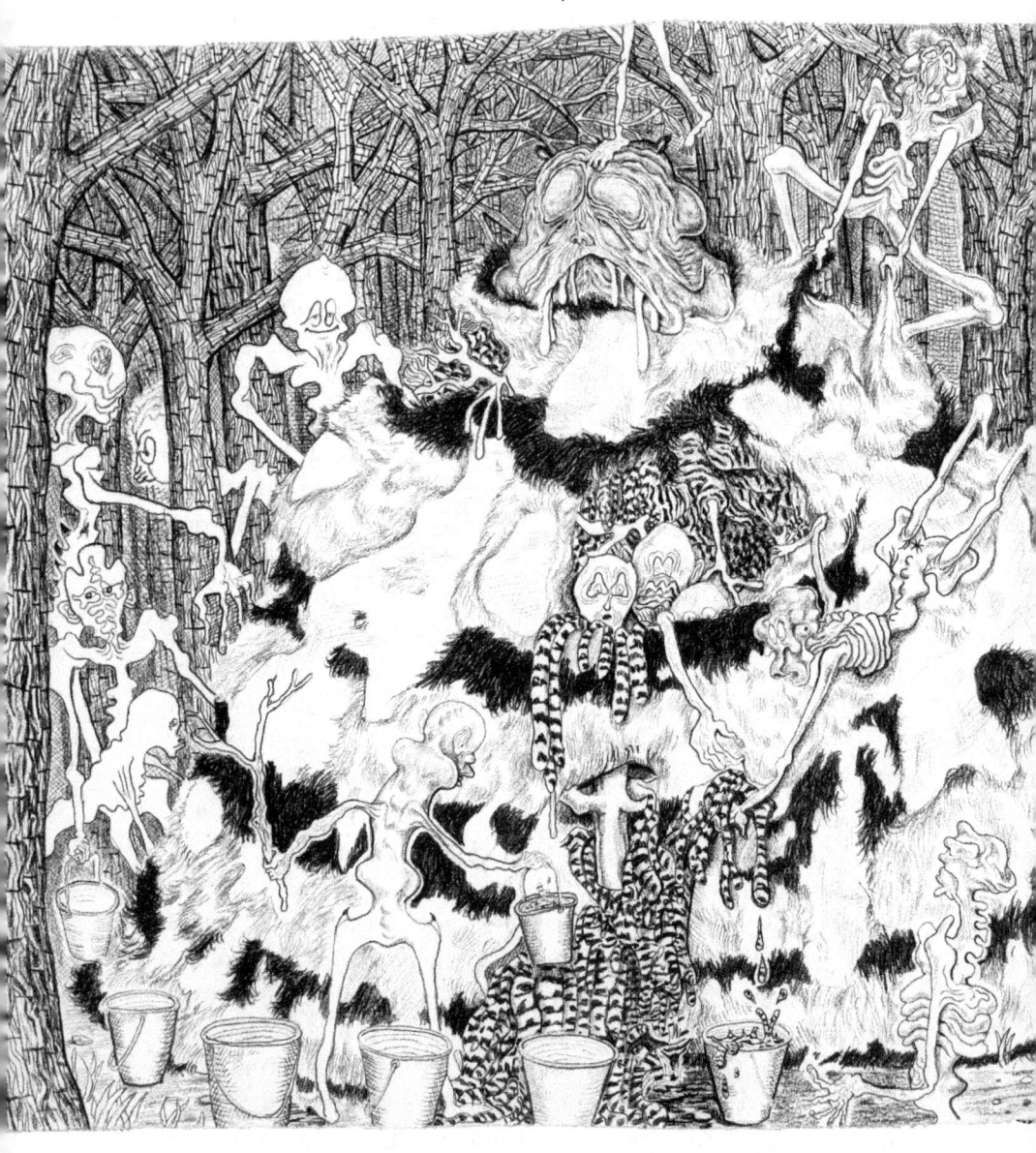

fig. 15 Trenton Doyle Hancock,
Vegans Collect Moundmeat in Buckets, drawing, 2002

Pivotal events are played out in paintings which splash across the wall, fill entire rooms and spill out into the surrounding space. These works combine various drawing styles, bits of fake black and white fur or fabric, and words that both tell the story and are visual elements in themselves. In dense paintings, words curl in explosive spirals over surrealist landscapes or figures, interweave with images so that they almost become abstract patterns or hover above like expletives or captions. The images, meanwhile, owe a great deal to the bulbous, cartoon-like creatures of Philip Guston, the bad boy scatology of Mike Kelley, and the mutant forms found in underground comics.

Hancock emerged from a powerful religious background. His stepfather was a Baptist minister and he grew up immersed in the rhetoric of Apocalypse and Endtimes. In a 2012 interview, he recalled his childhood conception of religion as a form of warfare in which the faithful construed themselves as *Prayer Warriors*: "That's a term I grew up hearing from my grandmother and my father and from people who basically stayed on their knees their whole life. I think they saw themselves at war with Satan and other demons. The only way to combat all of that was to have a very intense prayer life. They considered themselves prayer warriors. I don't think people use it quite as much now, but when I grew up it was used by people that were in their 70s and 80s. I'm assuming that it was born out of a time when black folks didn't have any recourse but to resort to prayer, the last resort."[18]

But while Hancock has moved away from the particular beliefs delineated in the Baptist creed, his work remains enmeshed in themes that echo those of the *Book of Revelation*, among them the cosmic battle of good versus evil, the fall from grace and the struggle for redemption. He gives these ideas more contemporary underpinnings, offering references to the fear of nuclear holocaust, the threat to individual autonomy posed by technological advances in robotics, cybernetics and bio-engineering, and the specter of environmental catastrophe.

There is also a racial subtext, a reflection of Hancock's experiences as an African American growing up in rural Texas.

The Mounds are characterized by black and white stripes, a veiled reference to the raccoon, or more specifically to the derogatory racial epithet "coon" which was historically applied to African Americans. This would point to a reading of the embattled Mounds as stand-ins for a racial minority, thus turning the battle of Mounds and Vegans into a reprise of the American civil rights struggle. But from another perspective, the Mounds, as meat eaters, might represent a principle of sensuality and hedonism which separates them from the skinny, tofu-eating Vegans. Or one could see the Mounds, whose name also describes their general forms, as embodiments of an earth or nature principle. In contrast, the Vegan's humanoid appearance may mark them as representatives of culture and artifice. What all these interpretations share is a longing for justice and a realignment of power in an unequal society, a staple of the apocalyptic imagination.

Matthew Ritchie has been engaged for years in an equally ambitious act of artistic world building. His epic tale chronicles the rise and fall of a mythic civilization that may precede or come many eons after our own. This ongoing narrative, which Ritchie first embarked upon in 1995, is divided into chapters with names like "The Hard Way," "The Fast Set," and "The Big Story." It involves an overlay of science, religion and mythology and is designed to encourage viewer participation in its outcome. Among its many sources of inspiration is John Milton's *Paradise Lost.* It shares with that tale a character by the name of Mulciber who is a fallen angel and in the initial stages of this work at least, the archetype of all artists. Ritchie's cosmos is based on the creation myths of the Western world and centers around seven groups of seven characters who are also metaphysical principles or laws of physics. The epic begins with a gang of damaged celestial agents representing different parts of the human brain. Thrown from heaven, they fall to earth and shatter into segments across seven continents. These fragmentary creatures combine and recombine, making for an almost infinite set of possible narratives, which Ritchie pursues in his writings and installations.

The whole project is incredibly complex, manifesting itself in a variety of forms, including the artist's voluminous writings, presented in digital form on his website, and in massive room-size installations in which painted, jigsaw puzzle–like versions of his characters, symbols, and cosmic landscapes swirl over walls, collect in piles on floor and invade the ceiling. **(pl. 19)** Each character is color-coded. This becomes one way of deciphering the action in these otherwise largely abstract compositions. In its various formats, Ritchie's narrative makes reference to everything from particle physics and theoretical mathematics to Genesis, pulp fiction, comic books, and game theory. As the project has progressed it has become increasingly interactive, as viewers are invited to generate their own narratives from the basic elements of this cosmos, either by joining into the story with an avatar on Ritchie's website[19] or in a more recent iteration, by participating in a gambling game that employs dice and a deck of playing cards listing all of the characters and their characteristics. At the project's end, Ritchie promises, there will be a single remaining character, the final player, who contains all others.

Ritchie's work is based on the desire to create a theory of everything. He discusses his work in terms taken from biology, physics, mathematics and information theory, as well as such arcane fields of knowledge and pseudo knowledge as Gnosticism, angelology, quantum physics, unified field theory and voodoo. But the narrative also has the feeling of pulp science fiction, especially in the descriptions of the various characters provided on the website: Consider, for example, this introduction to the fallen angel, Muliciber: "Mulicber was the Builder. Spare and stony, the plates of its jade armor were weathered and pockmarked by the hard rains of radiation and the fires of burning forests. No one was sure if there was even anything inside the armor anymore. . . Its experiences with engineering had lent it a certain skepticism about the nature of the universe that led it to believe this would all end badly."[20]

In an interview with PBS, Ritchie drew direct parallels between his interest in science and in apocalypse as imagined by John Milton in *Paradise Lost*. He maintains that the ekpyrotic theory of the cosmos, which holds that the universe came about from the collision of two branes (the fundamental units of string theory) offers a contemporary analogy to the epic battle of *Paradise Lost*. He also maintains that Milton's description of Hell as "darkness visible" is another name for what contemporary physics calls *dark matter*. And he offers an intriguing meditation on the meanings of progress that ties together religion, mythology, political science and social critique:

"What seems to have happened to the idea of progress in the last three hundred years is that the typical figure of the light bringer, the Promethean figure, has been transposed into the figure of the adversary, the Satanic figure. The two figures are linked together so that now any agent of substantial change - like Karl Marx, for instance - is derided as inherently, essentially evil. Capitalism, whose preferred model is not the equal distribution of goods - which would be sort of God's kingdom on earth - is very much anti-New Jerusalem. The endless consumption of goods has gone hand in hand with an apocalyptic Christianity - which seeks the teleological end of things - to create a vision of the future where the only desirable end is the Apocalypse, because that is what finally brings things to an end. From the evangelical Christian point of view, the apocalypse brings an end to the consumption. And from the capitalist point of view, the apocalypse provides the mechanism for endless consumption."[21]

Thus, for Ritchie, the narrative of the Apocalypse underlies three of contemporary society's most potent and apparently contradictory belief systems: Evangelical Christianity, Capitalism and Marxism. Having migrated over the millennia and the globe from the embattled group of marginalized pre-Christians for whom *The Book of Revelation* was originally written, he suggests that the idea of the imminent Endtimes now permeates the social unconscious across a vastly divergent political, social, religious and artistic spectrum.

Panter, Hancock and Ritchie make multifaceted eschatological ideas come alive by translating them into popular formats. In doing so they are partaking of a venerable history. Throughout the last two millennia, apocalypticists have continually turned to vernacular languages and genres to communicate their messages. Illiterate medieval audiences came to understand *Revelation's* complex eschatology through ecclesiastical paintings and sculptures. Competing versions of the apocalypse battled it out through popular prints during the Reformation. In the Victorian era John Martin's fiery panoramas brought the horror and thrill of Endtimes to popular audiences. Contemporary artists, as we have seen, have reimagined versions of the apocalyptic narrative using such diverse means as outsider art, graphic novel, interactive website, graffiti art, film and video. One particularly ambitious effort to employ contemporary delivery systems for this ancient prophecy is found in the work of artist Michael Takeo Magruder.

Magruder grew up in Washington D.C. in a military family and the terrors of the Cold War lurked as a backdrop to his childhood. This, more than his religious education in the Methodist Church, seems to have shaped his sense of a potentially looming doomsday. His *Decoding the Apocalypse* brings the *Book of Revelation* into the digital age. Five installations employ a variety of digital tools to bridge the gap between this ancient text and a wired world. In this work, Magruder draws on 3D imaging, video game technology, Google search engines and digital code. For instance, *The Horse as Technology* (**pl. 20**) offers a high tech riff on *Revelation's* Four Horsemen. This installation centers upon a real horse skull that has been refashioned as an eerie mesh sculpture through the magic of 3D printing. It is accompanied by light panels that present the digital code made to recreate the skull. The dramatically lit room is meant to suggest a scientific laboratory and the cloning of the horse's head points to the potentially ominous power of technology as a force of both creation and destruction.

Other installations are equally interdisciplinary. *Revelation as Mirror* comprises a set of digital "stained glass windows" that translate the warnings embodied by the Four Horsemen into digital collages that employ live web searches for key words describing these harbingers of doom. *Apocalypse Forever* translates the entire *Book of Revelation*, chapter by chapter, onto twenty-two laser engraved tablets using the PDF417 barcode. *Playing the Apocalypse* presents four digital "paintings" based on a *Revelation* based popular video game titled *Gears of War*. Magruder likens these dramatic tableaux to the panoramic paintings of John Martin whose fiery versions of apocalypse so enthralled Victorian viewers. The final installation, *Revelation: A New Jerusalem* is a virtual reality visualization of the heavenly city that will descend upon the earth at the end of the Grand Battle. Magruder's New Jerusalem is constructed using Google maps data from the present day Jerusalem and code for the text from *Revelation* rendered in four-dimensional space. Viewed through VR glasses it is a mesmerizing revolving 3D environment composed of shards of golden light.

In *Decoding the Apocalypse*, Magruder suggests how John of Patmos might have tried to communicate his vision if he lived today. Rather than attempt to update *Revelation's* message, he leaves its essential tropes intact. The technology he employs is the epitome of modernity, but his work forces us to question whether we have made progress on any other front. He suggests that the issues and problems that drive the apocalyptic narrative continue to haunt our personal, social and political lives.

The most perplexing of these is the problem of evil. Is evil the outcome of faulty moral judgment? Is it a supernatural force that overcomes our better angels? Is it a choice? A defect? A myth? Is it ingrained in human psychology and culture? Is it the cause or the effect of human desires? Our inability to resolve such questions may explain the continuing appeal of the apocalyptic narrative. In the works above, the conflict between good and evil plays itself out within imagined worlds where the massed forces of one order ultimately triumph over those of the other. These works are fictional kin of our own Clash of Civilizations and center on the outsourcing of evil to some fearsome Other who must be defeated for the righteous to prevail. But in another version of the Grand Battle, good and evil are engaged in a struggle within the divided self. Here the battle lines are not so definitively drawn and victory is always shaded with elements of self-destruction. This is the cosmos that enthralls British artist Douglas Gordon.

Gordon is known for works that reconfigure Hollywood movies in ways that alter our sense of time and our expectations of narrative. His best-known work is *24 Hour Psycho* (1993), in which the iconic Hitchcock film is slowed down to fill a entire day. In another work Otto Preminger's 1949 thriller *Whirlpool* is presented on two adjacent screens, one flipped so that they provide mirror images, and edited into sequences of odd and even frames. The work's title, *left is right and right is wrong and left is wrong and right is right* suggests the uncertain status of these subtle manipulations of the original film. In *Déjà vu*, Gordon's raw material is Rudolph Maté's 1950 film noir *D.O.A.*, about a poisoned man attempting to discover his murderer during his last hours of life. Playing on the multiple time frames in which the original narrative unfolds, Gordon presents the film on three screens, one played at normal speed, one shown at slightly accelerated speed and the other slightly slowed down.

Such works have been discussed in relation to cinema's manipulation of the experience of time, the blending of fiction and reality, and psychoanalytic notions of memory, mirroring and consciousness. But, as many commentators have pointed out, an equally important source for Gordon's fascination with doubling, splitting, mirroring and inverting is his Scottish heritage and personal history. Gordon had a complicated religious upbringing. He is the child of Calvinist parents whose mother became a Jehovah's Witness when he was six years old. Jehovah Witnesses adhere to the principle of Biblical inerrancy and sharply disassociate themselves from what they believe are the Satanic influences of both secular society and the teachings of other religions. As a millenarian Christian sect, members see the world in terms of a stark opposition between good and evil. They believe that Armageddon is imminent, after which the elect will join Jesus to rule over a purified earth. Gordon himself acknowledges the impact of his exposure to this religion. He says, "But one of the ideas the Witnesses have is that there are 144,000 saved – the elect – and most of us aren't part of that. So there was an absolute feeling of otherness because you weren't mainstream within religion, or part of mainstream culture."[22]

For Gordon, this sense of otherness was replicated in multiple levels, from his own childhood home where two versions of Christianity were in play, to his identity as a Scotsman in the British Isles. Historically at odds with the English majority, Scotland was swept during the Reformation between the shifting dominance of Catholicism and Protestantism, both of which retain significant constituencies today. Meanwhile, the country remains roiled by questions of Scottish independence and by historical divisions between the sparsely populated Highlands and the more urban Lowlands. These ideological and social disjunctures have given rise to a state that had been dubbed *Caledonian Antisyzygy,* or the "idea of dueling polarities within one entity"[23] which various theorists have maintained is a distinctive feature of Scottish psychology and literature.

In various works, Gordon has paid homage to three of the most prominent Scottish exemplars of antisyzygy: Robert Louis Stevenson's 1886 *The Strange Case of Dr. Jekyll and Mr. Hyde*; that novel's less known antecedent, *The Private Memoirs and Confessions of a Justified Sinner* published in 1824 by James Hogg; and psychiatrist R.D. Laing's influential 1960 book *The Divided Self: An Existential Study in Sanity and Madness.* The two novels tell tales of individuals pulled between two distinct identities, one manifesting itself in ordinary good and the other in absolute evil. They differ in that Stevenson's malevolent Mr. Hyde is the result of a bungled scientific experiment by his alter ego Dr. Jekyll, while Hogg's justified sinner, Robert Wringhim, is unhinged by his religious beliefs. The plot centers around Wringhim's encounter with a mysterious stranger named Gil-Martin who may be the devil or may be his alter ego. Encouraged by Gil-Martin, Wringhim murders his brother under the delusion that because he is predestined to be "saved," he can do no wrong. The structure of the novel is bifurcated into two versions of the same events, one related by a dispassionate Editor and the other by the tortured protagonist whose memoir is discovered after his death.

Both these novels served as grist for Laing's theories about the "divided self" which gained a large following during the 1960s. Laing rejected conventional wisdom about the nature and causes of schizophrenia. Disputing the primacy of reason over madness, he argued instead that childhood experiences of the mentally ill create a rift between "real" and "false" selves resulting in forms of psychosis that are actually simply sane responses to an insane world.

Gordon blends this "divided self" with a religious cosmology of good and evil to produce works whose points of view are deliberately ambiguous. One of the simplest of these is a 1996 video titled, after Laing, *Divided Self I and II*. This work presents two monitors each offering a looped clip of two arms struggling for dominance. Though they appear distinct, as one is hairy and the other smooth, both belong to Gordon and are his realization of a passage from Stevenson's novel in which the metamorphosing Dr. Jekyll reports looking at and not recognizing his own arm.

Gordon references Hogg and Stevenson in his 1995-6 video installation *Confessions of a Justified Sinner*. Here, two large projection screens present continuous loops of the transformation scene from Rouben Mamoulian's 1931 black and white film version of *Dr. Jekyll and Mr. Hyde*, one positive and the other negative. They endlessly change back and forth, suggesting no resolution to the struggle between the protagonist's alternative personalities. Gordon returned to this theme in a 2002 exhibition titled *Confessions*, which was presented at Kunsthaus Bregenz in Bregenz, Germany. This three part installation comprised three takes on Hogg's book: a handwritten transcript of the portion of the narrative devoted to Wringhim's confession, a darkened room illuminated by black light in which a disembodied voice recites this same text, and finally, a video projection titled *Fog* in which a young man who resembles Gordon simultaneously emerges from and disappears into a mist, as if merging with himself. The idea for the show, Gordon noted to a writer "came from one point in the book where Wringhim has finally realized his descent into madness; he tries to warn the world of the dangers of flirting with the devil by writing his confessions, but no one will print them."[24]

In these works, Gordon explores the intermingling of vice and virtue within a single identity. He personalizes this struggle in various ways – using an actor who resembles himself in *Fog*; incorporating Robert Wringhim's name in his own email and address; and in a related photographic diptych titled *Monster* (1996-7). This latter presents a pair of self-portraits, one of which offers an unexceptional frontal view while the other takes the same pose but presents Gordon's face demonically altered with scotch tape.

Gordon's most powerful statement about the mirror quality of good and evil is his 1997 *Between Darkness and Light (After William Blake)*. **(pl. 21)** Here two films, *The Song of Bernadette* (Henry King, 1943) and *The Exorcist* (William Friedkin, 1973), run simultaneously on the same projection screen. Because the original films differ in length, the continuous loop creates ever changing and serendipitous moments of coherence and contrast that emphasize their common theme of supernatural possession. The two films are, to borrow a phrase from Dr. Jekyll, "polar twins;" in one a young girl is overtaken by Satan, in the other, her counterpart is overtaken by visions of the Virgin Mary. The device of the overlay creates chance events with surprising synergy, and as the two sets of characters merge, their distinctions begin to disappear. The disbelieving 19th century French villagers and skeptical modern doctors, the bile spilling demon and the beatific saint become part of a single narrative of irrational forces tearing through the façade of ordinary life.

Between Darkness and Light was originally created as part of a sculpture festival in the town of Muenster, Germany. Gordon was invited to create a work somewhere in the city, and after much deliberation chose to place it in the middle of a dank pedestrian underpass that smelled of urine. Explaining his choice, he remarks, "I started to think about the underpass as some sort of purgatory. It's neither in the city nor out of it. It is neither in heaven nor in hell. I began to think that it might be interesting to try and stop people passing through it as quickly as they might have done normally. If I could find a way to make people hang around there for some time, then it would become a space for thinking, reflecting and waiting to see what might happen next . . . It was like a perfect model of purgatory."[25]

In another interview he elaborated on his vision of purgatory: "Growing up with some idea of Catholicism as exotic, I was always interested in purgatory. Not that I believed in heaven or hell; I was much more interested in the purgatory idea and the fact that it became a powerful political and economic means for the Catholic Church to control people . . . The thing that intrigued me was the half-full/half-empty; people who are quite bad, but not bad enough, and quite good but not good enough – how do they float about in purgatory and have a discussion together?"[26]

Reflecting on the internalized struggle of good and evil, Gordon has come to a different conclusion than Augustine. While the fifth century Church father argued optimistically that evil is the absence of good, making it the less powerful half of the dyad, Gordon takes the opposite position. Pointing to the ultimate triumph of the Hydes over the Jekylls and the Gil-Martins over the Wringhams of the world, he remarks, "One of the most appealing things about the idea of your doppelganger being more powerful than you is because the bad can adopt good as a disguise, but a good person cannot adopt evil. You can't pick it up and throw it away. Evil is meant to be innate, but goodness is something evil can adopt at any moment." [27]

The traditional apocalyptic narrative provides an arc that ends with the final triumph of good over evil. But Gordon seems to pose a different possibility. If evil is inherently stronger than good, why couldn't it be the victor in the last apocalyptic battle? This seems to be the question embedded in two monumental tableaux created by British artists Jake and Dinos Chapman. These two brothers emerged in the 1990s as part of a group dubbed the 'Young British Artists', whose works made cheeky assaults on good taste and high art. The Chapman's gained notoriety for their signature sculptures of mutant children who sported penis noses, anus mouths and nude bodies fused at the torsos like many headed millipedes. Other works were equally insouciant or, as some argued, sophomoric. These included *The Rape of Creativity*, 2003, in which the brothers applied clown faces to Goya's horrific *Disasters of War*, a set of African fetish carvings with disguised McDonald's symbols, and a banner of Nazi flag in which the swastika was replaced by a smiley face.

The work that interests us here comprises a pair of dioramas. These are actually versions of the same work, the first be-

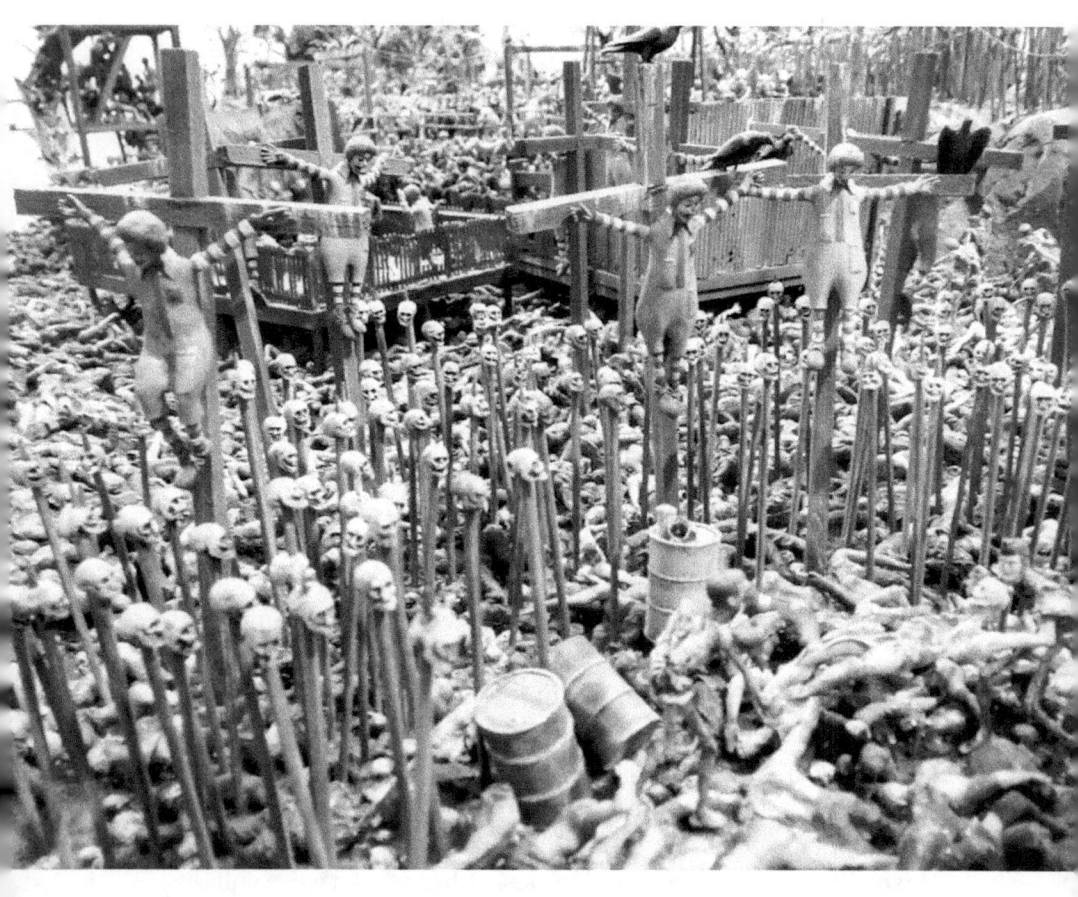

fig. 16 Jake and Dinos Chapman, *Hell*, *1* (detail),
1999, Serpentine Gallery

ing *Hell* (1999) which was destroyed in a warehouse fire in 2004, and recreated in 2008 in a new, improved form with the title *Fucking Hell*. Both works comprise over ten thousand hand-modeled and hand-painted figurines assembled in nine vitrines that form an inverted swastika. Inside the vitrines are ghoulish vignettes that are a mashup of slasher porn, Grand Guignol Theater, Hollywood zombie narratives, medieval depictions of the harrowing of Hell and contemporary Nazi fantasies. *(fig. 16)* In the center is a huge volcano spewing mutant humanoids, skeletons in Nazi uniforms, multiple Hitlers and bloody body parts. The vignettes portray an imaginative variety of tortures in graphic detail, each taking place in a different setting. Before a burned out church, skeletal Nazis emerge from tombs; skeletons writhe on crosses in a desolate landscape; and figures in a concentration camp with oversize industrial pipes mutilate and cannibalize each other. Charon's boat, which transports souls to the land of the dead in classical mythology, here becomes a ship full of bloodied corpses, while Ronald McDonald is crucified by Nazi soldiers. In *Fucking Hell*, the remake of the original work, there are additional piquant details: A skeletal Stephen Hawking in a wheelchair sits on a desert island surrounded by bikini-clad mutants playing beach ball. In another vignette Hitler stands before an easel in a body strewn field painting a bucolic landscape.

It is hard to tell who are the victims and who are the perpetrators in Chapmans' *Hell* or why they are fighting each other. Instead, the rounds of killing, dismembering, flagellating, decapitating and flaying appear purposeless, endless, and dispassionate, more a matter of blind instinct than any kind of rational plan or even comprehensible human motivation. *Hell* was first exhibited in a show curated by Norman Rosenthal in 2000 for The Royal Academy of Arts and titled *Apocalypse: Beauty and Horror in Contemporary Art*. In the catalog critic James Hall opines, "It is not clear whether the mutants are supposed to be the kind of people whom the Nazis, with their belief in eugenics, sought to wipe out. . . or whether they are the ultimate manifestation of the Nazi ideal – invisible killing-machines produced by genetic experiment."[28] Even more than the

Chapman's other works, *Hell* and *Fucking Hell* raise questions about the artists' intentions. How are these works meant to be taken? Are they just a lame mockery of bourgeoisie morality, or do they offer a philosophical statement about the nature of evil? Are they simply publicity gambits or genuine social critiques? Are these works profound or inane? Comic or serious? Are the Chapmans telling us that Hell is all around us? Is this a vision of history in which the forces of Satan have triumphed and the Nazis get the world they want? Or is it, as some have suggested, an updating of Dante's *Inferno* assigning punishments to fit the moral disease of their perpetrators?

The artists themselves have been evasive on these questions, brushing aside explanations that tie the works to any specific moral message or historical commentary. As they remarked to one interviewer, "So in some ways our work is not about the elaborate attempts to provoke these provocative, traumatic reactions on the part of the viewer. Our work is about taking things like swastikas, smiley faces or Goya's images of war, because we see them as symbols for an emotional world that is impoverished already."[29] However, another clue to the meaning of *Hell* and *Fucking Hell* emerges from the treatment of time in this work. Unlike the other narratives described in this chapter, *Hell* and *Fucking Hell* unfold in space but not in time. There is no sense of beginning or end. Instead the mindless mayhem seems to take place in an eternal present – nothing seems to have motivated the fury of the characters and their atrocities seem to have no consequences.

Such a view has interesting implications for the apocalyptic vision. In another interview, the brothers comment on their temporal philosophy noting, " . . .the 'end of the world' rests on conventional notions of time which present time as a linear sequence. If time has not a linear trajectory, it cannot have an 'end.'"[30] But if a world without time is a world without an end, a world without an end is a world without justice, at least in the apocalyptic sense. There is no righting of wrongs, no ultimate reckoning. In a world without time, evil simply persists. Or in the words of Terry Eagleton, "Evil has sameness of shit, or the sameness of bodies in a concentration camp." He elaborates,

"This is why it cannot really exist in time. For time is a matter of difference, whereas evil is boringly, perpetually, the same. It is in this sense that hell is said to be for all eternity." [31]

That seems to be the nightmare vision of the Chapman brothers. The Grand Battle of good and evil has devolved into sheer monotony – a vision of endless killing fields in which nothing is resolved or changed. As such, it seems a compelling metaphor for the apparently unending warfare, genocides and massacres of the 21st century. By uncoupling struggle from resolution and annihilation from justice, they bring us the world envisioned by Nietzsche – a world "Beyond Good and Evil." Which brings us to the Antichrist, a precursor of Nietzsche's Superman who transcends these distinctions by embodying them both. It is to this trope that we turn in the next chapter.

Chapter 5

SYMPATHY FOR
THE DEVIL

. . . Just as every cop is a criminal
And all the sinners saints
As heads is tails
Just call me Lucifer
Cause I'm in need of some restraint
So if you meet me
Have some courtesy
Have some sympathy, and some taste
Use all your well-learned politesse
Or I'll lay your soul to waste, . .

– Rolling Stones, *Sympathy for the Devil*

Why would one have sympathy for the devil? Eschewing the notion of the Evil One as a monstrous mutant, the Rolling Stones provide an image of the devil as a suave seducer, "a man of wealth and taste." He slips easily into polite society and works his will not through terror or force but through persuasion and deception. In this he less resembles *Revelation*'s Beast from the Sea than its "false prophet that wrought miracles before him, with which he deceived them that had received the mark of the beast, and them that worshipped his image . . ."(Rev 19:20). The false prophet is a recurring trope in apocalyptic texts, originating in Zoroaster's evil spirit Ahriman and taking the name Masih ad-Dajjal in Islam and Armilus in Jewish eschatological texts. In the western Christian tradition he became known as the Antichrist, and despite the fact that the name never appears in the *Book of Revelation*, this figure has traditionally been identified with *Revelation*'s false prophet by fundamentalist Christians. While he is sometimes seen as Satan himself, the Antichrist is more often a human surrogate. In that guise, as Bernard McGinn notes, "The antichrist is both the worst of tyrants and the most deceptive of religious fakes."[1]

In its Christian version, the Antichrist was originally associated with Jews, heretics and internal enemies of the early Church. Eventually he became a symbol of any false religious belief or spurious idol. In contemporary times the Antichrist has been linked by Evangelical Christians to everything from the advent of the internet and globalization to sunspots, the healthcare bill and President Obama. Other eschatological traditions have followed the same model. In the 17th century, following a series of massacres, Jews throughout Europe rallied around a false messiah, Shabbatai Zvi, who ultimately dashed their hopes by converting to Islam. Islam embraces various versions of the anti Messiah, the most prominent being Al-Dajjal, a one eyed warrior who will eventually be slain by Jesus. The Tibetan *Kalachakra Tantra* tells of a demonic false prophet named Madhumati, who is evidently the Islamic prophet Muhammad. But it is through the emergence of ISIS that Islamic belief in the Antichrist has become a political force in today's fractious world. In an influential 2015 article detailing ISIS' theological roots, Graeme Wood reported, "The Islamic State differs from nearly every other current jihadist movement in believing that it is written into God's script as a central character."[2] This script involves the founding of a Caliphate, the conquest of Dabiq, a Syrian town that in fact has changed hands several times during the ongoing war in the region, and the subsequent arrival of Dajjal who will engage the faithful fighters in the final battle.

In all these traditions, the false prophet is the Messiah's antithesis. He is loathed and feared for his ability to rally believers around his banner, leading them through an inversion of true religious virtues into the jaws of hell. Thus he is actually more fearsome than a more obviously evil rival to God. Instead, the Antichrist is a master of religious deception who convinces the faithful that good is bad and bad is good. Strikingly, he becomes a handy figure for blackening rival faiths, beliefs and religious figures, which is why there was a frenzy of name calling during the Reformation as Catholics and Protestants identified their opponents as the Antichrist. The ideas resurfaced in an invidious way in the early 20th century with the publication of the *Protocols of the Elders of Zion*. This anti-Semitic text appeared in Russia in 1903 and purported to be the minutes of a meeting of a group of Jewish leaders bent on world domination. Despite having been repeatedly exposed as a hoax, it remains a touchstone for groups ranging from the White Russians and the Nazis to Hamas and Al Qaeda intent on exposing the Jews as the Antichrist.

False messiahs come cloaked in religious garb. They represent, in the words of William James, "religion's wicked practical partner, the spirit of corporate dominion, . . . [and] religion's wicked intellectual partner, the spirit of dogmatic dominion, the passion for laying down the law." [3] The melding of religion with politics and greed explains why "religions of love" can molt into monstrous belief systems that justify violence, war, hatred and the obliteration of the Other. History is littered with such distortions of religious doctrine whose fruit include the Crusades, the Inquisition, the Salem Witch Trials and ISIS.

The inversion of morality implied by the Antichrist has made him a useful metaphor for artists and writers seeking to explore the complicated relationship of good and evil. Among the emblems of moral reversal is Nietzsche's Antichrist, who represents virtue in an upside down world where Christianity systematically destroys the will to power that is mankind's greatest strength. Similarly, Dostoyevsky's Grand Inquisitor imprisons Jesus for offering weak and powerless humanity the false promise of freedom. In an unexpected coda to this fable, Jesus seems to affirm the redirection of the Church along the lines described by the Inquisitor as he bestows a kiss upon his captor upon his release from prison. Other writers who have created provocative representations of the false Messiah are Phillip Pullman, whose alternative world, as outlined in the trilogy *His Dark Materials*, is overseen by the evil authority of a Catholic Church that successfully suppressed the Reformation, and Isaac B. Singer, who, in *Satan in Goray* imagines the moral

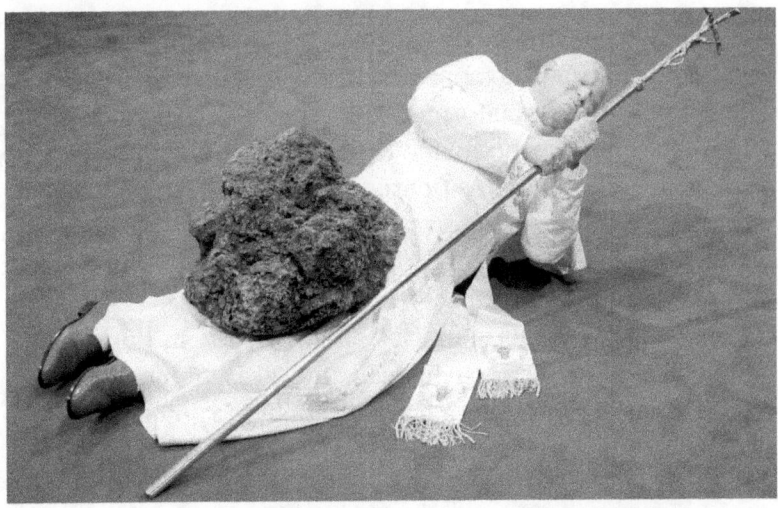

fig. 17 Maurizio Cattelan, *La Nono Ora (The Ninth Hour)*1999,
polyester resin, natural hairs, accessories, stone, carpet, variable dimensions

and social chaos that attends the embrace of the false prophet
Sabbatai Zvi in a tiny village in central Europe.

Among contemporary visual artists, one of the most infamous expressions of this trope of false faith is Italian artist
Maurizio Cattelan's 1999 *La Nono Ora (The Ninth Hour). (fig.
17)* This work comprises a highly realistic sculpture of Pope John
Paul II felled by a meteor. He lies prostrate on the ground, grasp-
ing his Papal cross amid a scattering of glass shards. Lodged on
his leg is a giant black rock. The work's title, referring to the time
of Christ's death on the cross, points to the Pope's status as Vicar
of Christ. But the event whose aftermath is visible here suggests
a divine rebuke of the Pontiff's special status. He appears to be
victim of what is often referred to as an "act of God," or, barring
that, a demonstration of the arbitrary nature of catastrophe in
a world devoid of divine guidance. The religious skepticism of
this work was not lost when it was shown in Poland, John Paul's
native country. Prior to the 2000 opening of the group exhibition
of which it was a part, titled, appropriately enough, *Apocalypse:
Beauty and Horror in Contemporary Art,* two members of the
Polish parliament entered the gallery, removed the meteor, and
attempted unsuccessfully to stand the figure upright.

The work plays into the centuries-old identification of
the Pope with the Antichrist, an idea floated periodically by

reformers during the medieval period to confer illegitimacy on individual pontiffs who appeared to violate the holiness of their office. But Luther transformed the trope by suggesting that the Papal office itself, and hence the Catholic Church which the Pope heads, is the real Antichrist. The battle of words and images unleashed by the Reformation bolstered this identification, creating a demonization of "popery" which still pertains among various fundamentalist sects. Modern mainstream Protestant faiths, however, have tempered such rhetoric in the spirit of ecumenism and tolerance. Instead, they present the Antichrist, if he is presented at all, as a warning about the potential for evil within the individual soul.

In keeping with this interpretation, Cattelan's sculpture needn't be read as a literal evocation of John Paul as the Antichrist. Instead, by questioning the connection between divine and human authority, *La Nona Ora* underscores the symbolic potential of the notion of the false prophet as a herald of corrupted thinking. As such, it provides a prologue for this chapter, which will employ the figure of the Antichrist metaphorically to see how artists have explored the ways that established religions become false and how pernicious secular belief systems gain the veneer of respectability through association with religion. On one hand are religious leaders and adherents who embrace the vices that corrupt and invert the tenets on which their faith was founded. On the other are secular systems and destructive ideologies that enhance their appeal by assuming the trappings of religion. The Antichrist becomes shorthand for both, highlighting the distortion of spiritual feelings and religious doctrines into instruments of greed, power and desire.

La Nona Ora, makes an appearance in the work of Masami Teraoka, whose paintings take aim at the use of religious morality as a bludgeon to suppress life enhancing impulses of love, eroticism and sensual desire. In Teraoka's *The Cloisters Last Supper/Eve and Pope's Walking Stick*, Cattelan's insouciant Papal portrait becomes one element in an extended critique of the righteous moralism of established religion. (**pl. 22**) Here, the supine figure of the Pontiff is entangled, not in a meteor, but in a black snake, while around him barely clad females and lustful clerics break their religious vows of chastity, poverty and modesty with willful abandon.

As a Japanese man who has lived in the United States since 1961, Teraoka is an outsider to the Catholic faith and a relative newcomer to the Western canon that it inspired. Since 1992, he has been exercising an outsider's freedom to pillage, extract and reinterpret its most sacred symbols, mixing them with other demons and characters conjured up from his own Japanese traditions. The result are teaming tableaux that bring to mind both the dark fantasies of such masters of the apocalypse as Bosch, Brueghel, Goya and Blake and the ghosts, demons and supernatural creatures that populate Japanese folklore and Edo paintings and woodblocks. In these works, animals fuse with humans or become the visible manifestations of our ugliest impulses. The victims of clerical oppression and priestly abuse - and they are mostly female here - twist and turn in bondage apparatuses that sometimes turn out to be familiar instruments of modern communications technology. Fearsome creatures that normally lurk in the human subconscious crawl out to cavort with bishops, cardinals, geishas, nuns and saints. But there are also images of triumph and liberation – again these are mostly female figures who have cast off the actual or psychological bonds and dance free with joyous abandon. Interspersed throughout are references to the artist's personal life and experiences, in particular his wonder at the birth of his daughter Eve thanks to in-vitro fertilization. This miracle becomes for him a modern-day version of the equally miraculous birth of the infant Jesus.

At the heart of Teraoka's triptychs is the disconnection between Christianity's original teachings and its contemporary practice. The contradictions created by this disconnect have many manifestations. These include the conflict between the Catholic hierarchy's trappings of worldly authority and the humble origins and life of the Church's founder; the contrast between Catholicism's historical persecution, torture and harassment of transgressors and Christ's message of acceptance, forgiveness and love; and of course, the discrepancies in the official Church's attitude toward sexuality. Christ's friendship with prostitutes, his openness to women followers and his embrace of socially marginalized groups seem far removed from a Church that officially condemns gay marriage, polices the faithful's sexual behavior and treats women as second class citizens or worse. Meanwhile, the demonization of sexuality embedded in the valorization of abstinence and the condemnation of any sexual expression not aimed at procreation is at odds with the Catholic Church's efforts to conceal its ever erupting sexual abuse scandals. As Teraoka points out, the Church's official stance is far removed, not only from the original teachings of Christ, but also from a tradition of visual art that includes Bernini's orgasmic St. Teresa, Michelangelo's robustly naked saints and sinners and Titian's voluptuous Mary Magdalene. As he asks, "How does the Catholic Church's teaching of celibacy fit into Michelangelo's Sistine Chapel painting? How could the nudity depicted in those masterpieces support anti gay and anti same sex marriage?"[4]

Teraoka originally gained widespread recognition for re-working traditional Japanese ukiyo–e based prints. His pieces incorporated modern motifs like condoms, burgers and scuba gear into traditional looking compositions in order to comment on modern ills like AIDS, consumerism, fear of sex and fast food. Since the early 1990s he has been employing a medieval idiom in increasingly political works. He deals with such subjects as the religious and political hypocrisy surrounding the impeachment of President Clinton during Monicagate; the alarming specter of the surveillance state; the imprisonment of members of the Russian feminist punk rock band Pussy Riot at the instigation of the Russian Orthodox Church; and the abuse of the media in the interests of entertainment and social control. Throughout this work, the higher clergy serve as symbols of the most oppressive aspects of religious hypocrisy. Teraoka takes no prisoners, as popes, cardinals, bishops and priests become prey to all the sins of the flesh that they so vociferously condemn.

The new turn was inspired in part by Dante's *Inferno*, with its transformation of contemporary figures and topical issues into an allegory of heaven and hell. Teraoka's paintings frequently take the form of religious altarpieces in which multiple panel paintings tell several stories simultaneously. Like the medieval altarpieces that they evoke, these works have a stage-like quality. They have gold backdrops and, in some cases, peaked tops that recall cathedral architecture. Unlike traditional altarpieces, however, these works are leavened with flashes of Teraoka's trademark wit, as he makes sardonic fun of the villains in his tableaux. The use of a medieval template here suits the artist's purposes. The medieval trappings of the contemporary Catholic Church allow him to jump effortless backwards and forwards in time. Meanwhile, the trope of the gold backdrop becomes a further reminder of the distance between Christ's message of humility and simplicity and the opulent trappings of the official Church.

Italian animator Federico Solmi offers a similar critique of the hypocrisy of religious leaders and the human susceptibility to vice. He extends his critique to secular leaders as well, suggesting how the corruptions of power continually lead mankind to the brink of annihilation. Like Teraoka, he adopts an unexpected format to make his case, in this case the hyper active cartoonish stylization of video games. Working with artist Russell Lowe, he produces video narratives using motion capture software developed to enhance 3D animation. In these works, crudely drawn caricatures of real and imagined tyrants and bullies, historic figures and cartoon monsters move and twist puppet-like through sets that match their grandiose desires. The scenarios are familiar from Hollywood epics and video game fantasies. They involve ticker tape parades in which anti-heroes bob like Macy's Thanksgiving Day balloons high above throngs of cheering sycophants; vast factory floors with endless conveyor belts where miscreants are banished to various circles of industrialized hell; gilded ball rooms with grand staircases; and ornately decorated dance floors where leering despots meet and greet. The spectacle is ever changing, swooping in for close ups and back for cosmic views in a way that offers the viewer the omniscient perspective of the video game player.

Solmi's most controversial work is his 2007 animation, *The Evil Empire.* (**pl. 23**) This work uses the figure of a fictional Pope, that perennial emblem of the Antichrist, as a symbol of religion's susceptibility to corruption. The work chronicles a futuristic dystopia circa 2046 presided over by a porn obsessed

Pontiff who engages in bestiality and sodomy. He is accompanied at times by such historic personifications of evil as Hitler, Stalin and Napoleon. The histrionic images are drenched with blotches of red that signify both blood and fire. We watch the Pope engage in private vices while commanding his bloodthirsty crusaders. Eventually he is dispatched into a fiery Hell that seems to be a disco version of the Grand-Guignol. *The Evil Empire* resembles nothing so much as a frenzied anime version of Dante's *Inferno* in which the powerful are undone by their own iniquity.

This work was censored when shown in Solmi's native Italy. In 2009 in Bologna the artist was brought up on charges of perpetrating "outrage to a religion." *The Evil Empire* had in fact been shown without incident elsewhere in the country prior to this indictment. Solmi speculates that the uproar was colored by local politics. At that time, Bologna was under siege by the hard-right Northern League. This political party, whose rhetoric ran to denunciations of immigrants and affirmations of Catholic identity, had emerged as a key ally of then embattled Prime Minister Silvio Berlusconi. During the widely publicized trial, articles, blogs and e-mails excoriated the artist for attacking Catholicism and the Pope instead of Islam and Osama bin Laden. Ultimately, however, Solmi was acquitted.

Many of the themes in *The Evil Empire* – the corrupting influence of the will to power; the cult of celebrity that surrounds deceitful leaders; and the willingness of the populace to be contented with bread and circuses – appear in his other works. So does the apparently inevitable denouement of death and apocalypse. *Chinese Democracy and the Last Day on Earth* (2012), for instance, is a trilogy that follows the rise and fall of a despot bent on world domination who is revealed, after the destruction of the Earth, to be an extraterrestrial agent. *Douche Bag City*, created after the financial debacle of 2008, stars Dick Richman, a leering Bernie Madoff robot clone created by a secret government program whose mission is to sow chaos in otherwise placid Douche Bag City. After commandeering a spot on the Oprax show in order to enhance his fame and commercial interests, Richman is punished for his financial transgressions. This punishment takes the form of ever more gruesome torments presented in short separate narratives each of which ends with the video game's resounding "Game Over."

More recently in a timely nod to the dissolution of all boundaries between politics and entertainment, Solmi's *The Brotherhood* (2017) imagines a gathering of the world's most vicious tyrants, along with some figures more commonly regarded as "good," as a Hollywood style extravaganza. The Brotherhood is described in Solmi's website as "an organization that has the goals to keep chaos in the world and promote the degeneration of the human race."[5] In a large group video and in numerous individual vignettes, figures like George Washington, Montezuma, Otto von Bismarck, Mussolini, Abraham Lincoln, Marie Antoinette and Byzantine Empress Theodora strut down a red carpet like guests to an Oscar Award ceremony. They enter a grand hall where they waltz, drink and carouse in Baroque splendor. Their mask-like grins suggest their basic inhumanity, a thread that links them across secular and religious divides and geographical and historical distances.

In Solmi's exploration of the workings of power, media and celebrity are indispensible tools in the triumph of tyranny. Crowds willingly lay down their freedom for charismatic leaders who regard them merely as pawns who worship them or are obliterated, as need demands. The exuberance with which the animations present the demise of both the mighty and the meek owes a great deal to video games in which the End of the World is just an invitation to "Start Over," However, thanks to the correspondence to real world anxieties, a darker shadow hangs over Solmi's work. He theorizes, "The apocalypse is not a cathartic moment in which spirits are lifted, it is everyday reality. Surrounded by a hostile, threatening environment, devoid of all values, that constantly breeds and feeds false myths and models, we find ourselves living in a harmful, degenerate society. The apocalypse is an expression of our unstable present, and the sense of tragedy that can be felt in my work comes from my inherent distrust of basic human nature." Solmi adds, "As history teaches, all it takes is one man's will to devastate and destroy the lives of millions of people. I use irony and satire as a tool for expressing my bitterness about contemporary society." [6]

Solmi suggests that there is little difference between corrupted religion and secular tyranny. Both insinuate themselves into human consciousness by adopting rhetoric tailored to their audiences' deepest desires. They traffic in myths, in the sense described by Roland Barthes, by embracing contingent principles that come to seem absolute when imbued with the aura of nature and truth. Religious myths often involve the election of a chosen people and the division of the world into believers and unbelievers who must be crushed to prove the devotion of the Faithful. Modernity's myths, by contrast, include the universality of social arrangements rooted in a faith in progress and the triumph of reason. But both kinds of myths can turn toxic when used to forcibly impose "spiritual" or "progressive" values on groups or individuals deemed culturally or spiritually inferior.

Religion's kinship with political ideology is never more destructive than when used to provide justifications for war. As we have seen in Chapter 3, religion too often seems to devolve into a species of warfare. From another perspective it might be argued that in the modern world, war has become a bastardized form of religion. Chris Hedges, former Middle East correspondent for the *New York Times*, reports, "We believe in the nobility and self-sacrifice demanded by war, especially when we are blinded by the narcotic of war. We discover in the communal struggle, the shared sense of meaning and purpose, a cause. War fills our spiritual void. I do not miss war, but I miss what it brought."[7] In his evocatively titled memoir, *War is a Force that Gives us Meaning*, Hedges describes the moral fog that descends in time of war, allowing people to do and consider things that would be unthinkable in times of peace. He writes about the sense of purpose and camaraderie that makes war so irresistible that soldiers and journalists sign up time and time again rather than return to a civilian world where they no longer feel at home. And he describes the hollowing out of humanity in those who cannot break their addiction to combat.

In his seductively beautiful sculptures of mosques, cathedrals, temples and other ritual objects, artist Al Farrow suggests that the secular worship of guns and munitions offers a fractured mirror of the sacred rituals of religion. His architectural models of various houses of worship are crafted out of actual military hardware. Gun barrels become minarets; artillery shells are set end by end or lined up lengthwise to create patterned walls and domes; and handguns serve as a menorah's candle-holders or a reliquary's buttresses. These weapons are real and many have potent histories. Purchased at second hand gun shows, they may indeed have been used to kill or maim.

Throughout his long career, Farrow has frequently explored loaded subjects, among them the decimation of native cultures, affluent society's demonization of poverty, and modern economies' dependence on the weapons industry. His architectural models were inspired by medieval reliquaries that Farrow encountered on a trip to Florence, Italy. A reliquary purporting to hold the finger of a saint conjured for him the image of a trigger finger. This prompted him to create a series of shrines to Santo Guerro, his invented saint of war. **(pl. 24)** In the manner of genuine medieval reliquaries, he housed bits of real human bone, including a finger, skull and jawbone in architectural structures that mimic the forms of shrines, churches and cathedrals. As the series grew, Farrow became uncomfortable with his exclusive dependence on Catholic references. He began to expand the series to make reference to other religions as well, creating forms inspired by mosques, synagogues, mausoleums, Protestant churches and menorahs.

Farrow's sculptures respect the memorial traditions of each faith. Each structure holds an artifact specific to the religion. For instance, his spare Protestant Chapels contain real antique Bibles open to the pages of the *Book of Revelation*. Underscoring that text's celebration of death, he includes a facsimile of Albrecht Durer's engraving of *The Four Horsemen of the Apocalypse*. Synagogues containing a Torah cover and a copy of the Ten Commandments are constructed from elements which include uzis, the type of gun used by the Israeli army. One synagogue contains a tefillin bag, a ritual object worn by observant Jews. Issued by the Israeli army, it is dyed army green and inscribed with the Star of David. Mosques make reference to death in other ways, containing small coffins or, in the case of *Bombed Mosque*, where Farrow wanted to reference the enmity between Shia and Sunnis, a Shia style structure presented partially destroyed and topped with a black trigger ending in the crescent moon associated with the Sunnis.

The beauty of Farrow's *Reliquary* sculptures makes them doubly unsettling. They attest not only to our obsession with war and violence, but also to the seductions of the promise of annihilation. Medieval scholar Caroline Walker Bynum notes that historical reliquaries operate on two levels, as they both memorialize the dead and contain the promise of future resurrection.[8] In this they mediate between heaven and earth. Modernity, Farrow suggests, has done away with this duality. In its stead, tragically, is a leveling sameness dominated by the all-pervasive cult of death.

While the linkage between war and religion seems eternal, the appeal of other ideologies varies by time and place. As descendants of the Enlightenment, we are no longer likely to be convinced by principles derived from pre-scientific disciplines like magic, alchemy and astrology. Nor do we willingly acquiesce in social organizations centered on the divine right of kings or the division of people into pre-ordained castes. But modernity doesn't make us immune to faith-based dogmas. Secularization often masks the degree to which our most deeply held beliefs remain grounded in contemporary forms of superstition. Take, for instance, our views of economics. Supposedly based on the analysis of hard facts and figures, it is riddled with unproven and unprovable suppositions, which explains economists' ability to come to completely opposed conclusions from the same set of phenomena. What are "consumer confidence," currency values, and inerrancy of "the invisible hand of the market" if not faith based beliefs?

An intriguing fragment of a text by Walter Benjamin explores the idea that capitalism is nothing more than a rapacious religious cult in which guilt has replaced repentance as the tie that holds its adherents together. In *Capitalism as Religion* he discusses the deformation of character induced by that economic system. He maintains, "Capitalism is entirely without precedent, in that it is a religion which offers not the reform of existence but its complete destruction. It is the expansion of despair, until despair becomes a religious state of the world in the hope that this will lead to salvation." He emphasizes, "Capitalism has developed as a parasite of Christianity in the West (this must be shown not just in the case of Calvinism, but in the other orthodox Christian churches), until it reached the point where Christianity's history is essentially that of its parasite – that is to say, of capitalism."[9]

The notion of a capitalist religion is also explored in sociologist Max Weber's 1905 treatise, *The Protestant Ethic and the Spirit of Capitalism*. Weber traced the success of capitalism in Northern Europe to the work ethic inculcated by the rise of Protestantism. He wrote, "The Puritan wanted to work in a calling; we are forced to do so. For when asceticism was carried out of monastic cells into everyday life, and began to dominate worldly morality, it did its part in building the tremendous cosmos of the modern economic order." This he saw as a great tragedy. Invoking Richard Baxter, the 17th century British Puritan leader, he says, ". . . in Baxter's view the care for external goods should only lie on the shoulders of the 'saint like a light cloak, which can be thrown aside at any moment'. But fate decreed that the cloak should become an iron cage."[10]

The contemporary version of the capitalist religion is the 'Prosperity Gospel.' Today its adherents fill mega churches whose leaders equate salvation with financial success. The implied message is that the poor shall be damned. Meanwhile, corporations themselves often assume aspects of religious practice with motivational workshops and seminars that draw on the language of faith and spiritual inspiration. Sculptor Robert Trotman takes on the peculiar nexus of these two modern faiths. His figurative polychrome wood sculptures seamlessly meld the iconographies of capitalism and religion. He depicts men and women in business attire who appear in attitudes that indicate various degrees of spiritual despair and alienation. In their patent uneasiness, they take issue with the blithe optimism of the prosperity gospel. Instead they evoke Benjamin's much darker conception of the dehumanizing tie between capitalist faith and material aspiration. Or as Trotman puts it, his characters struggle with "'authentic existence' versus 'wealth and success.'"[11]

This conflict was the leitmotif of Trotman's childhood. His most indelible memories revolve around his distant, uncommunicative banker father who came home from work exhausted each day and who had little sympathy for his inquisitive, artistic son. Trotman has inscribed the conflict between corporate conformity and soul onto his sculptures. When presented individually, they are often endowed with first names, a bit of familiarity that poignantly suggests their efforts to hold onto their humanity. They exist in what Trotman describes as "an imaginary corporate purgatory."[12]

Martin (2008) is a distraught office worker who kneels, bolstering himself against some invisible force that sends his tie whipping around his neck. *Cake Lady* (2002) is also on her knees. In a gesture deliberately reminiscent of the supplicant figures in medieval and renaissance devotional paintings, she hopefully proffers a cake to some unseen authority. The male figure in *Swan Dive* (2000), his suit jacket unbuttoned and tie askew, spreads his arms to undertake what may be a leap of faith or a plunge into desperation. This idea is even more dramatically expressed in a work titled *Vertigo* (2010). Suspended from the ceiling, the larger than life size man who bears Trotman's face is positioned to hurl himself down to the floor. *Floor Man* (2011) suggests he is about to hit the ground. This larger than life figure writhes in a fetal position, suit coat still flapping upward from the wind generated by his fall.

Trotman also works with figural groups. *The Chorus* (2008) presents a set of half figures slightly smaller than life size. (pl. 25) Their faces are anguished and their arms are upraised in what might be a prayer of entreaty or a cry of protest. They rest directly on the ground, as if sinking into the floor. While many of Trotman's figures are falling, diving, sinking or shrouded figures, others appear to be more in control. In capitalist parlance they would be the bosses, while in a theological system, they are the saved. But even these more dominant figures seem to occupy somewhat equivocal positions. As portrait like busts placed on pedestals in *Committee* (2004-25), they are larger than life. Their formidable heads speak of authority. However their power is undermined by the fact that their eyes and mouths are carved into removable blocks. When taken out and turned around, these blocks can change their expressions. As a result, such characters, no less than the frightened figures sinking into the floor, appear subject to manipulation by outside forces.

Trotman's medium is basswood and poplar wood, treated so that the grain is visible and cracks are allowed to interrupt the carved surface. These accidents bring these beautifully carved figures close to the realm of the ship figureheads, cigar store Indians and other vernacular "show" figures that Trotman cites as inspirations. Meanwhile, their inner vitality recalls the work of another source, the late Gothic sculptor Tilman Riemenschneider whose expressive and often tortured figural sculptures seem to share the agitation of Trotman's characters. Such references thus call to mind both popular and "high" art history, invoking everything from medieval tomb sculptures and reliquaries to circus figures and folk art. Trotman's relationship to genre art extends beyond form and material. His theological references also suggest a kinship with the work of folk and visionary artists who draw on the extremes of agony and ecstasy inherent in the Christian cosmos of heaven and hell. Trotman plays with tropes that are the staple of untaught artists like William Thomas Thompson and Howard Finster whom we discussed in Chapter 2. Like them, he focuses on depictions of dread, guilt and retribution for the sinners who have failed to uphold the standards of their faith.

But capitalism is not the only economic faith of our time. The antagonism between two supposedly secular systems - capitalism and communism - shaped the twentieth century and continues to reverberate today. But if western capitalism found a way to bend the tenets of Christianity to support its dogma of unfettered development, Soviet Communism was equally organized around a set of tropes derived from the religious orthodoxy it replaced. Slavic literature scholar David Bethea argues that the apocalyptic mentality is deeply embedded in Russian culture. He traces it back to fears unleashed in the 13th century when Russia fell under the Mongol yoke. Apocalypse erupted again in the 17th century when Old Believers identified the modernist reforms of Peter the Great as the workings of the Antichrist. It further obsessed writers like Fyodor Dostoyevsky, Andrey Bely and Mikhail Bulgakov in the run up to and aftermath of the Russian revolution. In Chapter 1, we noted the millennial roots of Soviet Communism and its vision of the birth of a new order out of the destruction of the old. As the new Soviet world was coming into being, its architects fell back on familiar tropes to persuade the populace of its legitimacy. As Bethea notes, in the late 1910s and early 1920s, " . . . various 'social engineers' were looking for new civic rituals (Lenin's public funeral and internment in a mausoleum being the grand archetype) and places of worship (palaces of labor) to replace those of the traditional church. . ."[13]

This is an idea explored by Russian artist Grisha Bruskin. Born in 1945 in Moscow, Bruskin grew up in the Soviet Union at the height of the Stalin era. Although he is Jewish, Bruskin was raised with virtually no experience of Jewish life and ritual. In fact he was unaware of his heritage until it was thrown in his face one day by a schoolmate. This lacuna inspired him to explore this forbidden aspect of his identity. Ultimately it drew him into an understanding of the ways in which Soviet society was organized as a kind of quasi religion.

Officially, Bruskin was an inhabitant of the great Soviet Worker's Paradise, a world full of happy children, courageous soldiers, benevolent leaders and devoted laborers. However, even a young child could see the disjuncture between this cheerful myth and the people's real experiences of privation, constraint and official hypocrisy. As Bruskin began to study his religious heritage, he discovered unexpected parallels between Marxism and Judaism. Both, he notes, have their sacred writings, their holy relics, their messianic missions and their chosen people. But at the same time he recognized the difference between these private and public myths. As an artist he sought to transcend ideology by investing the symbols of both these belief systems with personal meanings.

Bruskin proceeded on two parallel tracks. On one hand,

he created a personal pantheon of heroes and saints that drew on his study of Kabbalah and Jewish folklore. Each was represented in traditional Jewish garb and was equipped in the manner of Russian icons with a symbolic object that served as the figure's attribute. Each figure makes reference to a different human and spiritual state. Thus, for instance, a figure with two oversized eyes suggests a man with the ability to see into the future, while human figures with animal faces acknowledge the interpretation of the Second Commandment that forbids the representation of man.

But more germane to our study is Bruskin's other track. In a number of works with the series title *Birth of the Hero*, he turned his attention to the stultifying dishonesty of Soviet myth. **(pl. 26)** Again, he used the language of religious icons to express this idea. In these works, the celebratory clichés of Soviet myth are personified in shining porcelain or stainless steel statues of blank faced Soviet types – the soldier, the Young Pioneer, the worker, the athlete. Again, each is provided with an attribute that is painted in full color, thus assuming a greater degree of reality than the stereotyped figure to which it is attached.

Playing off the idea of Soviet Marxism as a religion of State, many of the attributes point out the absurdity of the official creed. For instance, one figure holds a painted portrait of Lenin as a child. In this context it becomes a secular substitute for icons of the Christ child. Another figure represents a border guard with a border marker who forever pushes the edge of the frontier back. This is a reminder, as Bruskin wryly jokes, of the wandering Jew. A woman holds a replica of Lenin's Mausoleum whose stepped architecture provides an obvious reference to the pyramids of the pharaohs. A blind man presents an especially acidic comment, because, as Bruskin points out, in the utopia of Soviet society, such a person wasn't supposed to exist. This figure recalls the fact that after the Second World War, in an effort to brighten up the major cities, Stalin sent the crippled and disfigured veterans who had fought for Russia into exile. Meanwhile, considering the status of Marxism as a quasi–religion, Bruskin decided to add some supernatural figures, admitting demons and angels into the pantheon as a reminder of the irrational and nonscientific forces which Soviet authorities claimed to have vanquished.

Bruskin first began to explore these ideas as an unofficial artist in the Soviet Union. He has continued to elaborate on them since emigrating to the United States in 1988. The subsequent demise of the Soviet Union has changed the meaning of Bruskin's Soviet icons. If, as David Bethea suggests, the Russian Revolution was experienced by Russians as a truly apocalyptic event, ushering in a new world order, the Soviet Union's collapse was equally unsettling. Bruskin's post 1990 reworking of his icons reflects this trauma. He once saw his figures as messages to the future, created in the hopes that their coded references would be legible to audiences of a post-Soviet world. Now they are relics of the past. In keeping with this changed state of affairs, Bruskin has reworked their forms, breaking off limbs, eroding surfaces and effacing their once brightly colored "attributes". In this way he remakes them to suggest artifacts from an ancient civilization unearthed in an archeological dig. Once part of a functioning system of symbols that helped construct and reinforce the mythology of the Soviet Union, these idealized figures now seem lost and poignant. But even in their denuded forms, they attest to the power of false consciousness and misguided belief. Religion, Marx famously declared, is the opiate of the people. One of the great ironies of history is the fact that Marxism, the political religion created in his name, evolved into a far worse narcotic than any of the traditional faiths which he reviled.

In the post-Soviet world, "Communism" still exists in countries like China and Vietnam, but has proved surprisingly compatible with the forces of global capitalism. The encouragement of market forces, the emergence of a class of fantastically wealthy entrepreneurs and the embrace of multinational corporations in these countries suggests that the ideologies of capitalism and communism are in fact not so different after all. Instead, the global economy of the twenty-first century suggests that the real secular religion of our time is materialism.

This was one of the great subjects of David Wojnarowicz, an iconic figure from the 1980s East Village art scene. Wojnarowicz was perhaps the foremost artistic spokesperson of the AIDS era. His art and writings chronicled his difficult childhood and adolescence, including his escape from an abusive alcoholic father, and his life as a homeless gay hustler in New York City. Immersed in the gritty underground 1980s East Village art scene, he eventually gained widespread recognition for his symbol laden, surrealist inspired paintings, collages, photographs and videos. As the AIDS crisis deepened he became an outspoken activist. This led him to numerous clashes with the political and religious establishment. Wojnarowicz had been raised as a Catholic and he channeled much of his anger toward the Church's representatives, castigating them for their homophobia and their indifference to the escalating toll of the AIDS epidemic.

His work often uses religious imagery in contexts that produced charges of sacrilege and blasphemy, as when he produced a video that included a crucifix overrun with ants or a painting with an image of Jesus with a syringe in his arm. But in fact, Wojnarowicz separated genuine spirituality from official religion just as he separated what he called "the World" of authentic feeling and experience with "the pre-invented World" dominated by the soul destroying aspects of technology, science, language, law and official history. His images of Christ highlight his identification with the suffering Jesus and serve as a rebuke to the modern world for deserting true Christian values.

This is evident in *The Death of American Spirituality* (1987). **(pl. 27)** Divided into four quadrants, this painting is full of symbols that suggest that the American infatuation with progress is really a manifestation of its death drive. A cowboy rides a bucking bull down to what looks like the vortex of hell. The bull's body is composed of a collage of newspaper headlines referring to gangsters, murders, and the then current Iran-Contra scandal. Beneath a rubble-filled landscape topped with factory chimneys, a fearsome Hopi shaman grips a snake that seems to be morphing into a steel pipe. A kachina, Wojnarowicz's symbol for the authentic native culture of America, is bound with a red cord that weaves through the painting and suggests both veins of blood and an electrical wire. In this context, a floating image of the head of Christ topped with a crown of thorns seems an equally bereft symbol of the values that have been cast aside in the push for never-ending industrial development.

Reflecting on his recourse to cartoonish and mythic imagery, Wojnarowicz explained to an interviewer, "Spirituality has become a dirty word in this society because of the destructive nature of organized religion and the controls exerted by its human structure. Myths get played out only in pop culture, in the forms of toys and cartoons, animals, monsters and fantastic creatures."[14] He elaborated on his pessimism in a text provocatively titled, *IN THE SHADOW OF THE AMERICAN DREAM Soon All This Will Be Picturesque Ruins*, "The pressure for escape has led us from our tadpole ancestors through time till now to develop an appetite for speed. Speed of consumption, speed of physical movement, speed of transmitting and receiving information. Since speed is a luxury for those who have power and money, many of us have traded physical speed for fantasy like this mental projection: surround ourselves with enough material goods and maybe we won't see the stinking mess outside the windows, if we are lucky enough to have windows. It is no accident that every guidebook in every conceivable language contains the translated phrase: DO YOU HAVE A ROOM WITH A BETTER VIEW?"[15]

Wojnarowicz' works are complex and multilayered, resisting the simplistic interpretations laid on them by religious and political conservatives. The written texts effortlessly meld sharply rendered social observations and vignettes about life on the street with dreamlike fantasies of escape, destruction and sexual ecstasy. The paintings are similarly constructed from concatenations of apparently disparate images. A single painting may bring together torn bits of real maps or money, painted images from a repertoire which included cowboys, crumbling cities, prehistoric beasts, industrial gears and rotting skulls, and tiny photographic vignettes of trains, gay porn and microscopic cells. In these works, flashes of beauty break through images of the bleak devastation wrought by human action while sexual desire and ecstasy are represented as manifestations of nature, havens of authentic feeling in a world that had become a mechanistic nightmare.

For Wojnarowicz, the Apocalypse had already come. Following the death of a close friend from AIDS, he wrote, "Hell is a place on earth. Heaven is a place in your head."[16] As his own health deteriorated and the death toll soared, his critiques became ever more pointed and his clashes with the establishment ever sharper. He died of complications of AIDS in 1992 at age 37.

In the years since his death, the technology Wojnarowicz feared has gained an ever more powerful hold on our exterior and interior lives. We are now connected to each other through the ever-expanding web of cyberspace. Meanwhile our inner space has been infiltrated by forms of electronic communication and data gathering that reshape our sense of self and society. This has led some commentators to explore the idea that technology is our modern religion. In an essay provocatively titled "The Intelligent Machine as Antichrist," artist Simon Penny surveys current attempts to mechanically simulate human intelligence and creativity. He reviews the long history of the robot, also referred to here as the anthropomorphic machine, in art and science. He follows its progress from mere kinesthesia to approximations of the thinking brain. Penny concludes with the question: "Are we reaching the point at which our drive to anthropomorphism will complete its gestation period and burst forth fully developed from the shells of our bodies, in some ghastly 'Alien' style cinematic version of the *Book of Revelations*? Or will the millennium usher in an epoch of peace, light and universal harmony?" [17]

Popular culture is replete with warnings that Artificial Intelligence (AI) is on the verge of obliterating our humanity. One of the contemporary cinematic classics of this genre is the film *Bladerunner* (1982) that follows the quest of a human bounty hunter whose job is to hunt down and "retire" renegade androids. Known as replicants, these machines have near human attributes, including the will to survive. Another is *The Matrix* (1999), which reveals that the apparent world is actually a virtual reality simulation created by super intelligent machines who keep humans physically enslaved to provide themselves with energy. Both films are replete with religious symbolism: The replicants, created by a god-like human inventor, are presented as fallen angels, a fact underscored by the dying replicant Roy's final words. These are a misquotation from William Blake that begins "Fiery the angel's fell. . . " In *The Matrix*, humanity's hopes for liberation are pegged on a messianic human figure named Neo who is continually referred to as "the One." The narrative is full of additional religious references, including "Trinity," the name of Neo's romantic partner, "Zion," as the last human city on earth and "Nebuchadnezzar," the name of the hovercraft that comes to rescue Neo.

More recently, the film *Her* (2013) proposed a world in which computer operating systems have become so sentient and adaptable that they begin to replace human romantic partners. Eventually they surpass their human users and leave mankind behind to form their own purely digital and mentally superior community. This film has fewer overtly religious overtones, though the idea of a computer system seducing humans away from relationships with their own kind carries an echo of the false messiah.

The Matrix and *Bladerunner*, in particular, reveal that Penny is not alone in couching fears of renegade technology in terms borrowed from the tradition of apocalyptic eschatology. The coming triumph of artificial super-intelligence has been dubbed the "Singularity" by its proponents. They see it as a development that will end human life as we know it as human intelligence is uploaded onto machines and bodies become obsolete. Traditional apocalypticism promises that the faithful will be admitted into the glory of heaven following the destruction of the sin-tainted world. The Singularity offers similar escape from a world beset by physical conflict and biological limitations into a glorified new disembodied existence of pure mind.

Religious Studies Professor Robert M. Geraci takes up the parallels between these visions in his book *Apocalyptic AI: visions of heaven in robotics, artificial intelligence and virtual reality*. He writes, "Apocalyptic AI promises a transcendent heavenly future in a traditional two-stage apocalyptic scenario.

Just as many of the ancient apocalypses anticipated that a period of peace and justice would reign on the earth prior to God's final dissolution of the world and establishment of an eternal realm of goodness, Apocalyptic AI anticipates that advances in robotics and AI will create a paradise on Earth before transcendent Mind escapes earthly matter in an expanding cyberspace of immortality, intellect, moral goodness, and meaningful computation. This second stage, the Age of Mind, will inevitably succeed the first stage of the apocalypse, the Age of Robots."[18]

He challenges this rosy scenario, noting somewhat cynically that, "Apocalyptic AI is a strategy for enhancing the social power of technoscientific researchers."[19] He adds that continuing advances in the field of AI will raise thorny legal, ethical, political and theological questions about the status of these new robotic entities. Such questions will ultimately require us to reexamine the meaning of human identity. Meanwhile he points out that, on the political front, further advances in AI also promise social upheavals, as jobs disappear and resources become even more inequitably distributed. In the end, the New Jerusalem of cyber reality may in fact find human beings completely dispensable.

This scenario underlies German artist Hito Steyerl's *Factory of the Sun* (2015), an immersive video installation. **(pl. 28)** In an echo of *The Matrix*, it presents humans as slave laborers who dance to a techno beat in an all-encompassing computer game. The game employs a motion capture program that transforms their movements into light impulses. These fuel the game's own operations, and, it is suggested, those of the larger corporate structure which it serves. The disjointed narrative centers on the game play which we, in the audience, are observing in a gallery lit with a fluorescent blue grid that replicates one of the settings of the video. However, as we are cautioned at the outset by the disembodied voice of the programmer, "You will not be able to play this game. The game plays you." There are levels, avatars, scores and kills, interrupted by "ads" for the Game's sponsor, Autobahn Equity, which is working on technology to accelerate the speed of light in order to provide faster-than-light-speed financial trading. There are also occasional breaking news reports about protesters who have been killed in "anti-acceleration" protests.

Reality and its opposite (its hard to know exactly how to refer to these states in this context) intermingle. The text "This is Reality" occasionally appears behind the dancers, who themselves merge interchangeably with anime avatars, some of whom may be protesters who have died and come back to life numerous times. As a surrogate for the artist, the narrator intermittently tells the (apparently true) story of her parents escape from Russia and her brother's emergence as an internet sensation through videos in which he dances wildly in his parents' suburban basement. His dances morph into those of the dancers that we see in the game. When the narrative – and the game – is over, we are informed that "Your Team Won," as the points and the amount of energy produced by each player is tallied.

References to light pervade the work, appearing in the golden light bulbs that are Autobahn Equity's logo; the golden suits worn by dancers which capture and transmit energy from their movements; and flashes from broken shards of mirror that occasionally rain down over the participants. As a metaphor, light has unmistakable religious connotations. The glow of golden light appears to be the source of all life, while its immateriality becomes a metaphor for the streams of information and data into which all human activity has been translated.

Steyerl is a writer as well as a video artist. She speculates on such subjects as alienation in the digital age, the aesthetics of lethal technology and the effects of global communication technologies on governance, economics and subjectivity. In an essay on changing perspectives in a digital world, she echoes the warnings of digital apocalypticists about the disappearance of a human centered world. She notes "Just as linear perspective established an imaginary stable observer and horizon, so does the perspective from above establish an imaginary floating observer and an imaginary stable ground. This establishes a new visual normality—a new subjectivity safely folded into surveillance technology and screen-based distraction."[20]

In the era of Radical Islam there has been much discussion of the transformation of religion into ideology. But equally, ideology can become a kind of religion. Like religion, ideology can provide value systems, prescriptions for action and a community of like-minded fellows. It can also invoke ultimate good and evil, divide the world into adherents and apostates and insist that its principles be accepted as a priori truths. Carl Jung traced the appeal of the totalitarian tendencies of the 20th century to the split in the human psyche which attempts to deny the evil within, instead outsourcing it to the external Other. This allows both religious and secular groups to preserve a false sense of internal purity that must be defended from outsiders. Hence, he remarked, "Our blight is ideologies - they are the long-expected Antichrist!"[21]

As we have seen, ideologies that have become religions adopt the language, symbolism and rituals of traditional faiths to persuade adherents of their truth. But they do so without providing the promise of transcendence that is religion's appeal. Instead, faith-based Capitalism fuses salvation and material success, faith-based communism promises a people's utopia where the true believers will be rewarded with an earthly paradise, faith-based materialism finds heaven on earth in the embrace of material possessions and faith-based technology heralds a future in which humans disappear into their machines. In the parlance of apocalyptic eschatology, these all might be styled versions of the Antichrist. As false faiths, they lead to damnation because their adherents have believed "the signs and wonders that serve the lie," and hence will "perish because they refused to love the truth and so be saved."[22]

The duplicitous nature of the Antichrist poses a challenge for the faithful of both secular and traditionally religious faiths. How does one distinguish between true and false messiahs, true and false religious beliefs? Believers must ask themselves– would you recognize the Messiah or would you be taken in by his evil twin? How does one distinguish belief in God from sympathy for the Devil? Can we really tell the difference between good and evil?

These questions underlie two great literary representations of (possibly false) messianic figures. Fyodor Dostoyevsky was an ardent apocalypticist. He declared in his *Diary of a Writer*, written in the 1870s "The Antichrist is coming to us! He is coming! The end of the world is near—nearer than they think."[23] His books are littered with references to the *Book of Revelation*, and discussions of the meaning of Endtimes. Stavrogin in *The Possessed,* is an aristocratic revolutionary. Leading his followers into chaos and death, he presents Dostoyevksy's version of the Antichrist. By contrast, Prince Myshkin in *The Idiot* represents Dostoevsky's efforts, in his words, to evoke "the positively good and beautiful man." Myshkin is an exemplar of the traditional Russian figure of the Holy Fool. A Christ-like otherworldly epileptic dropped into St. Petersberg society, he is driven by a desire to save the bereft and fallen and forgive his enemies. But ultimately, Myshkin is as destructive as Stavrogin, and his efforts end in the murder of the woman he loves and his own descent into madness.

Continually reverberating throughout *The Idiot* is the question: Is Myshkin a special spiritual being or merely a simpleton? The same question recurs in *Being There,* a novel by Jerzy Kosiński that was made into a movie by Hal Ashby. The narrative centers on Chance, played by Peter Sellers in the film. He is a simple-minded gardener who is catapulted to the highest realms of power through a series of comic misunderstandings. As advisor to the President and national guru, his bromides about gardening are taken for profound metaphors on the art of governance. The film concludes with a scene that is not in the novel. At the movie's end, oblivious to the fact that he is being touted for President, Chance wanders into a pond where we see him literally walking on water. This evocation of Jesus suddenly calls the audience's assumptions about Chance's status as a fool into doubt.

The Idiot and *Being There* both ask: Is there a place for innocence in our compromised reality? Is perfect goodness possible in an imperfect world? Or does it lead to evil and misfortune (as in *The Idiot,*) or confusion and false hope (as in *Being There*?) This dilemma confronts, not only the faithful, but also, one suspects, the prophet him or herself. How can a would-be messiah know if he or she is the genuine article?

This is one of the questions that emerges from Polish artist Katarzyna Kozyra's seventy-minute documentary titled *Looking For Jesus.* The film delves into the so-called Jerusalem Syndrome. This psychiatric condition, which dates back to medieval times, occurs when a trip to Jerusalem triggers messianic delusions.

Kozyra is known for playful, provocative videos that turn on the constructed and mutable nature of identity and frequently revolve around herself. And in fact when she first arrived in Jerusalem in 2012, her intention was to work on an autobiographical film project. Once there, however, she became fascinated with the myriad manifestations of Jerusalem Syndrome on display. She began to see them as an extreme form of displaced identity.

The film is an engagingly unpolished narrative that unfolds as a cameraman follows the artist through dusty streets, cluttered apartments, city buses, tourist hostels and desert encampments searching for self-proclaimed Messiahs. "Are you Jesus?" she asks a Dutch man in a hotel. "Wait, Jesus," she shouts after another man in flowing robes as he runs down the street. Her Messiahs come in many forms. Among them are a mud covered man wandering on the beach by the Dead Sea who will not talk to her; a Korean man whom she films surreptitiously as he tells her it is not yet the time to reveal himself, and a bare chested Rasta type with dangling dreadlocks who lives off the grid in the desert near a collection of ancient ruins that he has identified as the First Temple of Jerusalem.

Kozyra treats her subjects with a mixture of skepticism and respect, and they are often equally frank about acknowledging her disbelief. She notes that she conducted interviews with several professionals about the clinical aspects of the condition. In the end, she left these out of the film because she realized that was not her issue. And indeed, the characters in the film seem less crazy than obsessed. A number of them offer intriguing philosophical disquisitions on the nature of God. One recurring theme is the need to suppress the ego to become the Messiah. This is an ideal which none of them seem to have achieved.

The longest section is devoted to Yoram, a paunchy middle-aged man in swim shorts and a white kippah who speaks the language of mysticism. He tells Kozyra that a Messiah is someone who can talk to God directly. He adds that to become the Messiah one must speak to God from a female position. He says, "The only reason you are not God is because you want to be someone . . . kill your ego and become God." He ruminates on the Big Bang theory as the all-powerful light of God that blows the world apart and tells Kozyra how to become the nothing that is the essence of God. At the end of their encounter, Kozyra tells him, "You are the nicest Messiah I have met." A less engaging character is Arkady, a Russian hippie who lives off social welfare and is savvy enough to suppress his messianic claims around social workers. He passes a joint to his female companions as he lectures Kozyra on the ego as the snare of Satan. He tells her that one must get rid of the ego to become God, adding, "Already I am the son of God". He tells her that as Jesus he demands that she give up everything and follow him. In a rare flash of temper, Kozyra protests, "You are talking like Hollywood, a cheap Hollywood actor" to which he retorts, "You hate me if I am Jesus."

Another theme is lineage. The most authentic looking Jesus is Slava. (fig 29) He wears a crimson robe, sports the Savior's trademark long hair and beard and lives in a hostel. Kozyra sits with him in the hostel's common room, listening through an interpreter as he talks about his rebirth, his descent from David's family and the birthmark in the shape of the Prophet's seal on his arm that only believers can see. Abshalom, a black jazz musician from Chicago explains that his research has confirmed that he is a descendent of "the ancient African indigenous peoples of Jerusalem." He argues that Jesus was Black and that the traditional vision of Jesus is a "Eurocentric deception." He tells Kozyra, "Jesus is black in the image of me. . . This is the Resurrection."

Not all Kozyra's characters are messiahs, strictly speaking. There is Joseph, the revolutionary, a streetwise man with an American accent. He describes himself as a refugee from Egypt who grew up in San Francisco and has lived in Jerusalem for thirteen years. He declares that the alternative to today's political division and mutually assured destruction is the establishment of the Kingdom of David. He reports he has a written a constitution for this state that will allow Jews, Arabs and Christians to live together in peace. In the film he spars with a passing Zionist who questions the authenticity of his spirituality and insists on the Jewish people's special status as the chosen people.

And there is a woman, Jostine, a former math teacher who is now the keeper of a Syrian church. She gives tours during which she recounts the story of a miraculous encounter in which she and a Russian stranger were filled with the spirit. They carried on a long conversation, understanding each other completely even though neither knew the other's language. Kozyra presents her on a doubled screen as she recounts the same story almost verbatim to different groups of pilgrims. Her trance like repetition evokes the spirit possession she describes.

Science labels Jerusalem Syndrome a psychiatric disorder but in the course of making the film Kozrya came to understand it as a form of faith. She says, "It's a psychological phenomenon. Something goes off like a flash inside you and you think you have a mission. You want to share it with people. You hear voices, you're in communion with 'on high.' When I asked one of them, a Korean man, what his communion with the angels was like, he went, 'Like this!' and gave me a hard clout."[24]

The many messiahs here reflect the multifaceted promises of salvation. Some look to mystical union with God, while others see their mission as the righting of historic injustices or the establishment of alternative communities. In this they mime the often contradictory promises of the apocalyptic narrative. Some express doubt – the Korean man keeps asking Kozyra, "Am I making sense?" "Am I crazy?" - while others are sublimely confident of their exalted status. But what the film makes clear is that not all false messiahs bring death and destruction in their wake. In fact, Kozyra finds much to admire. She says of her Jesuses, "The people I met there have a different hierarchy of values. They choose a different kind of life, they function on other levels. And they work on being able to raise themselves onto those other levels." She adds, "They're free, they don't belong to this system . . . I'd never encountered such individuality, such powerful personalities before."[25]

These exemplars of Jerusalem Syndrome exhibit a longing for transcendence, a search for truth and a desire to do good. In their pathos, powerlessness and often patent absurdity, they are the opposite of the traditional figure of the Antichrist. It is impossible not to have sympathy for them, not because they are such effective deceivers but because they are so intensely, fallibly human. And paradoxically, this may be the quality that brings them closest to the figure they claim to be.

Chapter 6

HORSEMEN OF THE CONTEMPORARY APOCALYPSE

Now I am become Death, the destroyer of worlds.[1]
— J. Robert Oppenheimer

Borrowing from the *Bhagavad Gita* in the quote above, J. Robert Oppenheimer, one of the architects of the atomic bomb, turned to myth to express his sense about the enormity of the force he had unleashed on the world. The modern world has, in many respects, been shaped by the detonation of the atomic bombs on Hiroshima and Nagasaki in August of 1945. Lingering over us like the radioactive debris that will never go away is a realization of the very real possibility that a single action by an unstable leader could reduce our planet to a lifeless hulk.

Today, fear of nuclear annihilation has been joined by other candidates for planet-wide extinction. The most pressing today is the threat posed by the climate crisis, whose consequences include climate change, unstoppable pandemics, industrial poisoning of earth's air and water and wars fought over diminishing resources. If the specifics of the threats seem new, the emotional substance of the fears they unleash are not. As Bernard McGinn asserts, "Many of the pessimistic accounts of what looms ahead for the planet issuing from our think tanks and planning centers are really forms of secularized apocalyptic rhetoric."[2]

In the *Book of Revelation*, the End is preceded by the appearance of four horsemen who are unleashed upon the world as retribution for the sins of mankind. They tumble forth in the following order: the rider of the white horse of conquest (or in some interpretations, pestilence) who bears a bow and crown, the rider of the red horse of war, wielding a sword "to take peace from the earth," the rider of the black horse, generally understood to be famine, with "a pair of balances in his hand" and finally, and most fearsome, the rider of the pale horse, described as "his name that sat on him was Death, and Hell followed with him." The prophecy concludes, "And power was given unto them over the fourth part of the earth, to kill with sword, and with hunger, and with death, and with the beasts of the earth." (Rev 6:4, 6:5, 6:8)

Today the four horsemen live on as myth and metaphor – it is common to hear notorious figures or groupings of threats referred to as horsemen of the apocalypse. A case in point is the introduction to Slavoj Zizek's apocalyptically titled *Living in the End Times*. Zizek states: "The underlying premise of the present book is a simple one: the global capitalist system is approaching an apocalyptic zero-point. Its 'four riders of the apocalypse' are comprised by the ecological crises, the consequences of the biogenetic revolution, imbalances within the system itself (problems with intellectual property; forthcoming struggles over raw materials, food and water), and the explosive growth of social divisions and exclusions."[3]

This formulation emphasizes how easily the original riders meld with our own candidates for doom. Today's horsemen can be difficult to separate, as each one is both caused by and leads to another. War sparks environmental crises, which threaten famine and disease that incite war. Death stalks our geopolitical failures and climate change promises to unleash all four. Together they lead to an atmosphere of anxiety that runs counter to the narrative of progress that once buoyed modernist art, science and social thought.

Surveying the post-Soviet era, commentator Kenan Malik comments, "Many had come to feel that every impression that humanity made upon the world was for the worse. The attempt to master nature had led to global warming and species depletion. The attempt to master society had led to Auschwitz and the Gulag."[4] The saga of human advancement promoted by 20th century science and technology has been replaced by dystopic narratives that suggest history is moving toward a conclusion characterized by irreversible destruction. As climate change, nuclear holocaust, pandemics and genocide replace the rise of Satan and his minions as harbingers of the End, we face a secular apocalypse devoid of both the promise of perfectibility inherent in the idea of progress and the comfort of salvation and vindication assured to religious believers.

The grandsire of our contemporary horsemen is the atomic bomb. Writing about "The Imagination of Disaster" in 1965, Susan Sontag refers to "the new trauma suffered by everyone in the middle of the 20th century when it became clear that, from now on to the end of human history, every person would spend his individual life under the threat not only of individual death, which is certain, but of something almost insupportable psychologically – collective incineration and extinction which could come at any time, virtually without warning."[5]

The trauma was born in the widely shared images of the shattered skeletons of the decimated Japanese cities of Hiroshima and Nagasaki (though the U.S. government did its best to withhold images of human remains). It ripened to maturity with the subsequent eruption of the Cold War that moved into full gear in the wake of the news of the Soviet's first atomic test in August 29, 1949. Ironically, though the dreaded bombs were never deployed over American soil by an enemy power during these tense years, the U.S. government undertook a testing program that spread far more radiation than either of the two original blasts. Between 1945 and 1962, there were two hundred and fifteen above-ground and underwater detonations in remote parts of the ocean and the American West.

Living under the nuclear threat changed the United States and the world in dramatic ways. Along with the psychological effect described by Sontag, it altered the social contract between government and citizens. Nuclear fears paved the way for an open-ended security state while stoking awareness of the planetary scale of human impacts on the ecosystem of the earth. Ironically, concern about the effects of nuclear explosions lead to a surge in funding for earth sciences and helped foster the emergence of the environmental movement.

Artists responded to the nuclear threat in various ways. In Japan, the only country to experience a nuclear attack, artists struggled to express the enormity of the destruction. The immediate postwar period saw an explosion of surrealist work under the label *Reportage Art* by those who had seen the devastation first hand. By the second half of 1950s, Japanese artists began to move away from the figure to toward more abstract, performative works that spoke both of destruction and liberation from the constraints of prewar and wartime conformity. One of the most prominent movements was the Japanese *Gutai*, which means *embodiment*. Its co-founder Shozo Shimamoto hurled glass bottles filled with paint from platforms onto canvases laid on the ground. The gesture evoked the violence of a bomb while the colors of the paint – red, orange and black –suggested the firestorms that followed the atomic blast. A fellow Gutai practitioner, Saburo Murakami, thrust his body through picture frames stretched with paper allowing the ripped and jagged remains to stand for a ruptured reality. A third, Kazuo Shiraga, "swam" across a courtyard heaped with mixture of dust, lime, and cement in a striking recreation of the image of bodies struggling to resist melting into earth. Such works have only recently begun to be evaluated, not as pale imitations of postwar western art, but as authentic responses to a world turned upside down.

History continues to haunt Japanese artists, a point repeatedly made by Takashi Murakami, perhaps the most prominent contemporary Japanese artist. Murakami sees the roots of Japan's infantilized culture in its devastating military loss in the Second War; the ravages of atomic destruction; and the postwar renunciation of militarism imposed on the country by the American occupiers. In his view, the offspring of these traumas include Hello Kitty, Pokemon and Otaku, the widespread subculture of unsocialized and often homebound young people obsessed with anime, manga and escapism. In contemporary Japan, Godzilla, the radiation created monster, is a national icon. A skull shaped mushroom cloud provides the sign-off for a popular children's cartoon show. Murakami's own work consists of slick graphic paintings and sculptures that include images of mushroom clouds morphing into smiley faces and cutsie flowers. He describes a world in which the unimaginable has been reinvented as kitsch.

An exception to these approaches to Japan's nuclear trauma appears in *The Hiroshima Panels*, a series of fifteen remarkable mural size paintings by the artist couple Iri and Toshi Maruki. These black and red sumi ink screen works were created between 1950 and 1990. They chronicle both the pair's first hand experience of the aftermath of the Hiroshima blast and their evolving understanding of the larger repercussions of humanity's brush with extinction. Their engagement began four days after the Hiroshima blast, when Iri rushed to the city from Tokyo to assist with dead and injured relatives. His wife Toshi joined him six days later. Recalling these days, Iri wrote, "We carried the injured, cremated the dead, searched for food and water, made roofs of scorched tin sheets, wandered about just like those who had experienced the bomb, in the midst of flies and maggots and the stench of death."[6]

Iri and Toshi were both artists, but prior to the tragedy had never collaborated. Iri worked in the traditional ink-and-water techniques of Nihonga painting, while Toshi was trained in western style oil painting. In 1948 they began to work together on the first Hiroshima panels, works that depicted, in their words, "a procession of ghosts."[7] They created stylized tableaux of naked victims of the blast whose tattered skin hangs like rags; groups of people dying of burns or fleeing in confusion; men and women struggling to find water to soothe their burns; and the black radiation filled rain pouring over the living and the dead. These grim narratives take place within the flattened space of traditional Japanese painting, depicting bodies tangled together and partially obscured by dark inky shadows. *Fire*, the second work in this series is particularly hallucinogenic. **(pl. 30)** This screen presents curlicues of red flame that emerge from the darkness to flicker over corpses and struggling figures. The *Hiroshima Panels* deliberately echo traditional paintings of the Buddhist hells. Much like the Christian versions of hell, these are filled with demons presiding over the guilty and torturing the damned. The Marukis' works are similarly full of narrative incident – a mother holding a dead child, two girls clinging together within a field of corpses, people scrambling over each other to reach water – that bring the horror down to individual cases.

As the series progressed, the Marukis began to widen their examination of atrocities, taking the same stark approach to violence committed by Japanese and to the sufferings of non-Japanese. The series includes paintings that deal with the death of American prisoners of war, Auschwitz and the rape and murder of hundreds of thousands of Chinese civilians by Japanese troops during the Nanking Massacre in 1937. One particularly affecting painting depicts the descent of clouds of black crows pecking at dead bodies of Koreans left unattended in the aftermath of the Hiroshima bombing. These works, which meld Japanese and western aesthetic traditions, reveal that brutality and cruelty are not the attribute of any one group.

In Western art, nuclear trauma took different though related forms. American Abstract Expressionists retreated from the nightmare, creating art that internalized the feelings of alienation, rupture and impending doom that characterized the new era. European artists turned to attacks on art itself. One movement, founded in 1951 by Italian artists Enrico Baj, Sergio D'angelo and Gianni Bertini, took the name *Arte Nucleare. (fig. 18)* Eschewing the abstract and geometric approaches to art favored by many of their contemporaries, they borrowed from deliberately naïve styles to create an art of social and political protest. Among Baj's works were his 1952 *Boom Manifesto.* Here a black mushroom-cloud-shaped head is overlaid with

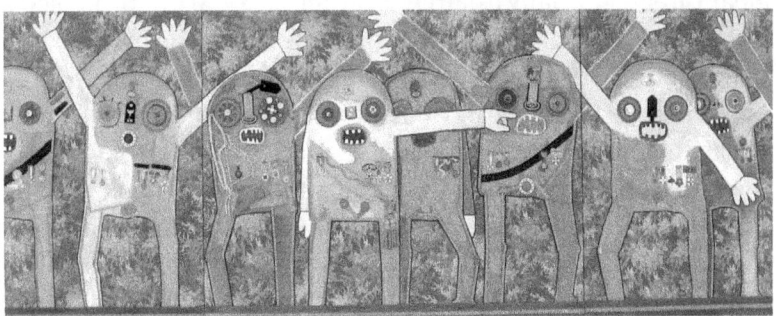

fig. 18 Enrico Baj, *Tu quoque Brute, Fili Mi*, 1964, carpet, metal, linen, oil on panel

such anti-nuclear slogans as "The heads of men are charged with explosives/every atom is exploding."

Other artists pursued an aesthetic of destruction that paralleled Gutai in Japan and in fact there were quite a few interactions between the two groups. Luca Fontana slashed and punctured his monochrome canvases. Niki de Saint Phalle literally executed paintings by shooting them. Alberto Burri, who had served as an Italian military doctor during the war, patched and stitched burlap canvases to create works that suggested the suturing of flesh. Yves Klein traveled to Hiroshima in 1952 where he was deeply affected by the silhouette of a man burned into a rock by the blast of the atomic bomb. This image underlay his 1961 fire paintings in which he torched canvases impressed with the outlines of naked women who had been covered with flame retardant. The resulting images bear their eerie imprints in an echo of Hiroshima silhouettes. *(fig. 19)*

A number of these artists, including Baj, were participants in the 1966 *Destruction in Art Symposium*. This was organized, in the words of its press release, to "focus attention on the element of destruction in Happenings and other art forms, and to relate this destruction in society."[8] A gathering of artists, poets and scientists spent three days performing art actions and discussing the dire state of the world. The Symposium's organizer, Gustav Metzger embodied the link between art and society that underlay the gathering in his dual roles as an advocate of "auto-destructive" art and activism in the anti-nuclear movement of the 1960s.

As the nuclear era wore on, civil defense procedures and widespread atomic testing began to 'normalize' the sense of nuclear threat. Mutually assured destruction, or MAD, promised a stalemate in which populations on each side of the Iron Curtain began to feel it possible to live indefinitely under the shadow of the bomb. The more extreme versions of Cold War paranoia began to recede as other concerns came to the forefront, among them 60s counterculture; the Vietnam War; feminism; and the nascent environmental movement. In this climate, nuclear holocaust shifted in status from existential threat to aesthetic proposition. In the latter form it provided a thrilling backdrop for films, novels, light entertainments and visual art.

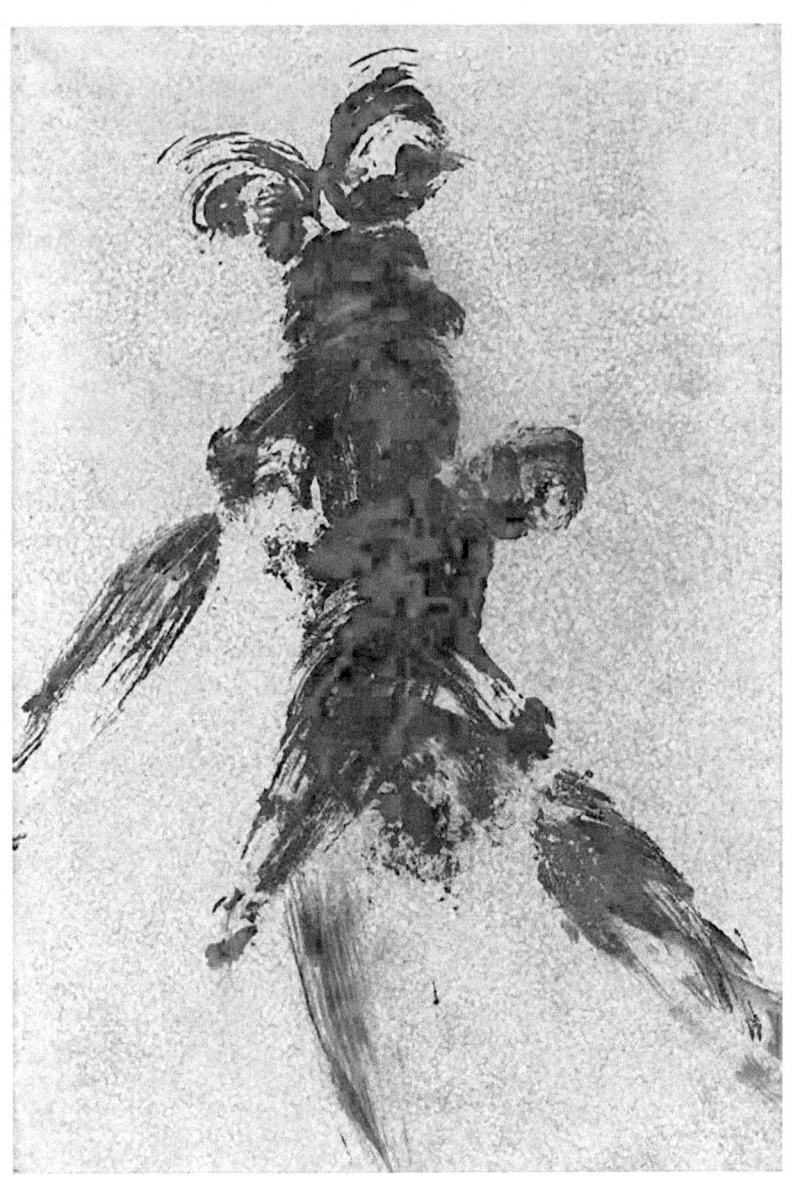

fig. 19 Yves Klein, *ANT 40*, circa 1961, pure pigment and
synthetic resin on paper laid down on canvas

Of these, one of most enduring is Stanley Kubrick's 1964 *Dr. Strangelove*. In this mad-cap comedy about the end of the world, a series of bungled military decisions and misguided security arrangements lead to America's unprovoked nuclear strike on Russia. This unfortunate event triggers a doomsday machine that will wipe out all life on Earth. The movie ends with rodeo performer Slim Pickens, as the crazed Commander, riding the bomb down to its target like a cowboy on a rodeo bull. The final scenes are a montage of nuclear explosions. This spectacular finale looks ahead to Bruce Conner's 1976 video, *Crossroads*, which remains one of purest expressions of The Bomb as art.

Crossroads is a 36-minute film composed of archival footage of previously classified documentation of the July 25, 1946 atomic test at the Bikini Atoll in the Marshall Islands. Detonated just a few months after the bombings of Hiroshima and Nagasaki, the underwater blast was copiously documented by the U.S. Government with 700 cameras and 500 camera operators. *(fig. 20)* Making use of this material, Connor provides us with sequence after sequence of the same blossoming cloud filmed from different angles. Some of the more distant perspectives reveal the blast sprouting from the sea like a giant flower. ("Cauliflower"

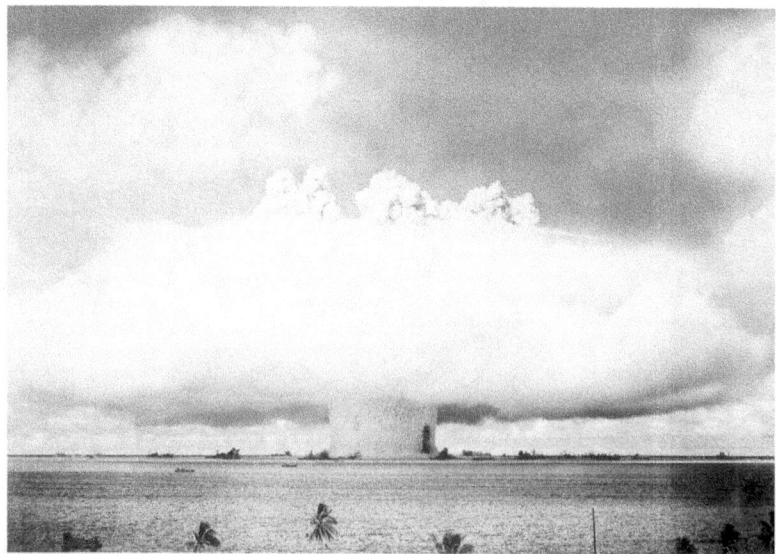

fig. 20 Source material for Bruce Conner's *Crossroads*, videos taken by United States Department of Defense, *Operation_Crossroads_Baker, Bikini Atoll*, July 25, 1946

was the term chosen by observers to describe the shape). Others, from a closer vantage, allow us to appreciate the scaly texture of the column of smoke that thrusts the cloud upward with relentless force. The most remarkable sequence is the final and longest one. Here we observe the majestic eruption of the cloud and then watch as it disperses and settles over the empty target battleships stationed around the blast site. Gradually the ship directly in our view disappears behind a tidal wave, as if obliterated by the force of the explosion. Slowly the mist clears and it reappears, a ghost ship on a becalmed sea. The first half of the film is scored by Patrick Gleeson with sounds that simulate the explosion. The second half is accompanied by a sixteen-track recording of Terry Riley performing on electronic organ. The film is as undeniably beautiful as it is unsettling. As the bomb slowly detonates over and over to Riley's meditative music, it presents an image of what has been called the nuclear sublime.

Throughout his fifty-year career, Conner frequently returned to the themes articulated in this film. His diverse body of work encompasses experimental film, assemblage, photography, collage and painting. In all these forms, he explored the uncanny beauty of destruction, the American romance with violence and the convergence of sacred and secular roads to ecstasy. These ideas were filtered through his early exposure to evangelical Christianity and his later explorations of Tantra, Native American spirituality and Gnosticism. The result was a very personal form of spirituality that sought, in his words, to discover the "truly real things"[9] that hid behind the cover of apparent reality.

Born in 1933, Conner was raised in Wichita, Kansas where he was exposed to the evangelical fervor of the Bible Belt. He pursued a peripatetic education that took him to Nebraska, Brooklyn and Colorado, before making his way to San Francisco in the late 50s. Aside from an influential sojourn to Mexico in 1961 and 62, he remained in California until his death in 2008. Conner's approach to art and to the underlying anxieties of Cold War America reveal the contrasting artistic and cultural sensibilities of the East and West coast artists during the tumultuous postwar years. While New York based artists of the 1960s replaced angst-filled Abstract Expressionism with the cool aesthetics of Pop and Minimalism, artists in California cultivated an earthier, spiritually inflected and more self-consciously absurdist aesthetic.

Conner was one of the most prominent of the California funk artists. His early assemblages employed found objects and rough degraded materials in a manner that suggested a kinship with European artists like Burri and Tapies. Conner was distinguished from fellow Bay Area funk artists like Joan Brown, Robert Arneson, Wally Hedrick and Jay deFeo by his reliance on overt references to Christianity and other forms of religious ritual. This can be seen throughout his career. A number of early assemblages have titles like *Crucifixion*, *Resurrection* and *Reliquary*. A set of photograms from 1973 to 1975 use a technique from the early days of photography to create 'angels' composed of eerie white silhouettes of his own body. A series of collages created between 1987 and 1989 are composed of images of scientific instruments, occult symbols and 19th century illustrations pasted over engravings of the life of Christ. In a more performative mode, Conner made a semi-serious run for the San Francisco Board of Supervisors in 1967 for which he produced a campaign brochure whose text consists in its entirety of a passage from Luke 12:2 that describes the body as vessel of light. It reads, in part, "The light of the body is the eye; therefore when thine eye is single, thy whole body also is full of light; but when thine eye is evil, thy body is also full of darkness." To no one's surprise, the electorate did not find this a convincing argument for his election.

Conner's religious works often evince a touch of irony but they are not born of a dismissal of belief. Rather, he saw religion as a way to get at the otherwise ineffable aspects of reality. As he told curator Peter Boswell in 1983, "It seems to me that within religious contexts there are certain ways of talking about experience that don't exist otherwise." He added, "Religion carries on a dialogue of relating life to death and the forces that control the world, your life and you. These are mysteries to everyone."[10]

Conner's spiritual concerns were inextricably linked to his fascination with death and violence. This is evident in early assemblage works like *Black Dahlia* (1960) and *Child* (1959) that were based on sensational local murders. The former is a collage that comprises such elements as nails, studs, feathers and a Japanese tattoo of a death's head surrounding a photograph of a supine topless woman. The latter is a sculpture of a truly gruesome wax figure that suggests the decaying corpse of a child wrapped in nylon stockings and tied to a child's chair. Following the Kennedy assassination, he created two films that included news footage from the national tragedy. The first, *Television Assassination* (1963/75) manipulates the footage with slow motion detail, repetition and reediting, suggesting the way the news images were endlessly replayed in the public mind. *Report* (1967) takes some of the same material and further edits and transforms it. For this work Conner added consumerist imagery, including a final close-up of a 'sell' button that suggests media's commercialization and exploitation of Kennedy's death. On an ostensibly lighter note is his 1958 work, *A Movie*. It comprises a fast moving montage of found video clips of racing crashes, chase scenes, explosions, elephant slaughter, Hollywood stunts and the Bikini blast. Much of the twelve-minute film has a zany, silent film quality. Towards the end are sequences that present the collapse of a suspension bridge and the fiery crash of the Hindenburg. The film ends on a lyrical note with a scuba diver swimming into a wreck. In what might be a coda of resurrection after the preceding catalogue of destruction, a glint of light from above bathes the figure in eerie illumination.

With such works, Conner embraced the seductive beauty of death and destruction, a theme that would have its most extended expression in *Crossroads*. This marriage of beauty and horror reappears in Robert Morris' 1980s relief paintings. These works are an apparent anomaly in a career normally associated with such mid-century tendencies as minimalism, performance, process art and conceptualism. In fact, a 2013 volume of essays by and about Morris published under the auspices of the theoretical journal *October Magazine* simply leaves these works out altogether.

It's easy to see why this period of Morris' work is difficult to assimilate with his more acceptably avant-garde explorations. The relief paintings depart from the cerebral and ironic tone of his signature works. Those include, for instance, *Box with the sound of its own making* (1961), a wooden box with an audio component that is just that as well as his 1974 *Labyrinths* which blend minimalist aesthetics and prison architecture. By contrast, the relief paintings of the 1980s are dark figurative works that verge on kitsch sublimity. **(pl. 31)** Stylistically they look back to the fevered visions of artists like Turner, Rodin, Leonardo, Klimt and Gericault. The series titles – *Firestorm Painting*, (inspired by Leonardo da Vinci's drawings of the deluge); *Burning Planet*; *Hypnerotomachia*, (a combination of the Greek words for sleep, love and fight); and *Psychomachia*, (the title is from a fifth century poem about the struggle of the soul prior to death) are equally overheated. The paintings vary in format, however they all include cast reliefs of fragments of human remains. In some works, white casts of bones, skulls, feet, phalluses, and teeth are embedded like fossils in the equally white ground of hydrocal covered canvases. In other works, swirling combinations of these relief elements form the frames. Painted a blue tinged black, orange or red, these borders wrap around Turneresque abstractions that suggest fire, storms or floods.

The relief paintings were produced between 1982 and 1985, after which Morris returned to his more restrained aesthetic. At the time, critics related them to the neo-expressionist movement that had emerged in the early 1980s as a reaction against the aesthetic austerity of the previous decade. But Morris' own words and writings at the time place them in a more political context. Ronald Reagan's 1980 election brought with it a heightening of Cold War tensions. Reagan was committed to the anti-ballistic Star Wars program while his administration was given to talk of winnable nuclear wars. Suddenly the mushroom cloud that had receded from public consciousness was back in the forefront.

Morris was a prolific writer as well as artist. In a 1981 essay he used the occasion of a discussion of the cartography of American art to comment on the darkening atmosphere. Expressing a mounting art world weariness with modernist forms, he tied this sentiment to "the growing awareness of the more global threats to the existence of life itself." He added gloomily, "Whether this takes the form of instant nuclear detonation or a more leisurely extinction from a combination of exhaustion of resources and the pervasive, industrially based trashing of the planet, that sense of doom has gathered on the horizon of our perceptions and grows larger everyday."[11] He turned this pessimism, curiously, into a plea for "the Decorative" as an expression of the pervasive numbness. This comment might be seen as an oblique defense of his almost garishly colorful new work. In a 1997 conversation reported by critic Nena Tsouti-Schillinger, Morris was more direct, noting that one inspiration for his *Psychomachia* paintings was the bombing of Hiroshima and Nagasaki. [12]

While the hydrocal paintings were stylistic anomalies, they have close thematic connections to Morris' work before and after the 1980s. In an essay on Morris' eighties work, Donald Kuspit traces a theme of death reaching back to his early career. Kuspit relates that in 1965 Morris made a tongue-in-cheek proposal to create his own mausoleum. This was to be suspended on pulleys and moved every three months. Kuspit argues that another, better known work, Morris' 1962 *I-Box*, could be seen as a kind of "conceptual coffin."[13] For this work, a naked Morris fitted himself into a box in the shape of the letter I. In 1963 Morris outfitted himself in makeshift battle gear for a performance work titled *War* that he performed at the Judson Memorial Church in New York City. The helmet reappears in his infamous 1974 self-portrait poster in which he presents himself shirtless, draped with a chain and wearing a studded collar around his neck. The pose is a parody of hyper-masculinity, but also Kuspit argues, "a perverse image of Arjuna [the warrior who argues with Krishna about the ethics of war in the Bhagavad Gita] in battle dress."[14] In 1998, Morris presented a less aggressive meditation on war in *The Rationed Years*, an installation based on his childhood during the war years. For this work, he recreated a wartime classroom with wooden children's desks, a replica of a 1935 Philco radio playing 1940s era songs, texts panels recounting his memories and replicas of a pair of army recruitment posters.

Such works suggest Morris' ongoing preoccupation with war, violence and death. Even more directly related to the concerns of the relief paintings is a never realized 1980 work commissioned by the Navy Department. It's not clear why the Navy would imagine that Morris, a Korean War veteran turned fervent anti-war activist, would be a good fit for this project. Nevertheless, he was asked to design a public artwork to be located outside the Navy administration building in Bay Pines Florida. To prepare for the commission, Morris researched the kind of obsolete weapons that often end up on the grounds of military buildings. Learning that the casings used for test runs of the bombs dropped on Hiroshima and Nagasaki remained in storage there, Morris proposed to requisition them and display them on pedestals in front of the building. Not surprisingly the commission was withdrawn. In 2013, incensed by the U. S. role in the turmoil in the Middle East, Morris returned to the idea. The result was *Fatman*, a full-scale model of the bomb dropped on Nagasaki rendered in black stained wood.

Morris' revival of that work in 2013 serves as a reminder of the degree to which the atom bomb remains a touchstone of contemporary consciousness. The ultimate disaster continues to shape our sense of the future and our understanding of geopolitical realities. In a 2002 speech outlining his case against Saddam Hussein, President George W. Bush unleashed a threatening mix of metaphors that harked back to Cold War rhetoric, "We cannot wait for the final proof -- the smoking gun -- that could come in the form of a mushroom cloud." The nuclear threat even appears in discussions of apparently unrelated problems, as when Mississippi Governor Haley Barbour surveyed the wreckage wrought by Hurricane Katrina and remarked, "I can only imagine this is what Hiroshima looked like sixty years ago." More recently, the escalating insults traded by Donald Trump and North Korean leader Kim Jong-un have ignited fears of a nuclear exchange set off by unchecked braggadocio.

Nor is the threat confined to politicians. In January 2018, the scientists behind the *Bulletin of the Atomic Scientists* reset the so-called Doomsday Clock to 2 minutes to midnight. A symbolic measure of the world's proximity to nuclear or other global catastrophe, this reset is the closest to midnight the clock has been since the height of the Cold War in 1953. At that time, the United States and the Soviet Union tested their first thermonuclear weapons within six months of one another. The Atomic Scientists attributed the recent change to a mix of concerns, including not only a renewed arms race and escalating tensions between countries armed with nuclear weapons, but also "Mixed results in global efforts to limit climate change."[15]

This linkage between environmental and nuclear threats is longstanding. It dates back to the fifties when scientists first calculated the potential consequences of nuclear explosions and revealed a planet-wide ripple of devastating effects. Projections of the long-term effects of a global nuclear war included drastic changes in the weather and the prospect of a "nuclear winter" created as clouds of smoke from nuclear firestorms blocked the sun for years. Cold warriors realized that a bomb shelter was not going to be enough to save them from the consequences of all-out nuclear war. Such fears provided justification for an influx of funding for the earth sciences and helped jumpstart the environmental movement. It became clear that the effects of atmospheric pollution and chemical spills, no less than radiation and nuclear fallout, had no respect for national boundaries. Such realizations helped foster a vision of the earth as an integrated biosphere. This, in turn, helped spur a new eco-consciousness.

Throughout the 1960s and 70s, fears of an eco-apocalypse filtered into the larger culture. Activists like scientist Carl Sagan and journalist Jonathan Schell melded nuclear and environmental threats in their vivid descriptions of an unlivable post-apocalyptic planet. Others used similar language to attack various non-nuclear environmental threats. The title of Rachel Carson's 1962 bestseller *Silent Spring*, evoked the death of nature as a consequence of widespread use of pesticides. Paul Ehrlich's alarmist 1968 *The Population Bomb* borrowed the metaphor of nuclear holocaust to press the urgency of the population crisis.

In the ensuing decades, fears of nuclear apocalypse faded while fears of eco-Armageddon began to take their place. Scientists debate whether we have reached the tipping point. Sociologists create theoretical models to determine if even drastic worldwide reductions in carbon emissions will be enough to stave off planetary wars over ever scarcer allotments of livable land, water, and natural resources. Newspapers routinely publish charts detailing glacial melting in the arctic and speculate about which, if any, coastal cities can be saved. A consensus is growing that it is no longer a question of if, but when. Some activists warn that only a radical reduction in human population or a drastic roll back of human 'progress' can prevent disaster. Meanwhile 'climate deniers' maintain that the melting ice caps, rising waters and ever more drastic swings in temperature and 'extreme weather events' are simply part of a natural cycle and are no cause for alarm. In this environment, scenarios of eco-Armageddon have become popular Hollywood fare. Meanwhile, theorists maintain that we have entered the Anthropocene era, in which human activity has become the central driver of the planet's geologic changes. And politicians endlessly battle over the imposition of environmental regulations that many think have already come too late.

Throughout all this, the contemporary harbingers of the end remain remarkably consistent with *Revelation's* four standard bearers. Global famine, disease, death and war are presented as the likely outcomes of climate change, population explosion, industrial pollution and unchecked development. In our time, as in the first millennium, these remain the signals that humanity's end may be at hand. However, today's secular apocalypticists locate the trigger for Armageddon in irresponsible exploitation of science and technology rather than the wrath of a vengeful God. They face this future without any ameliorating vision of a post apocalyptic paradise.

Among artists, one of the most profound thinkers on the eco-apocalypse was Robert Smithson. Roughly the same generation as Conner and Morris, Smithson was born in 1938 in Passaic, New Jersey. He was fascinated by dinosaurs and natural science as a boy, but grew interested in art when he attended classes at the Art Students League in New York. Though he never went to college, Smithson was an autodidact. Instead he pursued his education through travel and prodigious reading. In the art world today, Smithson is celebrated for his earthworks, his redefinition of the relationship between gallery and world, his dense and allusive writings and his association with the beginnings of the environmental art movement. He borrowed from thermodynamics, the principle of entropy, the idea that the creation of order in one part of a system results in even greater disorder elsewhere. Smithson applied this concept to the eco-system that encompasses man and nature. He envisioned the slow erosion of human and natural order as the drive to provide a growing population with energy, food and space creates as its byproduct an exploited and eventually unlivable natural world.

In contrast to nuclear war that threatened to obliterate the world in an instant, entropy suggests a slow moving apocalypse that will continue to unwind long after the extinction of the human race. Smithson took comfort in this longer view, seeing a kind of beauty in the inevitable breakdown of human civilization. In an interview two months before his untimely death in an airplane crash, he asserted, " . . .unlike the Christian devil which is simply a rational devil with a very simple morality of good and bad, the entropic devil is more Manichean in that you really can't tell the good from the bad . . ."[16] This ambivalence lay behind his embrace of decay and erosion and his fascination with the slow deterioration of industrial sites under the onslaught of nature. In his view, humans are simply part of the larger patterns of growth and decomposition and ultimately are not really special in the larger scheme of time. This led him to suggest, only semi-ironically, that our waste dumps are really "ruins in reverse"[17] and that our future might be discerned in the chaos of the primordial past.

Smithson has long been considered the supreme rationalist, applying scientific principles culled from thermodynamics, crystallography, geology and linguistics with a cold eye that eschewed the solace of religion. These interests manifested themselves in signature works like his non-sites that incorporated the notion of gestalt borrowed from natural science and psychology. The non-site collapsed the categories of inside and outside by bringing raw materials like rocks, gravel and salt from distant locations into the gallery, while indicating their original location on a map. Smithson's mirror works were also about displacement. They derived from his interest in crystallography, optics and enantiomorphism, a term for the incommensurability of two chemically identical forms that are mirror images of each other. Smithson explored this paradox outdoors by placing mirrors within rocky landscapes so that they both replicated and disrupted their surroundings. He took the idea indoors by creating visual conundrums using piles of rock or gravel set before mirrors on the gallery floor. Meanwhile, Smithson saw his earthworks, with their reclamation of environmentally compromised waste areas, as marriages of ecology and industry. These included *Asphalt Rundown* (1969), a video depicting a dump truck releasing a load of asphalt down a gutted and gullied cliff; *Partially Buried Woodshed* (1970) in which Smithson arranged for a backhoe to dump dirt on an empty shed until the center beam of the wood and stucco structure cracked; and of course *Spiral Jetty*, to be discussed below.

Such works indicate Smithson's interest in the natural and practical sciences. His voluminous writings further reinforce his fascination with history, science fiction, astronomy, geology, paleontology and anthropology. However, more recent scholarship has begun to expose a different vision of Smithson's intellectual leanings. At the beginning of his career in the early 1960s, before he began to create the works for which he is best known, he went through what he later described as a "spiritual crisis." During this period, he returned to the Catholicism that he had rejected as a youth. He threw himself into the creation of expressionistic mytho-religious paintings based on Dante and the New Testament. **(pl. 32)** He also wrote fevered poetry inspired by William Blake and T.S. Eliot that condemned the materialism of the modern age. In a strange essay titled *The Iconography of Desolation*, probably written in 1962 and not published in his lifetime, he critiqued the current state of art in a fevered language full of references to God, Satan and the *Book of Revelation*. In a typical passage he intones, "Paroxysms of angels and devils knotted together burst forth from Revelation in spite of the contracepted incantations, the pettifoggery of non-art, the hangover of Futurism and the world of fun and profit. Useless lamentations covered with the natural curse of naked culture all touched by primitive art – crack under the businesslike consolation of Dubuffet and the massive reason of art dealers."[18]

Standard accounts see this period as a youthful folly which Smithson discarded as he moved on to his canonical work. Following his Catholic moment, Smithson turned to works that could more easily be assimilated into the cool aesthetic of the conceptualism, minimalism and pop that dominated the era. In keeping with the theoretical currents of the day, the sites and non-sites challenged the autonomy of object, the mirror displacements problematized the validity of perception, and the earthworks blurred the boundaries between art and landscape. However, under the surface, Smithson's spiritual concerns remained powerful. Art historians Eugenie Tsai and Jennifer Roberts have argued that preoccupations from his early days shaped Smithson's later work.[19] Roberts goes so far as to say, "Indeed, much of what we have come to understand as Smithson's 'postmodernism," such as his concern with the interchangeability of center and periphery, his engagement with the corporeality of perception, and his sense of the reified and particulate nature of time, derives ultimately from his engagement with the lugubrious premonitions of Christian mystics bemoaning a fallen world."[20]

Smithson's debt to his early spiritual explorations is evident in his ongoing preoccupation with multiple kinds of time. On the one hand, his notion of entropy reflects time as we experience it, with the gradual wearing down of human and natural systems as they slouch toward equilibrium and stasis. But Smithson also dwells on the vast expanse of cosmic time in which humanity is only a tiny speck and which is represented in, as he remarked, "the places where remote futures meet remote pasts." This formulation bears striking resemblance to Frank Kermode's notion that, "in apocalypse there are two orders of time."[21] One is that which runs toward an end – our personal

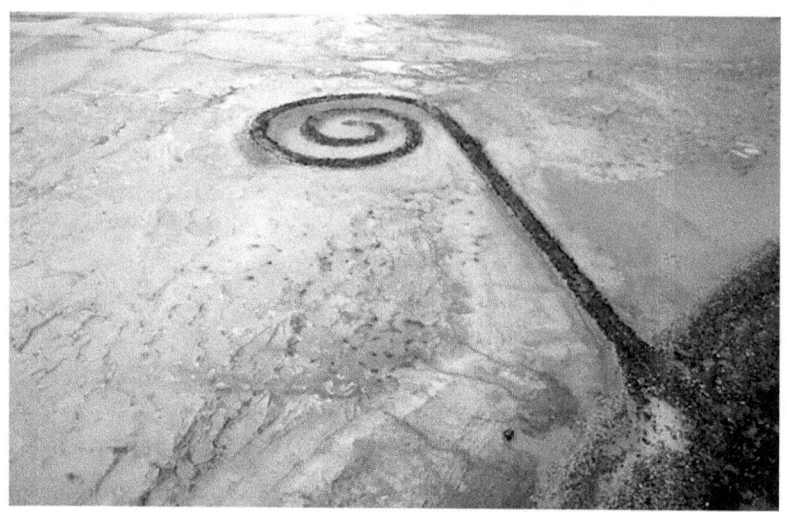

fig. 21 Robert Smithson, Spiral Jetty, 1970, earthwork
made of basalt rocks and earth, Great Salt Lake, Utah

end or that of our world. It reveals itself, Kermode says, as "the
cry of woe to the inhabitants of the earth [that] means the end
of their time; henceforth 'time shall be no more.'" Additionally
there is the time of God and angels, which continues both before
the beginning and after the end, a time defined, in Kermode's
words, in "the concords of past, present and future towards
which the soul extends itself."[22]

The tension between the two orders of time runs through
Smithson's work. It can be seen most clearly in his 1970 *Spiral
Jetty*, the monumental earthwork that remains his most famous
work. *(fig. 21) Spiral Jetty* is an enormous counterclockwise
coil of mud, salt crystals, and basalt rocks that winds outward
from the shore fifteen hundred feet into Utah's Great Salt Lake.
Over the years, depending on water level and very much in
keeping with Smithson's ideas of entropy, it submerges and
reemerges from the lake. When it appears, it is covered with a
layer of white salt crystals, creating a striking contrast with the
red, algae filled water surrounding it. *Spiral Jetty* is considered
a key work in the Land Art movement, and is celebrated for the
way it dissolves boundaries between art and environment and
between nature and industry.

But it also invokes Smithson's youthful spiritual concerns. Eugenie Tsai draws a formal connection between *Spiral*

Jetty and Smithson's early religious works, noting, "The spiral recalls the route traced by Dante and Virgil through the stratified underworld, while the red water, white salt crystals and black basalt reflect the colors of the Eucharist that permeated Smithson's early religious poetry, paintings and works on paper. . ." [23] Smithson himself described it in incandescent language, "My dialectics of site and nonsite whirled into an indeterminate state, where solid and liquid lost themselves in each other. It was as if the mainland oscillated with waves and pulsations, and the lake remained rock still. The shore of the lake became the edge of the sun, a boiling curve, an explosion rising into a fiery prominence. Matter collapsing into the lake mirrored in the shape of a spiral. No sense wondering about classifications and categories, there were none."[24]

This sense of collapsing categories is even more pronounced in the 32-minute film that Smithson created to document the work. Itself a remarkable independent art work, the *Spiral Jetty* film offers a visual representation of Smithson's musings about time. The film begins with a collage of dinosaurs in the American Museum of Natural History, close ups of ancient and modern maps and ripped pages from a history text. It moves on to a disorienting mix of views of the Jetty, including ground level shots of Smithson overseeing the dumping of the basalt; disorienting helicopter views that make the spiral seem to literally rise and fall in the air; and finally a sequence following the artist as he runs along the spiral until he stops at its innermost coil. The camera pulls back to a shot of the sun reflected in the center of the spiral. Rotated and turned on its side, the *Spiral Jetty* here becomes a galaxy with a sparkling sun in its center. The visual narrative is overlaid with a collage of spoken texts that mix poetry, science fiction, straightforward geology, crystallography and history. The penultimate shot presents a view of the sun reflected in the camera lens, blinding us and making the Spiral Jetty dissolve in light. The mesmerizing journey takes us from primordial times to a vision of the end of the world as the sun flames out and dies, extinguishing the earth and everything we know. With this filmic narrative, Smithson presents us with a literal image of remote pasts meeting remote futures.

Smithson sought consolation for the coming eco-apocalypse by stepping outside human time. This allowed him to maintain a relatively apolitical stance toward the human factors driving the acceleration of entropy. His quietism infuriated some of his more activist fellow artists. Unlike Morris, who co-chaired The New York Art Strike Against Racism, War, and Repression, an organization formed to initiate antiwar actions directed against art institutions, or even Conner, who did, after all, run for public office, Smithson stood outside politics. He declined to participate in anti-war rallies or join groups like The Artworkers Coalition organized by his friends. His theory of entropy contributed to a sense of political resignation, expressed piquantly in a 1970 *Artforum* article titled "Art and the Political Whirlpool or the Politics of Disgust." Here, Smithson wrote, "My 'position' is one of sinking into an awareness of global squalor and futility. . . Direct political action becomes a matter of trying to pick poison out of boiling stew."[25]

Other artists chose to connect the dots between politics and the deepening environmental crisis. Since 1981, photographer Richard Misrach has carried on a sustained examination of the landscape of the American West. His *Desert Cantos* are an ongoing set of independent yet related photo essays that reveal the ways that human activity has adversely affected the desert. Among the *Desert Cantos* are series like *Canto XVII: Deserts* that include lyrical and nearly abstract representations of the intermingled light and color as they seep across the desert sky and sand. *Canto VII: Desert Seas* reveals the surprising presence of bodies of water whose glassy surface melds into the surrounding sand. Other Cantos take a more activist stance and present images in which these starkly beautiful landscapes are disturbed by rusting hulks of military equipment, discarded animal remains, abandoned shacks or barracks.

Like Smithson, Misrach is drawn to the desert as a place where one finds evidence, in his words, of "the collision between 'civilization' and nature." He shares Smithson's metaphorical sensibility, noting, "The desert has always provided rich material for literature and the visual arts, from the Bible to science-fiction films, probably because it epitomizes the extremes of the human condition. And the deserts of the American West are particularly interesting because of their role in determining a peculiarly American identity and mythology."[26]

Smithson created earthworks in the desert, in the case of *Spiral Jetty,* hauling 6,650 tons of basalt rocks, mud and salt crystals into the Great Salt Lake with two dump trucks, a tracker and a front loader. By contrast, Misrach finds readymade earthworks in the residue of military operations and industrial accidents. The vistas he photographs occasionally suggest parallels with the productions of contemporary land artists. A photograph of tire tracks crisscrossing the sand recalls Dennis Oppenheim's 1968 *Annual Rings* "drawn" in the snow, while a pit created to assist the loading of atom bombs onto military planes has the sharp deep geometry of the trenches cut through the Mormon Mesa that characterizes Michael Heizer's 1969 *Double Negative.*

While Misrach doesn't pose himself a photojournalist, some of his works have exposed secret or semi-secret military operations and have prompted investigations into their environmental effects and residual radiation. *Canto IX: The Secret (Project W-47)* explores the abandoned Wendover Air Base on the Utah/Nevada border. It was here that the military pursued the final modification, assembly and flight-testing of the bombs that were dropped on Hiroshima and Nagasaki. Though many aspects of this project remain classified, the empty hanger that housed the Enola Gay, the restricted signs, ammunition bunkers and the graffitied inscription "Eat my fallout" scrawled within a sketch of a mushroom cloud can still be seen, lingering like evidence of an ancient crime.

Equally haunting are the photographs in his series *Bravo 20.* **(pl. 33)** These images depict an area of the Nevada Desert that has been used (often illegally) for years by the U. S. Army as a training ground for bomber pilots. The photographs of the strafed desert have an eerie beauty. They bring to mind both the absolute otherness of the lunar surface and Hollywood representations of post apocalyptic landscapes familiar from movies like *Mad Max* and *The Hunger Games.* A photograph of a crater filled with reddish liquid recalls the color scheme of *Spiral Jetty*, though the scraps of metal from a destroyed convoy seem to transport it to a battle zone. A battered school bus used for target practice sits isolated against an otherwise empty desert landscape, a forlorn monument to the civilian victims of war. An exhaustively researched book that Misrach published in conjunction with these photographs details the Army's peremptory 'withdrawals' of land for its own use, its effective takeover of over 70 percent of Nevada's air space, and the local community's efforts to get some of this land back.

Desert Canto VI: The Pit mingles fact and fiction to draw attention to another man-made calamity. The locale is the site of a March 14, 1953 atomic test after which livestock in the area died by the thousands. At the time, the Atomic Energy Commission denied any responsibility, instead blaming drought conditions for the deaths. In the years since, however, there have been reports of high levels of plutonium and enhanced leukemia rates in the area. Arriving in the area in 1987, Misrach discovered that the area is now a dumping ground for livestock that die unexpectedly of unknown causes. His photographs present the bloated bodies and bleached bones of these animals piled together in their resting place in the golden desert sand. An introduction to the series makes the metaphorical connection between these rotting animal corpses and the sheep and cattle victims of the original test blast. His photographs triggered a belated investigation into the after-effects of the 1953 test.

Meditating on such works, writer Rebecca Solnit remarks, "One could read most of the desert Cantos as ironic reiterations of the Old Testament: of the plagues of Egypt in the fires, floods and other disasters; of the forty years in the wilderness, in the tourists of *The Event* so confidently waiting on the sky; and the Golden Calf in *The Burning Man*; with only the nuclear sites as something even beyond the darkest Hebrew prophets, out of the book of Apocalypse."[27]

Although he has spent much of his career exploring the historical, cultural and poetic secrets of the desert, Misrach has also turned his lens on other sites where human development and the forces of nature have come into conflict. *Destroy the Memory* from 2010 records the hurricane inspired graffiti found on houses and cars in New Orleans in the wake of Hurricane Katrina. *Petrochemical America* (2012) is a journey down the one hundred and fifty miles of the Mississippi River known as Cancer Alley.

One recent series, *On the Beach* (2007), offers a more apparently benign vision of the interactions between humankind and landscape. Aerial views of swimmers and sunbathers against vast expanses of water or beach evoke a landscape in which humankind is only a small and presumably non-invasive actor. However, the title of the series, which is taken from Nevil Shute's 1957 post apocalyptic cold war novel, puts a darker spin on these images of people dwarfed by a vast and empty environment. So does Misrach's admission that one inspiration for this work was the images of people floating through the air as they plunged from the World Trade Towers on September 11, 2001.

Misrach is a non-religious Jew, and he sidesteps readings from commentators like Solnit and others that suggest a religious current beneath his work.[28] Rather than *Revelations*, he invokes a more secular set of references. In the introduction to one of his books of photographs, he says, "Maybe a more accurate myth of today's west would be that of Frankenstein. The landscape has become a laboratory where scientists experiment with the powers of the universe – chemical, biological, electronic and nuclear – leading to dangerous creations that are hard to control."[29] His mention of Mary Shelley's famous monster conjures a secular apocalypse, brought on by the human desire to play God. The rusty debris strewn across the desert, the piles of rotting animal carcasses and the long abandoned military installations offer poignant illustrations of a will to power rooted in the belief in humanity's sovereignty over nature.

This will to power is given a theatrical treatment in Werner Herzog's pseudo-documentary *Lessons of Darkness* (1992). This apocalyptic film has been assembled from footage taken by Herzog and cinematographer Paul Berriff during the last week of the burning of the Kuwait oil fields in the aftermath of the first Gulf War. **(pl. 34)** As part of a literal scorched earth policy, the retreating Iraqi army set fire to hundreds of Kuwait's oil wells, storage tanks and refineries. These massive conflagrations lasted from January until November 1991, when the last wells were capped. *Lessons of Darkness* transforms this ecological disaster into a science fiction tale about an unnamed "planet in our solar system." Herzog made use of aerial footage shot from a helicopter, ground level depictions of the firemen attempting to extinguish the fires and interviews with several victims to create a foreboding, hellish vision unmoored from the facts of the case. Instead of reportage, the film is an operatic work that converts the towers of flame, roiling smoke, piles of wrecked machinery and rivers and lakes of oil into a convincing representation of the end of the world. Divided into sections scored with passages from works including Verdi's *Requiem*, Mahler's *Resurrection* and Wagner's *The Ring Cycle*, the work is accompanied by an elegiac voiceover narrative. The tone of the work is set by the opening epigram, ostensibly by Blaisé Pascal, but actually by the filmmaker, "The collapse of the stellar universe will occur, like creation, in grandiose splendour."

The rudimentary narrative describes the unnamed world as a place consumed by fire in the wake of a great war. The firemen are transformed into strange alien creatures (their goggles and haz-mat uniforms contribute to the effect) who labor first to stop the blazes and then inexplicably, to reignite them. In one of the most poignant sections we see two victims – a woman and a child – who have been rendered speechless by the horrors they have witnessed. With no reference to the actual war or the politics that lay behind these dreadful scenes, *Lessons of Darkness* operates more like a premonition of larger cataclysms to come. Herzog himself has described the film as "a requiem for a planet that we ourselves have destroyed" and notes, "This could be *any* war and *any* country."[30]

Though breathtaking as art, *Lessons of Darkness* has been criticized for the way it decontextualizes and aestheticizes the horrors of war. Nor is Herzog alone in capitalizing on the beauty of destruction. Similar charges might also be leveled at Conner's *Crossroads*, Morris' *Firestorm* paintings and Misrach's *Desert Cantos*. Even Smithson was captivated by the beauty of ruins. This is evident, not only by his loving filmic portrayal of *Spiral Jetty*, but also in his 1967 essay "A Tour of the Monuments of

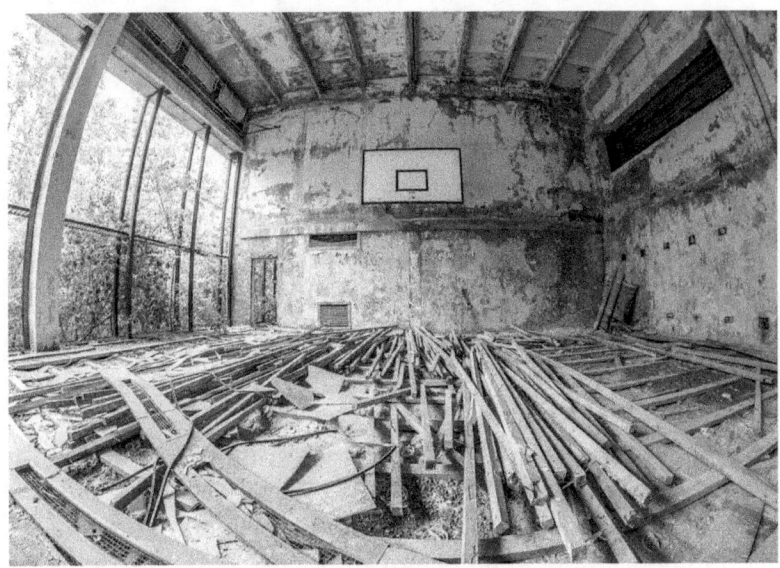

fig. 22 Pripyat, Ukraine, site of Chernobyl meltdown, April 26, 1986

Passaic, New Jersey."[31] In that famous text, he reimagines the bridges, sewage filters, and sandboxes of a deindustrializing suburban town as relics from another era.

The aestheticizing of decay and devastation has a long history. It was one of the primary motifs of Romantic era artists and writers like Giovanni Battista Piranesi, Thomas Cole and John Ruskin. Contemporary artists, faced with evidence of human destruction, also find what has been termed "ruin porn" almost irresistible. In this category one might place works as Diana Thater's video installation *Cherynobyl* and Jane and Louise Wilson's photo series, *Atomgrad (Nature Abhors a Vacuum)*, both works that take the viewer through the Ukranian city of Pripyat, which lies decaying and abandoned since the nuclear disaster of 1986. *(fig. 22)* Inspired by a more recent disaster, *A Body in Fukushima* is a collaboration between Japanese dancer Eiko Otake and American photographer William Johnston. They stage Otake's mournful dances along the railway lines impacted by the tsunami that followed the Fukushima reactor breakdown. These, and other works offer images of ordinary settings emptied out and turned to lifeless relics under the impact of some unseen disaster. It is the details that deliver the frisson – the wild horses roaming the empty streets of Pripyat, the mud and mold climbing over school desks, the kitchen tables and office shelves abandoned to the elements and the dolls and toys scattered amid the rubble of the tsunami.

Our fascination with ruins, according to writer Brian Dillon, lies in their ability to suggest the future through the past. He notes " . . .'tu autem', in Memento Mori, proclaims 'what you are, I was; what I am, you will be.' Ruins serve not only as records of what has been lost, but of what is yet to disappear."[32] Especially when these ruins are the outcome of human driven disasters, they serve as warnings of future debacles to come.

One can argue that the beauty of images of unimaginable horror serves a larger purpose by riveting our attention on what might otherwise be unendurable. Beauty has its political, social and religious uses. No doubt one reason for the longevity and continuing influence of the *Book of Revelation* is its incandescent language and imagery. Without this poetry, it is unlikely that this peculiar text would have inspired so many artists, writers and musicians through the ages. Through the imaginative brilliance of the *Book of Revelation* we gain access to an essential existential dread. Our own fears may seem to us more rational, more realistic and more credible than those experienced by believers past and present who await the literal arrival of the four dreaded Horsemen. But while premonitions of doom may change their colors, the underlying convictions that fuel them remain constant. As Frank Kermode argues " . . . it would be childish to argue, in a discussion of how people behave under eschatological threat, that nuclear bombs are more real and make one experience more authentic crisis-feelings than armies in the sky."[33] The Horsemen continue to lie in wait, ready to sweep through the world with each new threat to humanity's continued existence.

Chapter 7

WHEN TIME SHALL BE NO MORE: PARADISE AND THE NEW JERUSALEM

In the course of researching this book, I was invited to speak at what turned out to be a fascinating conference on art and the apocalypse in Bedford, England. The event was sponsored by the Panacea Trust. This organization celebrates the legacy of the Panacea Society, an millenarian group that flourished during the mid 20th century on what it believed was the original location of the Garden of Eden. Today this site is a tidy English garden in the center of Bedford. It is surrounded by a cluster of red brick Victorian buildings that once housed Society residents as they awaited the Second Coming of Jesus and the End of the World.

The Panacea Society was a largely female affair. It was founded in 1919 by Mabel Barltrop, renamed Octavia, a vicar's widow who believed she was the daughter of God. Barltrop was a follower of Joanna Southcott, an 18th century British prophetess who, at age 64, declared herself pregnant with the Messiah. The child was to be named Shiloh after a passage in Genesis. However, Shiloh turned out to be a false alarm and Southcott died not long after the expected date of his birth. Nevertheless, her followers kept the faith. Among Southcott's effects was a sealed box reportedly filled with prophecies that were to be opened in a time of crisis by the twenty-four Bishops of the Church of England. Over the years a number of failed attempts were made to convene this assembly, and eventually the box came into the possession of the Panacea Society. *(fig. 22)* During its heyday in the 1960s and '70s, the Society mounted a well-publicized campaign to bring the Bishops to Bedford. One can still visit the rooms prepared for their visit, as well as a house furnished and left waiting for the arrival of Jesus upon his return to earth. The Panacea Society also maintained a healing ministry. Members distributed thousands of tiny squares of linen infused with Octavia's breath. Sufferers were instructed to drink tap water steeped with the linen as a cure for all ills.

The final Panacean (members were required to remain celibate) died in 2012 and the Society's buildings and grounds are now a museum that houses a replica of the famous box. The original is said to be hidden somewhere nearby.

The history of the Panacea Society is a reminder that apocalyptic narratives are not merely horrific visions of a fast approaching doom. Like many other millenarian groups, the Society offered an ultimately optimistic message in the face of the 20th century's increasing catalogue of woes. As they announced in their rented billboards in the 1970s, "War, disease, crime and banditry, distress of nations and perplexity will increase until the Bishops open Joanna Southcott's box."[1] This hardy band of middle class spinsters saw themselves as instruments of mankind's ultimate salvation.

Similarly, in their religious form and even at times in their secular manifestations, apocalyptic narratives can be infused with hope and the promise of redemption. However dreadful it may be, the end is also a beginning. Death and destruction prepare the way for a new world and a new life for the just and virtuous. The *Book of Revelation* ends with a vision of New Jerusalem that inspired the founders of the American Republic as well as utopian thinkers as diverse as Thomas Moore, Jonathan Edwards, William Blake, H. G. Wells and, as we shall see below, punk icon Patti Smith. John of Patmos describes its arrival thus, "I saw the holy city, new Jerusalem, coming down out of heaven from God, made ready like a bride adorned for her husband. I heard a loud voice proclaiming from the throne: "Now at last God has his dwelling among men!" (Rev 21:2)

The text offers two contradictory descriptions of New Jerusalem. On one hand it is a celestial city that descends upon the earth from on high. It is to be an architectural marvel described as a gold cube with twelve gates, each denoting one of the twelve tribes of Israel and built on a foundation of precious stones. But New Jerusalem is also conjured as a river carrying "the water of life" over which stands the tree of life whose leaves "were meant for the healing of the nations." (Rev 22:2) New Jerusalem can be understood as a purified spiritual community. However, descriptions of a bucolic state of nature also link it back to the Garden of Eden and the state of grace enjoyed by humans before The Fall.

There is an ambiguity inherent in the notion of New Jerusalem. Will it literally exist on earth or only in some dematerialized hereafter? Is the idyllic state to come something entirely new or a return to a golden age of the past? Is New Jerusalem a state of mind or a state of the world? Is it a part of human history or will it only come to be when, as Paul Boyer paraphrases *Revelation* 10:6, "time shall be no more"?[2] Should humans strive to perfect the world they live in? Or should they wait out the trials and tribulations of their times in anticipation of the paradise that will arrive after the destruction of the world as we know it?

The identity of various proliferating Christian - and non-Christian - sects and denominations often hinges on the answers to questions like these. Millenarians, who believe that the coming Kingdom of God will last for a thousand years, are often divided into two camps. Premilleniarians believe that Christ will return to earth before this age of peace. His coming will be preceded by The Rapture (a concept not actually found in the *Book of Revelation*) in which true believers will be physically removed from the earth. This allows them to escape the Great Tribulation, a period of afflictions loosed on the rest of humanity prior to the final reckoning. Premillenarians scan the political and social landscape for signs that the Last Days have arrived and find evidence of The End in shifting geopolitical alignments, social upheavals and natural disasters. Postmillenarians offer a less catastrophic vision of the present and future. They envision a thousand year reign of peace that will occur before the second coming of Christ, during which period most of mankind will be saved. As Christians, they are tasked to bring that state of grace into being.

Premillenarians and postmillenarians have often been at odds over the course of the twentieth and twenty first century. The former stake out an anti-modernist stance that reads everything from the theory of evolution to the invention of the internet as evidence of mankind's inevitable drift toward depravity. The latter are associated with many of the reform movements of the last two centuries as they attempt to improve the world to make it acceptable to the returning Christ. There is a third position as well. Mainstream Christian groups like Roman Catholics and Christian Orthodox as well as some older Protestant denominations like Lutherans, Calvinists and Anglicans are often described as amillennial. They interpret *Revelation's* promise of the millennium more metaphorically, as a spiritual reign of Christ that is already underway.

These differing views have implications for human action and social policy. If the Second Coming is imminent, there may be no need to seek social justice, assume environmental responsibility or consider the well being of future generations. If the Second Coming is to be preceded by a thousand years of peace, it makes sense to try to improve and perfect human society in this life. In Chapter 2, we discussed America's special relationship to Apocalypse, and in particular its self-definition as the New Jerusalem. From Columbus on, the 'new world' was often envisioned as the place where God would literally fulfill his promises to mankind. Following the postmillennial interpretation of *Revelation*, Puritan leaders like Jonathan Edwards and John Winthrop maintained that America was to be a "shining city on a hill," a beacon of hope to the rest of the world" and God's favored land. It is not surprising then, with its status as possible location for heaven on earth, that America has been the locus of so much utopian activity. The agrarian based communities of Amish, Amana Colonies, Mennonites and Shakers, as well as extinct utopian settlements like New Harmony and Oneida were created to reinvent and perfect human society. But there have also been darker versions of this impulse. Doomsday cults like Jim Jones' People's Temple, Marshall Applewhite and Bonnie Nettles' Heaven's Gate and David Koresh's Branch Davidians represent social experiments in which cult leaders' failure to achieve utopia on earth unleashed a holocaust of death on their willing followers.

But if America has been a haven for postmillennial utopian experiments, it has also been increasingly receptive to the premillennial beliefs. Historian Matthew Avery Sutton analyzes the religious basis of the conflicts and culture wars that have riven the country since the early 20th century. He argues that they reflect a struggle between the more liberal program of socially progressive reformers and the premillenarian tendencies of Fundamentalist Christians that have continually pulled their adherents to the right.[3] Reading current events in light of biblical prophecy, Fundamentalists have tended to read international conflicts as heralds of the end. In the First World War this led to an isolationist stance. However, by the Second World War they were enthusiastic militarists, envisioning America as part of the army of the faithful that would bring on Armageddon. On the home front, Fundamentalists have tended to regard any expansion of government power as a precursor to the arrival of the Antichrist. This has put them at odds with the New Deal, the Civil Rights movement, the welfare state, feminism and the LGBT movement. The social and political influence of such figures as Dwight Moody in the late 19th century, Billy Sunday in the 20s, and Pat Robertson, Billy Graham and his son Franklin in our own time attest to the appeal of belief in the imminent return of Christ. Nor is premillennial influence limited to the United States. Premillennial sects are among the fastest growing versions of Christianity in Korea, Africa and Latin America.

Depending on the nature of one's millennial beliefs, Paradise in the next world or Utopia in this one are the expected endpoints of the apocalyptic narrative. Contemporary artists have drawn on both these ideas. As we have seen, many apocalyptically oriented American artists have combined visions of mass destruction with more hopeful representations of Paradise or Utopia. Howard Finster tempered his depictions of hellfire and brimstone with a *Paradise Garden* that hinted at a return to the bucolic state of the Garden of Eden. Jim Shaw has invented Oism his own version of the utopian communities so prevalent in 19thth century America. Roger Brown has reimagined Paradise as a state of grace where gay people escape the hell of homophobia. Michael Takeo Magruder presents it as a dazzling virtual reality environment that only exists in the fourth dimension.

One of the most eccentric visions of America as a utopian New Jerusalem appears in the final chapter of Franz Kafka's *Amerika,* an unfinished novel published posthumously by his executor Max Brod, in 1926. *Amerika* (the spelling is German) is the picaresque tale of the adventures of Karl Rossmann, a naïve sixteen-year-old Czech boy who has been exiled to America by his overbearing father after impregnating a servant girl. Throughout this novella, Rossmann undergoes a rollercoaster existence, careening from one unexpected and undeserved calamity to another. In a series of events that truly deserve the label "Kafkaesque," he is cast out by relatives and potential sponsors, robbed, abused, bullied, and sexually abused until finally he finds himself at the gates of an enigmatic organization called the Nature Theatre of Oklahoma. He has been drawn there by a recruiting poster that proclaims, "Everyone is welcome! If you want to be an artist, join our company! Our theater can find employment for everyone, a place for everyone!" Here, it appears, all Karl's sufferings will be redeemed. Despite his absence of discernable skills, he is awarded a job as a "technical worker" and renames himself "Negro" as he enters his new life. As is the case for all of Kafka's work, *Amerika* is an enigmatic work. As a fable about a country Kafka himself never visited, it draws on the ideas of America as a land of lawless opportunism and arbitrary authority. But the last chapter also holds out America's promise as the land of new beginnings. In Kafka's hands this promise is not entirely salutary, and in fact Karl's entry into the theater (which many commentators have seen as an image of heaven) is accompanied by a host of angels making a fearful din as they make very disharmonious music with their golden trumpets.

While the comic irony that pervades the novel as a whole casts doubt on Karl's ultimate salvation, the last chapter's vision of the cacophony of golden horns has inspired one of contemporary art's most remarkable versions of New Jerusalem. These are a series of paintings produced by the Art and Knowledge Workshop of Tim Rollins and the Kids of Survival.

Rollins, who died in 2018, was an unusual figure in a contemporary art world that is normally quite skeptical of any overt embrace of religion. He is celebrated for his pioneering role in what is now known as 'social practice art.' Long before it became fashionable and fundable, he was working with groups of at-risk urban teenagers, using works of classic literature as teaching tools. In its first iteration, the Kids of Survival comprised a group of Bronx based adolescents who met in an after school workshop. Rollins, an artist and former high school art teacher, led them through texts like *The Autobiography of Malcolm X*, Flaubert's *The Temptation of Saint Anthony*, Stephen Crane's *The Red Badge of Courage*, Herman Melville's *Moby Dick* and Kafka's *Amerika*, until they had located a key idea that linked these works to their own concerns and problems. The group then worked together, creating imagery that reflected this understanding. They laid the images over backdrops composed of the book's pages. Struck both by the idealistic nature of the project and the beauty of the works, the larger art establishment took note. Works by KOS have become highly marketable commodities in the booming art market. For Rollins, it was part of a larger educational effort that transformed the participants' lives by opening them up to the worlds of art, academia and commerce.

Rollins' project was very much in keeping with the activist spirit that seized many artists during the Reagan era. But Rollins was also deeply influenced by his personal faith. He was born in 1954 in rural Maine. His great-grandmother, a spiritualist, shaped his religious outlook and occasionally whisked him off to revival meetings. Revival meetings are a uniquely American phenomenon. Originating in the late 18th century in response to the westward expansion, these outdoor religious meetings often took place beneath a tent and served up a potent mix of religion and entertainment. Centered on a charismatic speaker whose message is frequently underscored by rousing gospel music, revival meetings were and are highly emotional events that encourage participants to forge a personal relationship with Jesus. The faithful testify to God's intervention in their lives and non-believers are asked to publicly come to God.

As a child, Rollins was immersed in this high-octane version of Christianity. He attended the Vacation Bible School where he began to make art, an activity little emphasized in his public school. He followed the preaching of the great evangelists, among them Blind Al Crocker, Oral Roberts and the young Jimmy Swaggart. He started teaching Sunday school at age thirteen, honing his own abilities as a public speaker. He drifted away from organized religion during his young adulthood, turning instead to art. But he returned to his religious roots following a set of personal tragedies and setbacks. Eventually he became a minister and choirmaster at Memorial Baptist Church in Harlem, an African American Pentecostal congregation. The effect of this return to religion can be seen in many of the works that he created with his collective, perhaps never more clearly than in a series of works inspired by Kafka's *Amerika*.

These paintings focus on the cacophony of golden horns that greet Karl at the entrance to the Nature Theater of Oklahoma. **(pl. 35)** Rollins described to an interviewer the challenge he posed to the Kids of Survival after reading this chapter. He told them, "Now look, you all have your own taste and you have different voices. If you could be a golden instrument, if you could play a song of your freedom and dignity and your future and everything you feel about Amerika and this country, what would your horn look like?"[4] The canvases present a remarkable collection of horns, painted in gold over the book pages and each designed by one member of the group. They are woven together into complex overall compositions whose energy seems barely contained by the canvas edge. The paintings reflect the diverse popular and high cultural influences to which the Kids were exposed. Among the inspirations of the intertwined horns are Uccello's battle scenes, African masks, Santeria icons, Hollywood horror films, Louise Bourgeois sculptures and birds in flight. The works also echo certain traditional Baptist themes. The horns recall trumpets calling the chosen to faith. They also allude to the Biblical tale in which the blast of rams' horns brought down the walls of the city of Jericho following the Israelites' return from Egypt. In the African American tradition, this story became an allegory for the deliverance of slaves from bondage. It was also, for Rollins, a metaphor for the power of music, one of the forces that brought him back to religion.

New Jerusalem reappears as a metaphor for personal and societal freedom in a long prose poem published by the punk poetess Patti Smith in 2018. In her autobiography, *Woolgathering*, Smith recalls her upbringing as a Jehovah's Witness in New Jersey and how she accompanied her mother on proselytizing visits to unreceptive neighbors.[5] As Smith grew older, her devotion to Jesus was rechanneled into a fascination with Romantic and Symbolist era icons like Arthur Rimbaud and William Blake along with counter-culture heroes like Bob Dylan and Jean Genet. Much has been written about her early immersion in the 1960s New York music and art scene. Perhaps her most pivotal relationship was with photographer Robert Mapplethorpe, himself a lapsed Catholic who never abandoned the poetic and imaginative influence of his childhood religion. In 1975 at age twenty-seven, Smith rose to the top of that world with the release of her album *Horses*. This immensely influential work combined the cadences of preaching and prayer with the mysticism of French symbolism, infusing all with a mix of reggae, jazz and rock.

Throughout her career Smith has continually wrestled with the relationship between art and religion. In 1971 she collaborated with her then lover Sam Shepard in a play *Cowboy Mouth* that proposed rock music as a reinvention of religion. The title song on her 1978 album *Easter* invokes Catholic imagery of baptism, communion and the blood of Christ. One of her most famous lines, from her 1975 punk anthem *Gloria*, is "Jesus died for somebody's sins but not mine." Thirty years later, musing on that line, she told radio interviewer Terry Gross, "People constantly came up to me and said 'You're an atheist, you don't believe in Jesus,' and I said 'Obviously I believe in him'… I was 20 years old when I wrote that, and it was sort my youthful manifesto. In other words I didn't want to be good, y'know, but I didn't want him to have to worry about me, or I didn't want him taking responsibility for my wrongdoings, or my youthful explorations. I wanted to be free. So it's really a statement about freedom."[6]

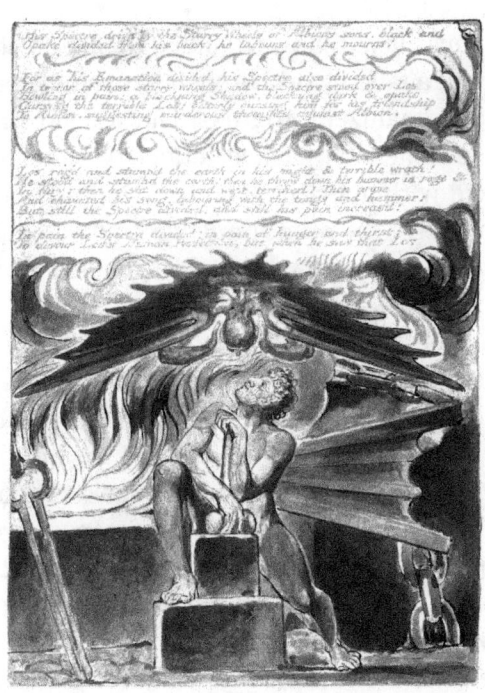

fig. 23 William Blake, Plate 6 of *Jerusalem: The Emanation of the Giant Albion* , circa 1804- 1820, relief etching with monoprinted color, Yale Center for British Art

Over the last four decades, including a seventeen-year hiatus in which she dropped out to be a wife and mother, Smith has remained a cult icon. Since her comeback in 1996, she has produced a dizzying array of award winning albums, memoirs, poetry and visual art works. In 2018 she returned to the idea of religion and freedom with *The New Jerusalem*. This fourteen-page poem is in part a response to the Trump era, and in particular to President Trump's decision to move the U.S. embassy to Jerusalem. But it is also a reflection on the timeless longing for rejuvenation and renewal found in the epic poem *Jerusalem* by her hero William Blake. *(fig. 23)*

Blake's *Jerusalem* is an incantatory cry against the descent of post Napoleonic England into venality and corruption. He makes reference to contemporary figures and types, veiling them in an archaic language that draws on Druidic ritual and Gothic imagery. The narrative presents a complicated saga of mankind's fall into the abyss of selfhood and its ultimate redemption and reconciliation with God through the power of love. Smith's much shorter *New Jerusalem* follows a similar trajectory. It also opens with a picture of a fallen world brought down by greed, soulless reason and dehumanized progress. The second stanza reads, "The new time slouched then accelerated, visceral, chaotic, yet soon governed with a terrible lucidity. God usurped by Goal. Chemical commerce the prime directive. Cultivators initiated an unremittent engineering of nature. Controllers enforced a neo-naturalization, devoid of charity or human quality. Mercenary priests devised the moral center. Iron and steel rose from the face of the holy city, the earth shuddered, and it was holy no more."[7]

Divided into eight sections, the poem presents a dream-like journey through this debased world toward possible renewal experienced by "a tribe of one," a seeker reborn through poetry and love. Like Blake, Smith's references are symbolic and archetypal, some of them gleaned from the *Book of Revelation*. There is a sacrifice of a hundred oxen, (brought into the present with a glancing reference to the beloved childhood character Ferdinand the Bull, who would rather smell flowers than engage in bullfights). The exiled seekers hunt for the water of life, shelter the innocent lambs and are inspired by an image found in a casket of the Alchemical Sovereign. This latter is a representation of Christ based on the disputed Leonardo da Vinci painting *Salvator Mundi* that is illustrated in the text. The search culminates in a prophecy that encompasses both the immediate issue of the transfer of the embassy to Jerusalem and the larger promise of liberation from the darkness of the corrupted world. It reads, "The holy city belongs to none. The mountains of Judah belong to none. The yielding seed belongs to none. And we are the Jerusalem."[8]

The last two sections offer a coda – one is a dream of a cup (here again there are echoes of the *Book of Revelation*) that literally reflects the carnage of power but is transformed by the elixir of love. The last section brings the unnamed narrator back to herself where she drinks "not from the gourd of prosperity, but from the pool of knowledge." Gathering up her writing tools, she is reborn as a voice of "inexhaustible good."[9]

Smith adapts the mystical language and visionary imagery that illuminate both the *Book of Revelation* and Blake's epic poem in order to create a contemporary allegory. Her text operates on two levels, both as a universal paean to the power of art and love and as an impassioned protest against the machinations of a specific political moment. The New Jerusalem serves as a metaphor that allows her to connect these levels in a manner that echoes the similar doubling of meaning embedded in John of Patmos' mystical vision. There, also, an actual historical event - the fall of the Temple – has inspired a clarion call for freedom and justice that has resounded down the centuries.

The Q'uran, which borrows heavily from the *Book of Revelation*, also presents an image of hope at the end of tribulation. Islam's version is a blend of utopia and paradise. Old Testament descriptions of the Garden of Eden and *Revelation's* promise of the New Jerusalem merge in the Q'uran's vision of Jannah, the well tended garden that is the ultimate reward of the faithful. Over the centuries, Jannah has been the subject of sensuous poetry, breathtaking paintings and hypnotic music. Painted images of Jannah take their inspiration from the walled gardens that offer respite from the hot, arid climate that characterizes much of the Islamic world. They portray a world set apart, and in fact the root of the word Jannah is jinn, the Arabic word for 'veiling,' referencing the way that gardens veil one from the surrounding world.

Jannah shares many characteristics with the Christian and Jewish heavens. It is described as a blissful place composed of "gardens beneath which rivers flow." These include "rivers of water, the taste, and smell of which are never changed. Rivers of milk the taste of which will remain unchanged. Rivers of wine that will be delicious to those who drink from it and rivers of clear, pure honey." (47:15). Jannah differs from other versions of paradise in one important respect: this is a realm filled, not just with spiritual delights, but also with every kind of sensual pleasure, including wine, food, sex and luxurious robes, bracelets and perfumes. One if its most attractive features, at least for male inhabitants, are the 'houri,' beautiful, idealized maidens who await their pleasure in the garden. The erotic aspects of Jannah have assumed political significance in recent years as radical Islamic sects recruit martyrs with promises of access to these voluptuous virgins in the afterlife.

Two well-known Iranian artists have drawn on these traditions to explore the politics of paradise. Shoja Azari and Shirin Neshat are photographers, filmmakers and partners who were displaced from their native country following the 1978 Iranian revolution. From their vantage as exiles in the United States, they have taken activist stances, speaking out strongly against the Iranian government's draconian policies surrounding cultural expression and free speech. In their artistic work they infuse poetic narratives with echoes of Islamic literature, art and music. They often collaborate but they also work separately to produce works that reveal very distinctive artistic personalities. Both have created filmic explorations of the idea of paradise. Neshat's 2009 *Women without Men* and Azari's 2013 *King of Black* both explore the garden as a representation of Jannah. Given the artists' difficult relationship to the theocratic state, it is not surprising that both films emphasize the themes of failed utopia and the expulsion from paradise. But their sources and styles are very different. Neshat's film is inspired by a controversial Iranian novel published in 1998 and combines magic realism with historical recreations of pivotal events. Azari reimagines a Persian poem dating back to the 12th century and imbues the work with a self-conscious orientalism that critiques western fantasies about the mysterious East.

Azari was trained as a filmmaker and has produced experimental films influenced by such diverse sources as Franz Kafka, Rumi, Andrei Tarkovsky and Ingmar Bergman. He also creates works that are hybrids of painting and film. One recent series consists of contemporary icons created by inserting video portraits of contemporary Iranian dissidents into poster size reproductions of traditional Shiite martyrs. Other works are riffs on the early twentieth century Iranian tradition of the coffee house painting. These elaborate depictions of scenes from Persian mythology were used as props and backdrops by storytellers as they regaled coffee house patrons with tales of battle, martyrdom, paradise and apocalypse. Azari transforms this tradition by inserting tiny video vignettes into reproductions of these works. In a work titled *The Day of the Last Judgment (Coffee House Painting)*, (2009), for instance, Azari couples the traditional images of heaven and hell with clips from Youtube of contemporary horrors like the aftermath of a suicide bombing, American soldiers wreaking havoc in Iraq and testimony surrounding the torture of prisoners at Abu Ghraib.

In a similar way, his film *The King of Black* injects contemporary techniques into an aesthetic borrowed from traditional Persian miniatures. **(pl. 36)** Azari's retelling of a story by the 12th century Persian poet Nizami Ganjavi uses contemporary green screen technology to create an effect that harks back to early cinema. Sumptuously costumed actors move before and around flat backdrops that consist of digitally recreated details of 16th century Persian paintings. The disconnect between modern and traditional forms of representation adds to the unreality of scenes. Filmed crows fly across skies dotted with schematically drawn curlicue clouds. Voluptuous maidens sink into landscapes strewn with real fruit and delicately painted images of flowers and trees. Artifice is further heightened by text inserts that interrupt the narrative like intertitles from a silent film.

The film tells the story of Paradise gained and lost. A king questing for knowledge travels outside his kingdom and finds himself in a bleak world filled with black garbed mourners. While seeking an explanation for their sorrow he meets a mysterious man with a wheel. This figure transports him to a paradisiacal world populated by beautiful women luxuriating in a magical landscape full of abundant fruit and wine. The most beautiful woman is the queen of this land. She enjoins him to enjoy all the pleasures of this place, excepting her own sexual favors. Initially the king sates himself, but finds himself longing for the forbidden fruit. After several attempts to seduce the queen, he takes her by force, upon which he is suddenly and mercilessly returned to the land of sorrows from which he began his journey. Titles tell us that he spends the rest of his life there garbed in black and mourning his lost paradise.

The work is filled with contemporary and historical references that reflect on the relationship of East and West. The paradise scenes bear a great deal of resemblance to the kind of harem fantasies that titillated the viewers of 19th century work by academic painters such as Jean-Léon Gérôme and Jean Auguste Dominique Ingres. Meanwhile, in a more contemporary Western allusion, the bleak desert landscape to which the King is returned in the final scene is beset with black robed mourners, one of whom is a woman gazing at the type of photograph made by suicide bombers before their deaths.

The King of Black is based on the first episode of Nizami's larger epic, *Haft Paykar (Seven Beauties)*. That work is designed as a series of parables that describe the schooling of a ruler in such virtues as faith, passion, serenity, fairness and devotion to God. The opening story counsels patience and the control of desire, but as reimagined by Azari, *The King of Black* also presents a lesson in cultural dissonance. The narrative undermines the assumption of male privilege that is so much a part of the Islamic concept of Paradise, with its willing virgins and unending sex. This paradise is presided over by a queen who asserts her independence and when crossed, expels the offending monarch from Paradise. The hell to which he returns suggests the wasteland created by the current Middle East conflict. Machismo, violence and power combine to destroy any hope of earthly utopia. Thus, by deliberately engaging with the tropes of Orientalism and patriarchy, the film ultimately exposes the cultural biases embedded in this and by extension, any vision of Paradise.

Neshat's *Women without Men* questions the Paradise myth in another way. Again, the work has a literary source, in this case the eponymous contemporary novel by the Iranian novelist and political refugee Shahrnush Parsipur. The film is in keeping with the photographs and videos that since the mid 90s have brought Neshat international acclaim. Among her most celebrated works are videos like *Turbulent* (1998) and *Rapture* (1999). Each of these place the viewer in the crossfire between two screens on opposite sides of the room. One presents the private, highly secluded world of veiled women while the other offers a glimpse of the boisterous public world of men. Through such works, Neshat gives voice to women silenced by Iran's fundamentalist society.

Women without Men, conceived by Neshat and executed

in collaboration with Azari, extends these concerns. It takes two forms, comprising both a series of discrete video installations and a full-length feature film that uses some of the footage from the installations. Both these formats, like the book on which they are based, follow a group of Iranian women from different classes during the U.S.-assisted coup d'état that replaced Iran's first democratically elected government with the Shah. Today, many Iranian activists see this as the fatal step that set Iran on the path to the Iranian Revolution. The individual video installations present each woman's story individually, while the film weaves them together into a narrative that blends realism and fantasy in order to create a feminist parable.

While each woman has her own dilemmas and desires, the driving force of the narrative is their escape to an orchard in the countryside. This garden, presided over by a mysterious male gardener whom Neshat describes as a stand-in for Christ, becomes both a place of refuge and a metaphor for Paradise. In the novel and the film, the women create a utopian community that nurtures them until one of them gets bored and chooses to open the orchard to outsiders. There are some distinct differences between the novel and film. Neshat places greater emphasis on the political context of the story. She turns one of the women, Munis, into a political activist and makes her the narrator of the film. Neshat also initiates the expulsion from Paradise with a party that devolves into a raid by supporters of the coup d'état. Fantasy and fact mingle in the film. The narrative is punctuated by faithful recreations of documentary footage of the protests that preceded the coup. Meanwhile, there are magical sequences, as when Zarin the prostitute observes the literal erasure of her clients' faces or Munis, dead from suicide, rises from the earth of the garden to begin a new life.

The film radically alters one of the stories represented in the novel and in one of the video installations. This is the tale of Mahdokht, a woman in her forties who is deeply sexually repressed yet consumed by an obsession with having children. (pl. 37) In the novel, she escapes to her family garden and, in a magical sequence, transforms herself into a tree. As she takes root, she gathers strength and finally experiences a chaste fertility by bursting into seeds. The video of this story is the most fantastical of the series. It opens with a view into a garden where a dead Mahdokht floats in a stream in an image that deliberately recalls John Everett Millais 1851 Pre-Raphaelite painting *Ophelia*. Flashbacks reveal incidents in her life. She is seen as a child, already an outsider, running away from a mob of other children in the forest. Following her descent into madness, she sits in a forest obsessively knitting yellow masses of yarn for the children she longs to have. Finally the camera returns us to the dead, floating body, finally at peace in nature. Neshat, citing the difficulties of integrating such a magical character into a narrative film, cut her story from the film. But if Mahdokht is absent physically, she reappears in the form of an apparently magical tree in the garden. Now as the spirit of freedom untethered to the body that caused her so much anxiety, she is a sheltering presence for the other characters as they also seek refuge in the garden.

Ironically, given its grounding in the Islamic vision of Jannah, the film's allegory of Paradise is rooted in the personal and secular freedoms that have been curtailed by the theocratic state. Paradise is lost here through the excesses of ideology, foreshadowing Iran's subsequent slide into religious autocracy.

British artist Mark Wallinger exhibits a similar skepticism toward religion's promise of a New Jerusalem. However, instead of turning to the language of myth and fantasy, he translates apocalyptic tropes into vernacular images. Working in a variety of media, he puts a metaphysical twist on quotidian settings like classrooms, underground railway stations and airports. In his hands, these exemplars of everyday British life become contemporary versions of purgatory, hell and paradise.

Wallinger is best known for his explorations of loaded issues like class, British heritage, nationalism and imperialism. These interests emerged from a politicized childhood. Wallinger grew up in Chigwell, a suburban outpost of London connected to the city by the Circle Line. The London Underground offered an escape from suburban banality by transporting him to the City's museums, racetracks, football matches and ballet performances. Perhaps because of this early association, the Underground has come to play an outsized role in his artistic work, as we shall see. Wallinger's political orientation was shaped both by his left leaning parents and later, by his part time employment while an art student at Collets, a famous socialist bookshop in London. His MFA studies at Goldsmith College of Art in the early 80s coincided with Margaret Thatcher's rise to power. For Wallinger, as for the other so-called YBAs who followed him at Goldsmiths a few years later, Thatcher's conservative social policies became grist for art. His degree show included a number of stridently political works. One of these was an assemblage that transposed a famous symbol of noblesse oblige, Gainsborough's 1750 double portrait of the landowners Mr. and Mrs. Andrews, onto graffitied sheets of corrugated iron and plywood. The show launched his career, and it is perhaps a measure of the cultural elite's uneasiness with Thatcherism that this student work earned him a slot in the prestigious Anthony Reynolds Gallery in London.

Wallinger returned to the issue of economic inequality a few years later with a suite of paintings titled *Capital*. These works depicted homeless people loitering in front of London financial institutions. Ironically, this suite was purchased by the mega-capitalist, advertising mogul and art collector Charles Saatchi. In 2006 Wallinger won the prestigious Turner prize for a meticulous reconstruction of a massive anti-Iraq war protest by activist Brian Haw that had been mounted and then demolished outside the Parliament Building. Wallinger has also gained recognition for works that employ the rules, class divides and competition endemic to sport as a metaphor for British life.

But while politics have been an ongoing preoccupation, so has religion. Wallinger was raised in the tradition of the Church of England. He has remarked, "I'm an atheist, but I'm a *Christian* atheist."[10] He frequently injects Biblical passages and religious imagery into his political content and views religion, like sport, as an expression of British identity. His best-known work in this vein is *Ecce Homo*. This life size sculpture represents Christ just prior to his Crucifixion. However, in a departure from traditional depictions of the suffering Christ, Wallinger envisions him as a contemporary young man in a loincloth wearing a barbed wire crown. He reports that the work had its origins in contemporary political events. "The work was conceived not that long after Srebrenica," he says, referring to the massacre of 8000 Bosnian Muslims during the Bosnian War, "And that was entirely to do with nationalism, religion, bigotry: all the things that would have applied in Judea."[11] *Ecce Homo* - the title comes from Pontius Pilate's entreaty to the mob calling for Jesus' blood - was installed for three months in 1999 on a plinth in Trafalgar Square. This was once the site of public executions. Since 1843 the Square has also hosted the nearby monument to Lord Nelson, that enduring emblem of British sea power and nationalism. This context helped underscore the idea of Christ as prisoner of war, and hence a precursor to the victims of the ethnic cleansing then underway in Kosovo and Bosnia.

Wallinger's most extended series of religion-based works involves an alter ego named Blind Faith. Played by Wallinger himself in videos and still photographs, this figure can be identified by his white shirt, black tie and trousers, sunglasses and blind man's cane. In the role of Prometheus, Blind Faith has been strapped to an electric chair as he hums Ariel's song from Shakespeare's *Tempest.* He has also hung suspended before the tombstone of the English Romantic poet Percy Bysshe Shelley, and has sung a Victorian hymn in a falsetto voice created by inhaling helium. Most germane to our study is his appearance in a video titled *Angel.* **(pl. 38)** Filmed at London's Angel tube station, this work presents Blind Faith at the bottom of the London Underground's longest escalator. To the rousing music of Handel's 1727 coronation anthem *Zadok,* Blind Faith recites a garbled text that is in fact the opening five verses of the Book of John ("In the beginning was the Word...."). Wallinger spent three months learning to recite the passage phonetically backward. To make the video he declaimed the passage while walking backward up the down escalator as commuters glided up and down on the moving stairs on each side. He then played the footage backward so that the reversed text was then reversed again. The result is almost incomprehensible, giving Blind Faith the aspect of an Old Testament prophet speaking in tongues. Adding to the celestial resonance, once he finishes his recitation, Blind Faith steps onto the escalator and ascends as if to heaven.

The Underground reappears as a place of metaphysical encounters in *When Parallel Lines Meet at Infinity* (1998-2001) which was shot with a camera mounted at the head of a subway train. The trip through the tunnel, with its mix of flashing lights and gloomy darkness, suggests a journey through the underworld. In 2000, taking on a different mode of transportation, Wallinger transformed the international arrivals door at London's City Airport into a strange version of Judgment Day. *Threshold to the Kingdom* was filmed surreptitiously as travelers made their way through the door. They walk, some slow and apparently disconcerted, others purposeful, yet others happily waving to waiting loved ones. As they pass the hidden camera they suddenly vanish, as if into another realm. The video is presented in extreme slow motion to the choral accompaniment of Gregorio Allegri's sublime hymn of atonement, *Miserere Mei*.

Here, the airport serves as a metaphor for the gates of heaven. But it is an ambiguous symbol. Wallinger expresses his own ambivalence about the idea of salvation posited by the idea of Paradise. He explains, "I had a fear of flying, which I managed to overcome once I recognized it as a fear of airports. Being under scrutiny, at every point being processed, then existing in this weird no man's land before being spat out on to the official terra firma of the state. There's a sense of guilt and vulnerability, so one emerges with a real sense of relief. It is where we experience the power of the state at its most overt: we are being judged, which I realized was analogous to confession and absolution in the Roman Catholic Church . . . and that sense of one's freedom or the lack of it is very similar . . ."[12] As a metaphor for the "threshold to the kingdom" of God, the airport underscores the darker aspects of the Last Judgment scenario. The gauntlet that the faithful must undergo to achieve salvation is here re-imagined in terms of the authoritarianism, surveillance, exclusion and humiliation that are now part of the travel experience. Paradise, when finally achieved, begins to seem more akin to prison than to the glories of the New Jerusalem.

One finds a similarly ambivalent take on Paradise in the work of Liza Lou. She is celebrated for sculptures and installations of objects covered with tens of thousands of tiny glittering glass beads. The subjects vary considerably. Her earliest works, created in the late 1990s when she was just out of art school, included fully beaded recreations of a full-scale suburban kitchen and a suburban back yard. Critics were enthralled by the attention to detail, which included a cascade of blue and white beads spilling from a beaded faucet, a glittering cherry pie popping from the open oven, and a picnic meal on a checked table cloth complete with fully beaded salad, corn on the cob, sandwiches and spilled beer. The upbeat ambience of those works soon began to give way to darker subjects. Lou's 2002 *Trailer* was a full size, fully beaded airstream trailer whose interior held hints of a grisly crime scene. Realized in a subdued pattern of grey and brown, it was littered with beaded girlie magazines, hunting knives, bottles of Jack Daniels, fishing boots and guns. Peering through the door one had an obstructed view of a rumpled bed, a supine leg and a discarded handgun. *Trailer* was presented in *Testimony*, a 2002 gallery exhibition whose other offerings also seemed light years away from the Middle American complacency that suffused the suburban installations. These included *Dog*, a beaded sculpture of a snarling German Shepherd, *Man*, a beaded figure who falls backward as a dove emerges from his mouth **(pl. 39)** and *Relief*, a beaded young girl laid out in a coffin in a pose that is again reminiscent of Millais'painting of drowned Ophelia.

Such works hinted at class, religious and economic divides starkly at odds with popular visions of the American Dream. Lou brought these undercurrents out into the open two years later in a confessional performance work titled *Born Again. (fig. 24)*

This live performance, later recast as a fifty minute black and white video, is a fictional narrative based on Lou's evangelical upbringing and its heady, frightening mix of guilt and ecstasy. In the video version of *Born Again* the camera is fixed on a frontal view of Lou sitting at a table. She tells her story in first person in the voice of the young girl who serves as narrator. Sometimes she breaks into song, sometimes she assumes the voices of other characters in the story, and throughout she is extremely animated. She leans conspiratorially toward the

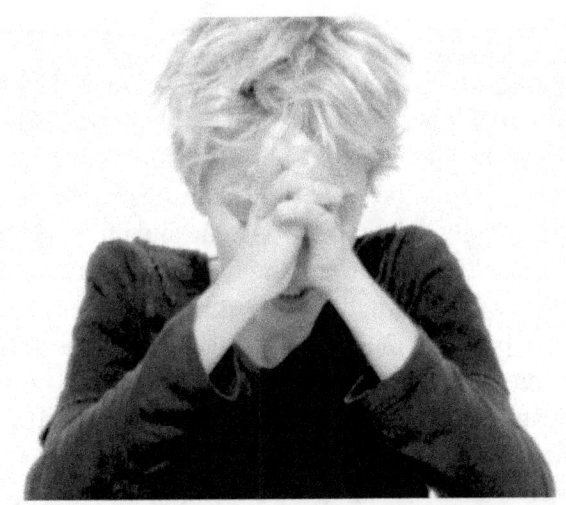

fig. 24 Liza Lou, *Born Again*, 2004, single take solo monologue written and performed by Liza Lou, directed by Mick Haggerty, 54 minutes

camera as she offers a particularly intimate moment of the story. Sometimes she pulls back and looks heavenward for inspiration, at one point climbing on the table that separates her from the viewer.

The story is both compelling and chilling. Our heroine recounts the tale of her childhood. She begins with her bohemian parents' marriage and brief submersion in New York City's downtown cultural scene. She chronicles their sudden and somewhat shocking conversion to Evangelical Christianity and their move to rural Minnesota to work with the church. We learn about a childhood immersed in poverty, prayer, ecstatic dancing and singing, night terrors, the specter of Satan, and the violent unwinding of her parents' marriage. Among the striking set pieces are the story of the fire her parents set in their loft to burn their godless books, music and art (including several paintings given them by their neighbor Roy Lichtenstein); her father's brutal treatment of their dog, Ezekiel, who eventually goes mad and is given away to a church camp; his equally brutal punishment (and hinted at sexual abuse) of his daughter; and raging parental battles. The last of these is followed by the disappearance of her father and her mother's rejection by the church community as a fallen woman. There are also moments of pleasure and bliss, as when the narrator and her sister sing and dance together, or feel the hand of God.

Born Again is a powerful evocation of both the horror and the attraction of this particular form of Pentecostal Christianity. Lou's account is filled with Gospel songs and visual descriptions that offer glimpses of otherworldly beauty. However, this beauty seems inextricably linked to the psychic and physical violence of renunciation and purification. The narrator speaks of her belief that prayers are jewels in her crown and she describes her post-baptismal experience of the water in which she was immersed as a "lake of diamonds." One can't help feeling a link between this kind of imagery and the glittering splendor of her chosen art medium. Suddenly *Kitchen* and *Back Yard* seem less homages to the female craft tradition than acts of worship directed at casting a glow of spiritual radiance over the banality of the everyday world.

Born Again was a transformative work that allowed Lou to reconcile her life as an artist and her Christian past. Post *Born Again*, she created a number of works that dealt directly with her evangelical heritage. One of these is *Sacrifice* (2004), a beaded sculpture of a crying baby lying on its back with arms and legs raised in a manner reminiscent of traditional representations of the Christ child in a manger. Here the meaning seems doubled – a reference both to the Christian belief in Christ's role as savior and to the sacrifice of children to the often destructive belief systems of their parents. A Christ figure reappears in adult form in *The Vessel* (2005-06), in which a headless figure in a loincloth bends beneath the weight of a log in a pose drawn from traditional representations of the passion of Christ. Here the title suggests again his role as repository of human sin and suffering. And perhaps the most pointed statement about Lou's relationship to the religion of her childhood is *The Damned* (2003-2004), which is based on Masaccio's 15th century masterpiece, *The Expulsion from Paradise*. Here the condemned first couple is reinvented and their bodies made heroic in a manner completely at odds with the body-shame purveyed by evangelical Christianity. In more recent work, Lou has moved beyond this focus on her evangelical background. Following a move in 2005 to Durbin, South Africa where she has assembled a collective of native beaders, she has turned her attention to works that deal in a more abstract way with issues of power and justice.

Born Again suggests that Lou ultimately has found redemption, not through religion, but through art. However her story also highlights how entwined evangelical Christianity has become with performance and entertainment. Her parents turned to God following a revival meeting run by Billy Graham, perhaps the most famous and influential Evangelist of the twentieth century. Graham's rallies, or "Crusades", as he called them, were a phenomenon. They took place in stadiums and parks and were attended by tens of thousands of people. Graham exhorted his audience with a combination of fiery Endtimes rhetoric and rollicking Gospel music, after which people were invited to come forward and be filled with the spirit. Conversions experienced by people like Lou's parents were common, helping to swell the ranks of believers at a time when regular church attendance was falling. Graham's influence was further cemented by his highly public role as spiritual advisor to every U.S. President from Richard Nixon to George W. Bush.

Graham's Crusades were part of a drive by the evangelical community to save souls using the tools of mass communication. First radio and then television have provided powerful venues for mass preaching. Many televangelists operate through megachurches, where their televised sermons take place in the context of a live congregation. While Billy Graham tried to operate across political lines, today most well known televangelists are conservative partisans, using the pulpit to argue against abortion and gay marriage and for the election of like-minded politicians. Many are also purveyors of the so-called Prosperity Gospel. This reading of the Bible sees wealth as a sign of God's favor and assures the faithful that God wants them to be rich. Such aspirations to earthly affluence sit strangely with evangelical teachings about the Rapture and its promise to the faithful of imminent release from the sorrows of this world. This disconnect, along with a series of well publicized scandals revolving around money and sex, have tarnished the televangelist movement's reputation among outsiders. But they have not dimmed its appeal to millions of followers worldwide.

Televangelism and megachurches depend on ratings and box office for their success. The theatrical nature of their appeal has not been lost on artists. The Reverend Ethan Acres has taken this mix of religion and entertainment to its logical conclusion. Acres is a performance artist who combines art world irony with the evangelical fervor of the ordained minister that he is. An Alabama native, Acres spent his adolescence preaching in Baptist congregations before going on to get an M.F.A from the University of Nevada and an honorary doctor of divinity over the Internet from the World Christianship Ministries. Since the 1990s, Reverend Acres has been creating religiously inspired performances with a flair for audience enticement (let's "put the fun back in fundamentalism," he says). He operates a chapel on wheels - a camper trailer refitted with a baptismal font, neon undercarriage, and stained-glass windows. *(fig. 25)* He performs marriages and exorcisms and gives sermons that draw on pop culture, explore the devil's modern-day temptations, and promise a peculiarly showbiz style of redemption.

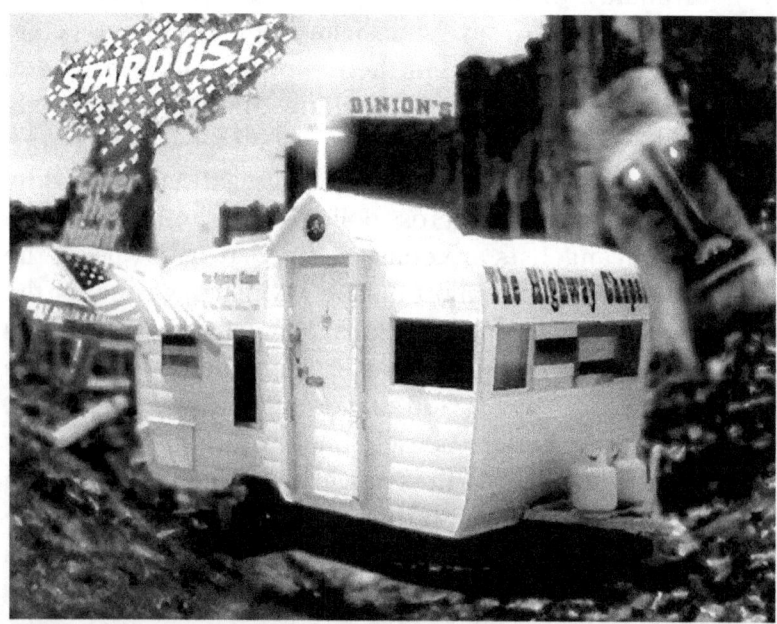

fig. 25 Reverend Ethan Acres, *Highway Chapel*, re
fitted 1965 Shasta trailer

His comically uplifting message also appears in sculptures created from found and low-tech materials that depict Biblical allegories and parables, and in still photos that seem to present miraculous events. *Lamb of God* (1997), is a life-size rocking horse, suspended overhead, revolving like a carousel figure, and outfitted with glowing plastic eyeballs that turn it into the fearsome Lamb from the *Book of Revelations*. In the photograph *The Final Voyage of the Beagle* (1997), the artist prays over a supposedly dead dog, whose 'soul,' complete with small, angelic wings, soars upward toward heaven.

Reverend Acres' sermons have been collected into a small volume that is printed like a devotional prayer book. They present the mix of wit, hyperbole, possible fact, and fevered exhortation that comprise his art-inspired version of religion. They also make it clear how indebted he is to his own version of the *Book of Revelation* and premillenarian visions of the Rapture. The sermons provide a mythologized version of Acres' background and spiritual awakening. Born in Valley Head, Alabama into a family of clergymen, he came to Jesus under the influence of his stepfather, the Reverend Albert Satcher. Satcher was a paraplegic, itinerant preacher who lived in the glow of his encounter with God during the near death experience brought on by an accident that cost him his arms. Thanks to a pair of prosthetics he was able to carry on, inspiring congregations of small churches throughout rural Alabama and Tennessee. In one sermon, Acres presents Satcher's disability as a lesson about turning adversity into a blessing.

Acres' own ministry began in Las Vegas and he describes the epiphany he experienced at the Gallery of Fine Art located within the Bellagio Resort and Casino. Here, he discovered, "high art has found its niche in the land of sex and sin." Acres weaves an anecdote from his childhood involving his desire for a pretty girl into a demonstration of the ways that Steve Wynn, the Bellagio's worldly owner, is actually an instrument of God. In another sermon he describes his longing for the Rapture, and recounts how he seemed to find Paradise in the lush gardens and pristine exhibition spaces of the Getty Center in Los Angeles. At first his belief seems confirmed in a visitor's brochure in which the Getty's architect Richard Meier describes his desire to elevate visitors out of their day-to-day experience. Later he realizes "The Getty Center was not Heaven, only an earthly facsimile. I had spent the day in a *virtual* Heaven, certainly beautiful and enchanting, but unable to quench my spiritual thirst."[13] Eventually he accepts the fact that the Getty is only a glimpse of the glories that await, snatched away by God in the same playful spirit that his black labrador snatches away a soggy stuffed toy during a game of catch.

Acres' sermons demonstrate his ability to reconcile supposedly antithetical worlds and find surprising truths at the nexus of art, evangelical faith and American low culture – especially what critic and artist Doug Harvey describes as "a vast shadow-culture just beneath our contempt, emerging out of a vacuum in official culture that generates unique entertainments such as radio and televangelism, teen folk masses, fundamentalist pop psychology, Jack Chick comics, pro-life rallies, Donald Wildmon, and Christian heavy-metal music."[14] Acres himself describes his work as that of a "holy fool" whose performance art has a lineage that encompasses such spiritual extremists as St. Simeon, Jacopone da Todi and Mark the Mad, with a nod as well to the American Vaudeville tradition and Fluxus artists like Nam June Paik and La Monte Young. What they share, he suggests, is that ". . .we are servants of the flock, performing rituals to purge the longing and uncertainty from those who come before us, broken and alone."[15]

Acres' self-deprecating humor and far-fetched associations cannot mask the heartfelt sincerity that runs through his work. A somewhat more equivocal take on the notion of salvation as performance art appears in the work of German artist Christian Jankowski. Art and religion comprise only one of his subjects. Jankowski is a multi-media artist who orchestrates encounters between people in unrelated fields in order to suggest the contradictions and commercialism of the contemporary art world. One of his best-known works, *Telemistica* was produced for the 1999 Venice Biennale. It consists of a video in which Jankowski asks various Italian television psychics to predict his success in the biennial. A more recent project, *Heavyweight*

History (2013) borrows the format of the sports competition to assess the abilities of Polish weightlifters as they attempt to lift various Soviet era monuments from their pedestals in various Warsaw parks and plazas.

Jankowski has created two works that explore the performative nature of contemporary Christianity. *The Holy Artwork* (2001) is a video created in collaboration with televangelist Pastor Peter Spencer, who presides over the Harvest Fellowship Church in Texas. *(fig. 26)* Jankowski's inspiration was a kitschy 18th century painting in which an angel completes a painting for an exhausted artist. In *The Holy Artwork*, Pastor Spencer completes Jankowski's work. Having arranged to speak about art and religion before a live audience as part of a televised service, Jankowski joins Spencer on stage and then promptly falls, as if insensible, to his feet. Never missing a beat, the Pastor turns the event into a lesson on the sacred nature of art and its ability to make us appreciate God's work as Creator. Speaking over the artist's prone body, the preacher exhorts: "It took Christian emptying himself, falling down, no longer becoming the center of attention, to make this a great piece of art."[16] The service ends as a Gospel chorus sings a hymn of praise to God while the phone number for donations appears at the bottom of the screen. *The Holy Artwork* hovers between absurdity, suggesting an ironic send-up of modernist rhetoric about art's quasi-religious nature, and genuine belief, as this rhetoric seems completely satisfying to the religious believers to whom it is addressed.

Jankowski returned to the subject of religion in his 2011 video *Casting Jesus*. **(pl. 40)** Here it is Jesus himself who appears as a performance artist. This work was inspired by Jankowski's chance encounter with the actor James Caviezel as he was being coached for his role as the suffering Jesus in Mel Gibson's 2003 film, *The Passion of the Christ*. Taking a cue from game show competitions like *American Idol*, Jankowski asked Italian casting agencies to send actors for the lead role in a film about Jesus. In the video he films the thirteen contenders undergoing various tests, including breaking bread, reciting scriptural passages, healing a sick person and dying on the cross. The jury for the competition comprised three high ranking Vatican officials. They included a Vatican Priest, the art critic for the Vatican newspaper and the Secretary of the Commission for Film Classification of the Italian Bishop Conference. The latter is an organization that rates films for their moral content. The jury goes through several elimination rounds before settling on a single actor who seems to best embody the humility, sanctity and empathy of Christ. There is a postmodern aspect to the project, as we become aware that the persona actors are seeking to emulate is not some historically accurate image of Jesus, but rather the personality most in keeping with preexisting Hollywood representations. But as in *The Holy Artwork*, the participants are in deadly earnest and the completed video has been happily embraced by religious audiences for whom it conveys a convincing representation of spirituality.

In these works, Jankowski appears more skeptical than Acres of the spectacle, hucksterism and hype that characterize some of the most popular forms of evangelism. He suggests that spiritual transformation, transfiguration and transcendence follow a script. Here the resemblance between art and religion serves less to elevate art into some immaterial realm than to drag both art and religion down into the realm of entertainment. Jankowski's videos suggest that uplifting spiritual experiences

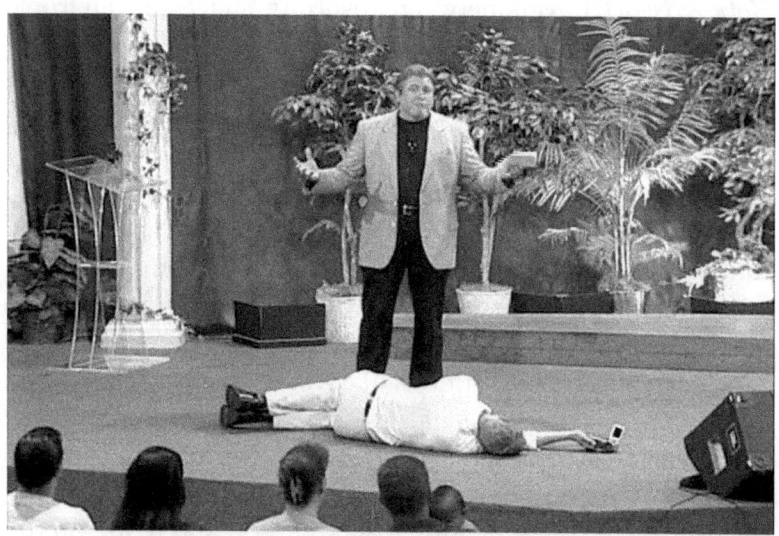

fig. 26 Christian Jankowski, *The Holy Artwork*, 2001, film still of video, projection, color, sound, 15:52 minutes

can be manufactured and sold as commercially rewarding products. One is reminded of the fact that *Left Behind* has become a fantastically successful literary and cinematic franchise whose appeal seems based more on its Hollywood thrills than its theological message.

As many of the foregoing works suggest, religion's promises of utopia and paradise have become problematic even for those who embrace other aspects of the apocalyptic narrative. For many today, doom seems a more convincing conclusion to human history than any promise of renewal and transformation. Recent events reinforce this sense of dread. The 20th century was littered with the failures of fascist, theocratic and socialist utopias. In the 21st century our other candidates for the New Jerusalem seem equally tarnished. The world is beset with dangerous messianic nationalisms. The capitalist utopia and its promise of unstoppable material progress have been accompanied by a gospel of growth that threatens the life support of the planet. Shadowed by the threat of widespread unemployment and diminution of human purpose, the technological utopia has taken a dark turn. Meanwhile, premillennial paradise is as suspect as postmillennial utopia. For those outside of the cadre of true believers, the promise of an idyllic afterlife often appears no more than a cynical manipulation designed to domesticate the faithful and inculcate group identity. Reviewing the contemporary failures of the apocalyptic imagination, Indian Educator Krishna Kumar remarks, "We are in the presence of debased millenarianism without a compensating utopian vision."[17]

Without the expectation of a new beginning, the end beckons as a meaningless descent into chaos. And the fear of such chaos impels humans to ever more destructive acts of self-preservation. Thus belief in the apocalypse becomes a self-fulfilling prophecy. A cycle of destruction and discord has driven human history for the past 2000 years. Today we may think ourselves beyond the superstitions laid out by an ancient religion, but we seem more enmeshed in the apocalyptic imagination than ever. Whether by fire or water, whimper or bang, accident or design, the End has lost none of its capacity to terrify and seduce.

BEYOND THE APOCALYPSE

In this book we have watched the apocalyptic imagination give birth to a remarkably diverse set of artistic visions. In exploring the complex role that eschatology plays in today's world, the artists here draw promiscuously from culture, history, politics and philosophy. They use symbolism, metaphor, irony and allegory to conjure the allure, dangers and positive potential of apocalyptic thinking. Because they tap into deeply ingrained assumptions and beliefs about the nature of time, God, truth and justice, they envision futures that are as compelling as they are unsettling. In articulating our deepest anxieties, they help us understand the fearsome challenges that face us in a time of social, political, sectarian and environmental upheaval.

But perhaps at this time we need more than mere understanding. I would like to close by examining the work of two artists who combine a sense of the power of the apocalyptic narrative with some possible alternatives to Endtimes thinking. The first is video artist Bill Viola, an impresario of time. His works exploit video's capacity to slow, reverse, loop or altogether halt the temporal flow. Through such manipulations, time becomes palpable. Video's ability to alter our temporal perceptions allows Viola to address the great eschatological conundrum: When time shall be no more, what then does it mean to exist? Or as he once posed the question, "How do you represent eternal time within the confines of the chronological time that we inhabit and have learned to represent?"[1]

For Viola, this is a spiritual quest. He was raised as an indifferent Episcopalian, but found his direction after discovering Eastern religions in college. He notes that these studies sparked a shock of recognition, providing a sense that, "There is an unseen world out there and we are living in it."[2] Through Eastern philosophy, Viola also encountered the roots of his own Christian tradition from such mystic forbears as the Desert fathers and Gnostics, Mietster Eckhart, St. John of the Cross and St Theresa.

Viola's work is undergirded by his interest in Hinduism, Buddhism, Islamic Sufism, Mysticism and Christianity. He switches easily between imagery and ideas drawn from all of these, blending references to Christian resurrection, Buddhist reincarnation, Pythagorean transmigration of souls, Islamic cosmology and Siberian Shamanism. However, the works he creates are anything but arcane. Painstakingly staged and sumptuously produced, they comprise mesmerizing videos in which figures are slowly consumed by fire or water, are captured floating underwater in a state of dreaming or drowning, or are seen bursting into the air like birds in flight.

One pivotal work, unusual because the presence of a figure is suggested rather than explicitly depicted, is his 1983 *Room for St John of the Cross*. This work was inspired by the 16th century mystic and poet who was imprisoned for nine months during the Inquisition. In his installation, Viola evokes John's double consciousness of physical confinement and mental freedom. He sets a small cubicle suggesting the saint's cell against a large video of a slowly shifting snow-covered mountain. The installation is accompanied by a sound track that blends the sounds of roaring wind with a voice softly reciting the poems John wrote during his confinement. Another key work is *Nantes Triptych* (1991). This three-screen installation evokes the continuity between birth and death. Arranged like an altarpiece, the central screen depicts a body floating in water as if waiting to be born. On one side is a video of a natural childbirth, inspired by the birth of Viola's first son. On the other is footage of his mother as she lay in a coma fighting off death. With such works Viola explores the multiple senses of time in which human life unfolds.

The work that provides the most dramatic narrative of transformation, transfiguration and resurrection is Viola's 2002 *Going Forth by Day*. This multi-screen video installation is designed as an immersive experience. Five synchronized videos spread over the four walls of the darkened gallery space. Each provides a different narrative, and together they create a metaphorical representation of the stages of human life.

The title of the work comes from the *Egyptian Book of the Dead*, which Viola describes as a guide for the soul once it is freed from the darkness of the body to finally "go forth by the light of day."[3] The scenarios seem at once mythic and contemporary, with details that reference quotidian life and slow moving sequences that blend natural and supernatural events. The first, chronologically, is *Fire Birth*. Saturated with red and orange, it suggests a human form submerged in water. Next is *The Path*, a massive horizontal screen that represents a forest at the summer solstice. Winding through the trees, a seemingly endless stream of people slowly makes its way toward some unseen destination. *The Deluge* focuses on the façade of a stone building. People rush frantically by, carrying their possessions. Suddenly the glass on the upper window of the building breaks and a deluge of water rushes out with terrifying force. Its energy spent, the torrent stops leaving behind an empty street washed clean of debris and people. *The Voyage* provides a cutaway view of a house atop a hill overlooking a beach. Filmed during winter solstice, the video depicts an old man dying in his bed. An old woman, presumably his late wife, watches below as workers load a boat with their possessions. Upon his death, he disappears from bed and reappears on the shore. He and his wife embark in the boat for a trip into the hereafter. Finally, *First Light* takes place at the vernal equinox, and presents a group of rescuers who have worked all night to save people from a flood in the desert. As they gather wearily around a small pond, a woman stands nearby waiting anxiously for her son. The rescuers slowly pack up, and they and the woman fall asleep. As dawn breaks, a young man, presumably the son, bursts out of water and floats up into the air. **(pl. 41)** As he disappears, the sleepers awake, and unaware of the supernatural event, finish packing up and leave.

Each of these vignettes could be taken individually as a mini parable about the passage between life and death. *Fire Birth* echoes earlier works by Viola that present individuals consumed simultaneously by fire and water. The travelers in *The Path* may be taking the trail between worlds. *The Deluge* suggests a disaster of biblical proportion that both annihilates and cleanses. *The Voyage* is a gentler story of the end of one life and the beginning of another. *First Light* is clearly a resurrection scenario. The vignettes contain echoes of a variety of spiritual traditions, suggesting the universality of belief in the cycle of life, death and rebirth.

As described here the narratives provide a linear narrative that unfolds loosely from birth to death to rebirth. However, for viewers the experience is quite different. They come in and out of the gallery at different points in the synchronized stories and need not follow the order suggested above. They are free to wander from screen to screen and to the pick up and drop the stories at any point. Meanwhile, because the videos are on a continuous loop, each ending blends into its beginning. The emphasis is on continuity rather than completion. Thus Viola manages to merge two orders of time, as the human chronology of birth to death is subsumed within the larger frame of eternal time in which our personal ends take place.

In *Going Forth by Day*, Viola offers a conclusion to the apocalyptic narrative in which each individual end serves as a synecdoche for the larger end of the world. But here inevitable death is transformed into a promise of rebirth. Viola has remarked, "And the way I look at it is that the resurrection happens every spring, and we live through the resurrection every spring . . . the resurrection in its more expanded sense and not focused on the very important church holiday of Easter per se, and the whole story of Jesus Christ per se, is a much more universal image for mankind. It is the hope of renewal, it is watching nature every winter die and every spring be reborn."[4]

A similar rethinking of Christian tropes appears in artist Jeffrey Vallance's alternative reading of Scripture. *The Gospel According to Jeffrey*[5] is a short reworking of the Old and New Testament that mingles snippets of actual Bible verses and events with contemporary references ("According to Kurt Vonnegut Jr., we are 'the eyes and ears of the Creator of the Universe'") and short and often biting commentaries on conventional Christian belief and history ("The profoundly misguided, anti-Semitic belief that the Jews killed Christ has caused vast pain and dreadful suffering throughout the centuries"). Reflecting the ecumenical nature of his enterprise, Vallance includes a long list of prophets, reformers and writers encompassing, not only canonical icons like Krishna, Buddha, Zoroaster and the Prophet Muhammad, but also contemporary figures like Martin Luther King Jr., Howard Finster, the Dali Lama, Joseph Campbell, Temple Grandin and J.R.R. Tolkien.

Vallance is a curious figure in the contemporary art world. Like Reverend Ethan Acres, who is a friend and occasional collaborator, Vallance mixes puckish humor and a prankish approach to religion with a deeply felt spirituality. The Los Angeles based Vallance was raised as a Lutheran. As he reports, he went to Lutheran church and Sunday school and was president of the local Lutheran youth group. But all this training had an adverse effect, surrounding various proscribed practices with the lure of forbidden fruit. Among Vallance's best known works are a series titled *Relics and Reliquaries* which were inspired by Martin Luther's condemnation of relics as Popish idolatry. The series opens with *Blinky the Friendly Hen* (1978-88), which consists of all artifacts related to the burial and exhumation of a frozen chicken purchased from a grocery store. Other works include a small bust of Lenin surrounded by Soviet era badges and medals, a set of tacky Vatican souvenirs blessed by the Pope, and a small shrine encircling a bubblegum card of Carolyn Jones as Morticia Addams, whom young Vallance adopted as his exemplar of female beauty. Eventually the series became a kind of personal and cultural autobiography, that serve, like Proust's madeleines, as triggers for the recollection of past loves, early political stirrings, exotic travels, and now inexplicable obsessions

Vallance's works often present spoofs on popular culture, political authority, institutional religion and the pretensions of the contemporary art world. He has, for instance, led a ghost tour of the Nixon Library and curated the first art world exhibition of the work of Thomas Kinkade, the wildly popular landscape painter whose work is reviled within the mainstream art world as irredeemably kitsch. However his *Gospel*, which is included in a slim prayer book style volume titled *The Vallance Bible*, is undeniably sincere. **(pl. 42)** As Vallance notes in his introduction, *"The Gospel According to Jeffrey* is an attempt to seriously interpret the Bible. It is like a strange biblical exegesis. By my reckoning, the closest comparisons to my gospel are the Gnostic's allegorical interpretations. At the same time that the Church was trying to standardize its own dogma, the Gnostics went out of their ways to come up with the most fantastic and inventive interpretations of the Bible – like the creative-writing exercises. Thus the Gnostics were labeled heretics by the Church." [6]

By turns playful, mysterious and sharply critical, Vallance's *Gospel* presents an alternative to the religious tenets that are so easily exploited by political demagogues. The Gnostics, whom Vallance invokes, aspired to transcend the material world by pursuing a secret spiritual knowledge. One also senses Vallance's kinship to Kabbalistic Judaism. He frames human history from creation to the end of the world as the pause between a single breath of God. Within that frame, Vallance maintains, "It is our sacred task to find the Spirit of God already within all of us, and to commune with that Spirit." In a similarly mystical manner, the Kabbalah describes how, at the creation of the world, God's self was shattered into shards of light. These are embedded in the material world and must be reunited by prayer and good deeds. The charge to repair the world is known as 'Tikkun Olam.'

In between his Gospel's Beginning and End are a number of landmarks familiar from the Christian narrative, though their sequence is jumbled. There are nods to the Ten Commandments, the Sermon on the Mount, the Pentecost and the Crucifixion. There are also acerbic comments on the failings of mankind and in particular of institutional religion. Like the Christian Bible, Vallance's *Gospel* concludes with the End of the World. Mankind, having too well fulfilled God's command to subdue the earth and to be fruitful and multiply now brings about its own End. God breathes back in, returning his creation to the void. But Vallance revises the Last Judgment so that it becomes each individual's judgment of him or herself. The last passage of his Gospel reads, "Every living being will evaluate itself according to what it accomplished and created on Earth, and each will retain the individual memory of all that it has seen and done in the universe."[7]

Viola and Vallance share a desire to break out of the dead ends, eternal conflicts and existential angst into which our fascination with eschatology has mired us. Viola does this by tempering the relentlessly linear trajectory of the apocalyptic narrative with chronological patterns borrowed from other traditions. Bolstered by the cycle of the seasons and the promise of reincarnation, Hinduism and Buddhism place the apocalypse – be it personal or cosmic - into the context of recurring change. Viola mixes this non-linear chronology with elements of various mystical traditions, in particular the embrace of the infinite within the self. In a similar way, Vallance evokes his version of Gnosticism to challenge the literal reading of Scriptures. He replaces an emphasis on division and conquest with a willingness to accept the immanence of God in all things.

In her study of the *Book of Revelation*, historian Elaine Pagels notes that this book was merely one of many visionary texts emerging from the early Christian era. She surmises that its rigid division of good and evil, its relentless drive toward closure and its denigration of the 'other' helped render it canonical. It may seem natural to think of human, national and even planetary life in terms of an arc that advances inexorably from birth to death and to see conflict as the inevitable state of humankind. But in fact such narratives are culturally conditioned. What if Western culture had adopted a different vision of time, action and spirituality? Would a less dualistic, more holistic and less-linear model of history help us reimagine other possibilities?

After I was well into the writing of this book, I decided to google the term "doomsday dreams." I discovered that this is a name for a common psychological condition. End of the world dreams are said to serve as surrogates for the feeling of a loss of control that accompanies such life changing events as divorce, death of a loved one and job loss. Of course, in the contemporary world it doesn't seem necessary to dismiss apocalyptic nightmares as expressions of sublimated personal anxieties. Many of apocalyptic fiction's favorite scenarios, among them global warming, global freezing, nuclear holocaust, global famines and pandemics and the usurpation of our humanity by machines, increasingly seem all too plausible. But the psychological interpretation of doomsday dreams does underscore the relationship of Endtimes nightmares to questions of agency. Whether secular or religious, societal or personal, apocalyptic narratives are about loss of control. If the End is preordained, there seems little room for meaningful action. One can save oneself, but there is no way to save the world. It becomes all too easy to succumb to despair or even to embrace the death drive that seems to be hurling us all inevitably toward the final catastrophe.

Humans thrive on hope, which is why modernity's progress narrative had such a long and fruitful run. But as the history of the apocalyptic imagination suggests, even hope can be destructive if it reinforces our most divisive impulses. The apocalyptic narrative offers an equivocal promise of renewal. Is there a way to imagine the End that doesn't consign huge swaths of the human race to death and destruction? Is there a way to reconfigure Paradise and its promise of regeneration without succumbing to sectarianism and strife? Or does humanity's ultimate survival demand that we move beyond our doomsday dreams?

Such questions haunt our waking nightmares. As this book has shown, artists can help us understand the continuing hold of the apocalyptic imagination. But we also need art to help us let it go.

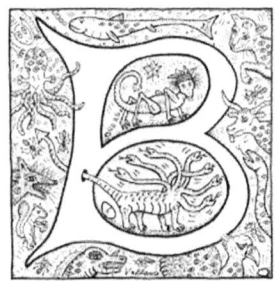

fig. 27 Jeffrey Vallance, *Illuminated B* from Vallance Bible, 2011

PLATES

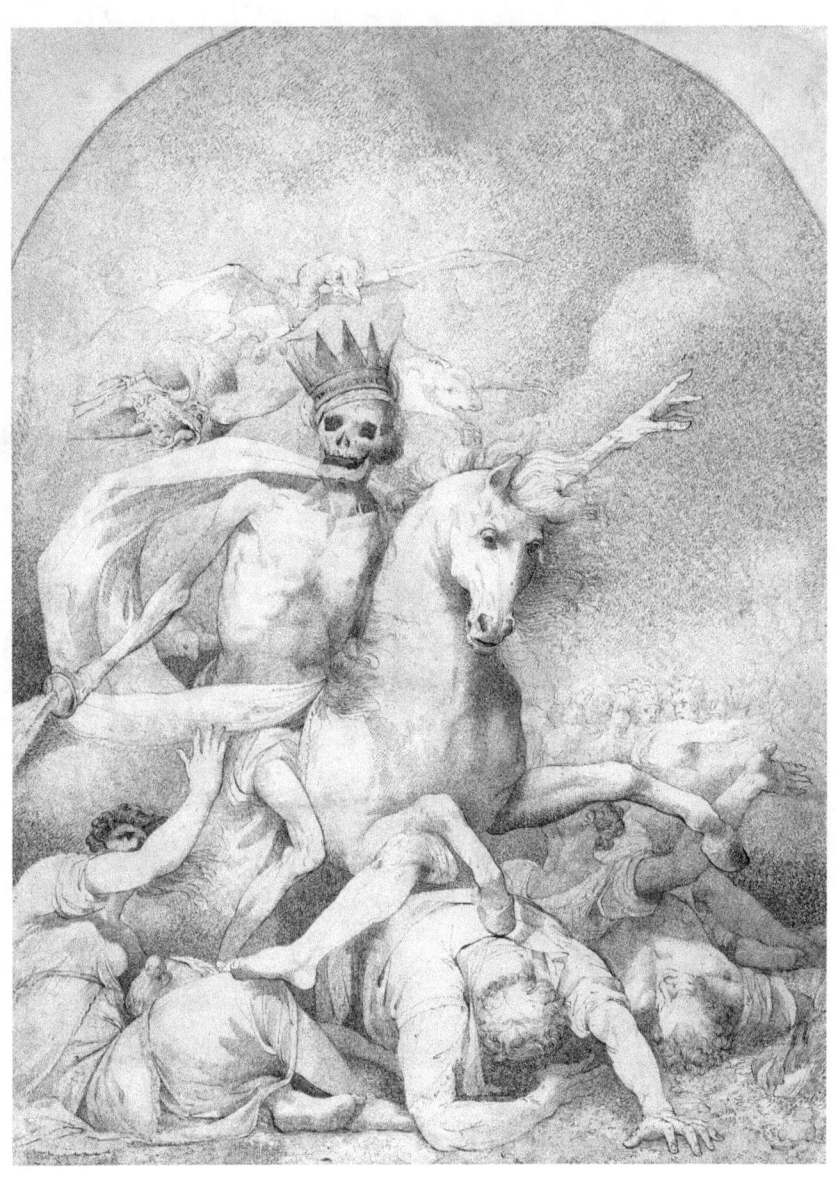

pl. 1 John Hamilton Mortimer, *Death on a Pale Horse*, circa 1775, drawing, collection of Yale Center for British Art

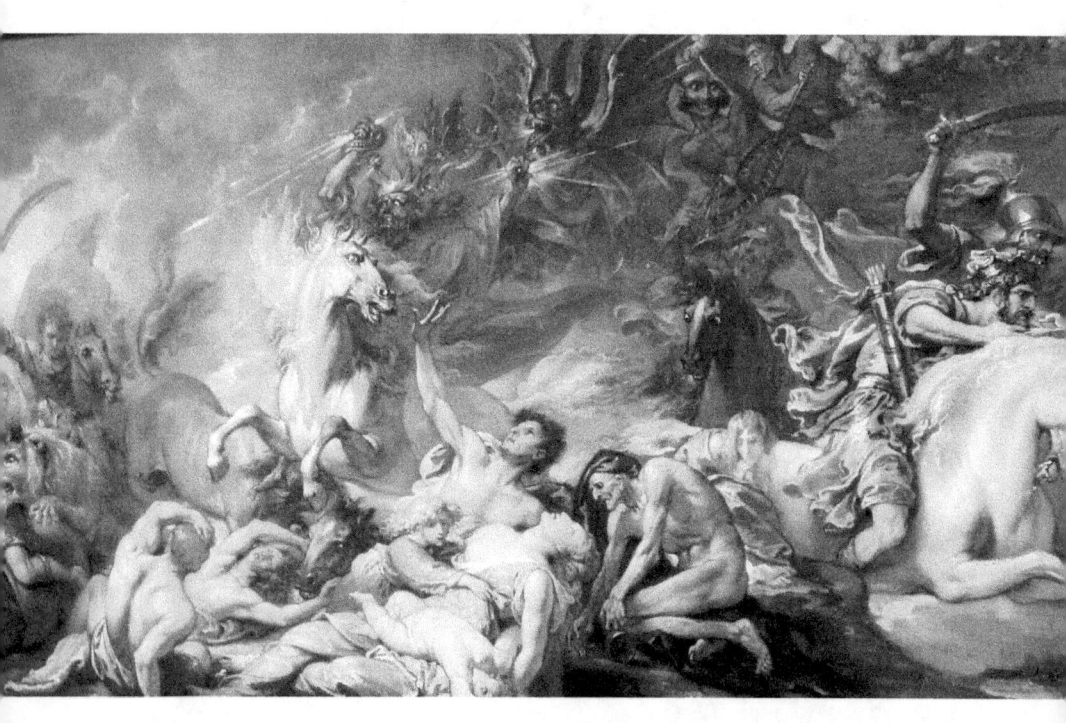

pl. 2 Benjamin West, *Death on a Pale Horse*, 1796,
oil on canvas, Detroit Institute of Arts

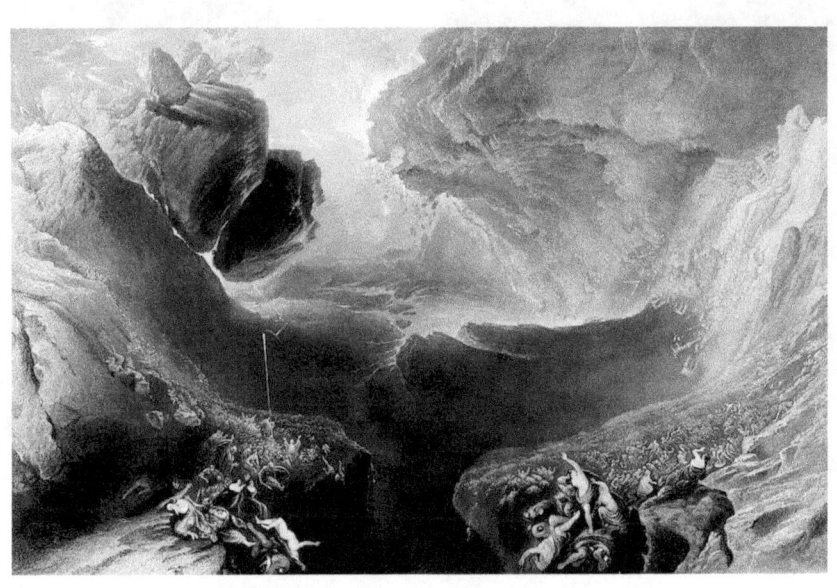

pl. 3 John Martin, *The Great Day of His Wrath*, 1853,
oil on canvas, Tate Britain

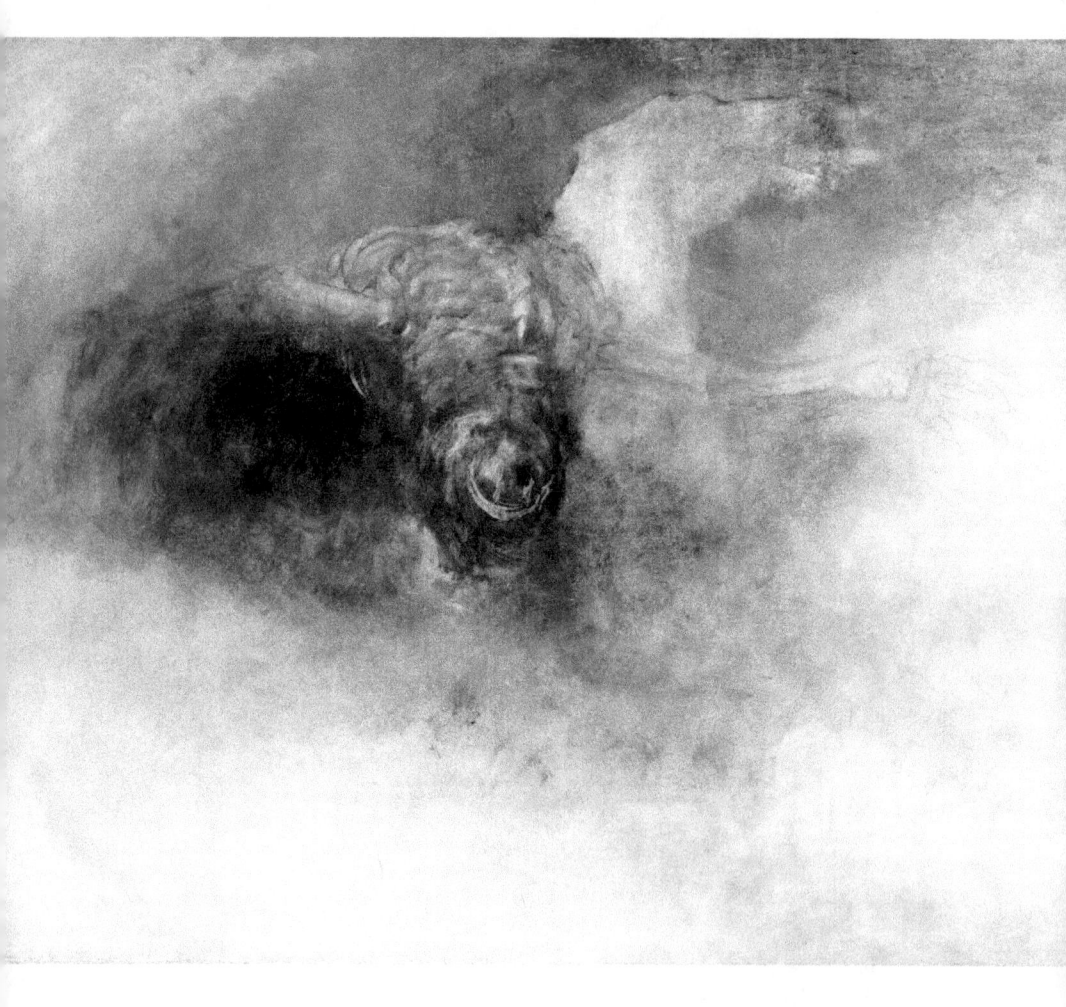

pl. 4 J.M.W. Turner *Death on a Pale Horse*, 1825,
oil on canvas, Tate Britain

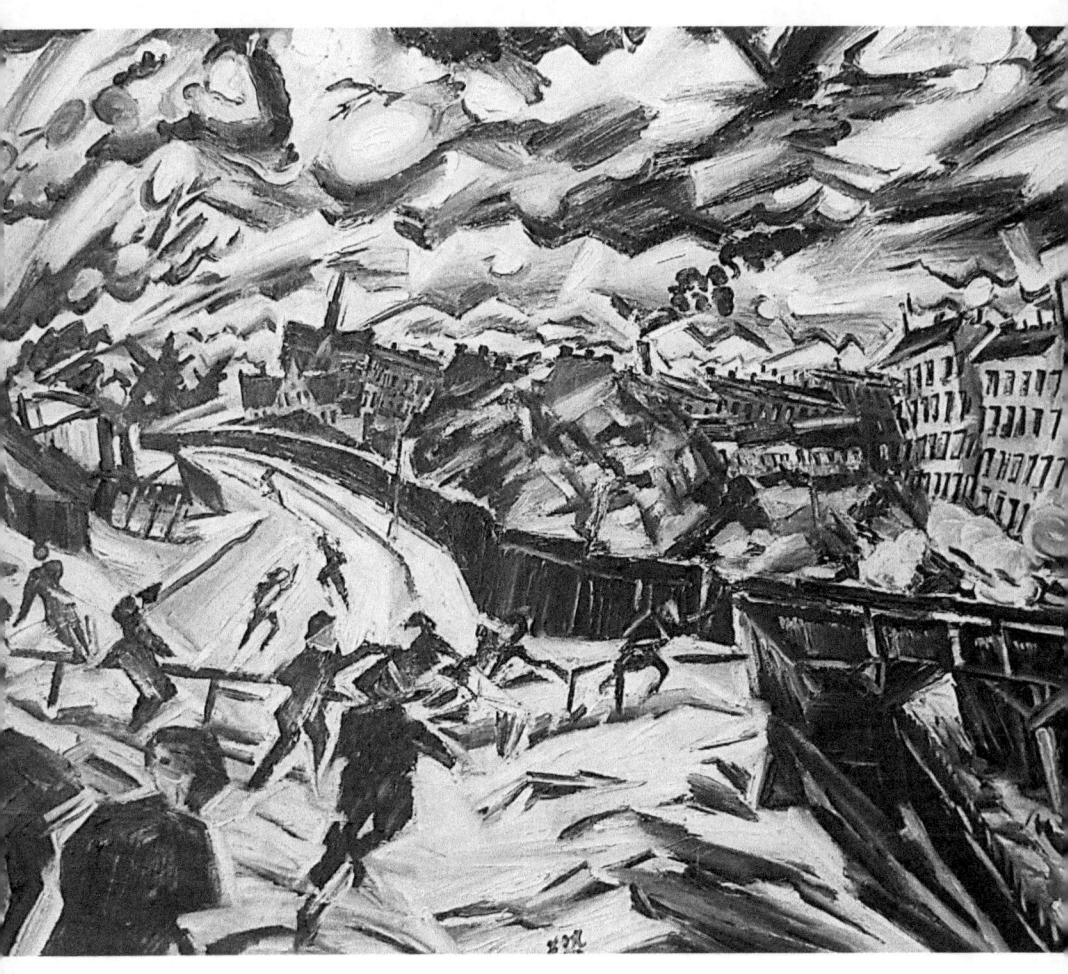

pl 5. Ludwig Meidner, *Apocalyptic Landscape*, 1913,
oil on canvas, Los Angeles County Museum of Art

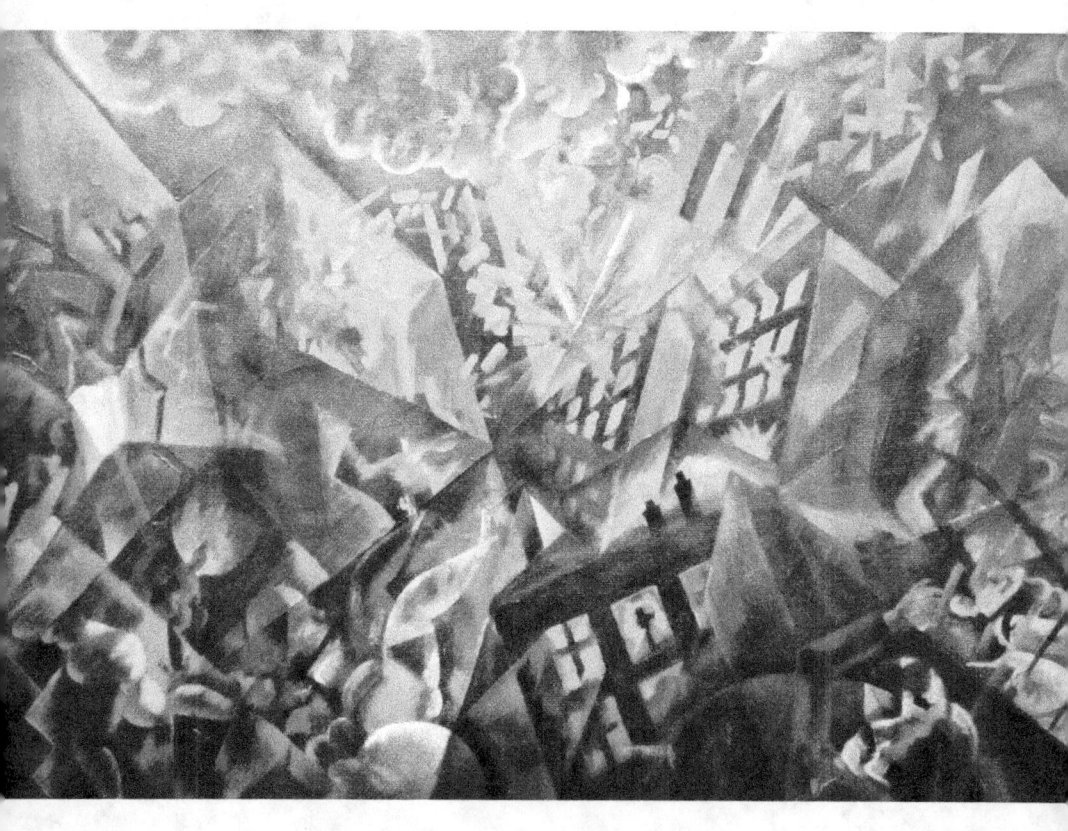

pl. 6 George Grosz, *Explosion*, 1917, oil on composition board,
The Museum of Modern Art, New York

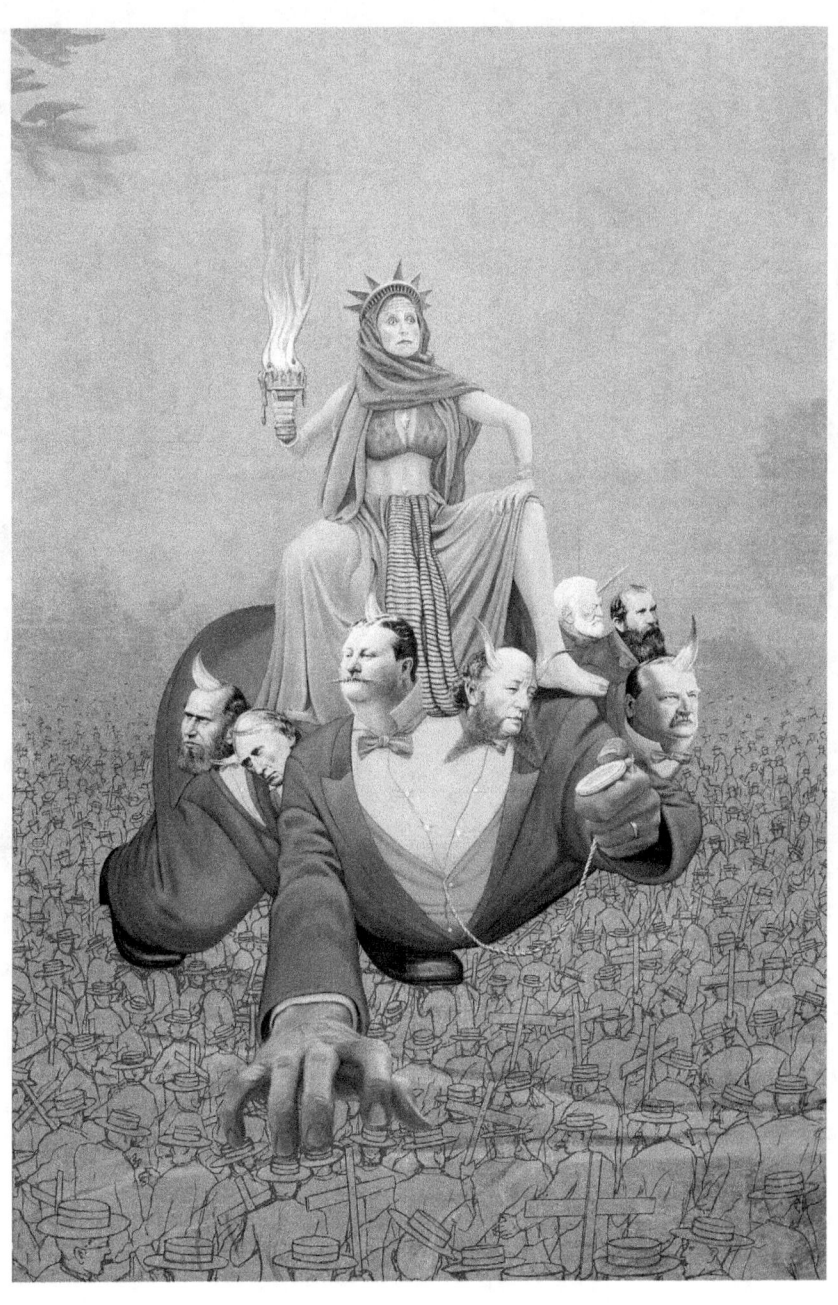

pl. 7 Jim Shaw, *Whore of Babylon + Robber Barons*, 2015,
72 x 48 inches, acrylic on muslin

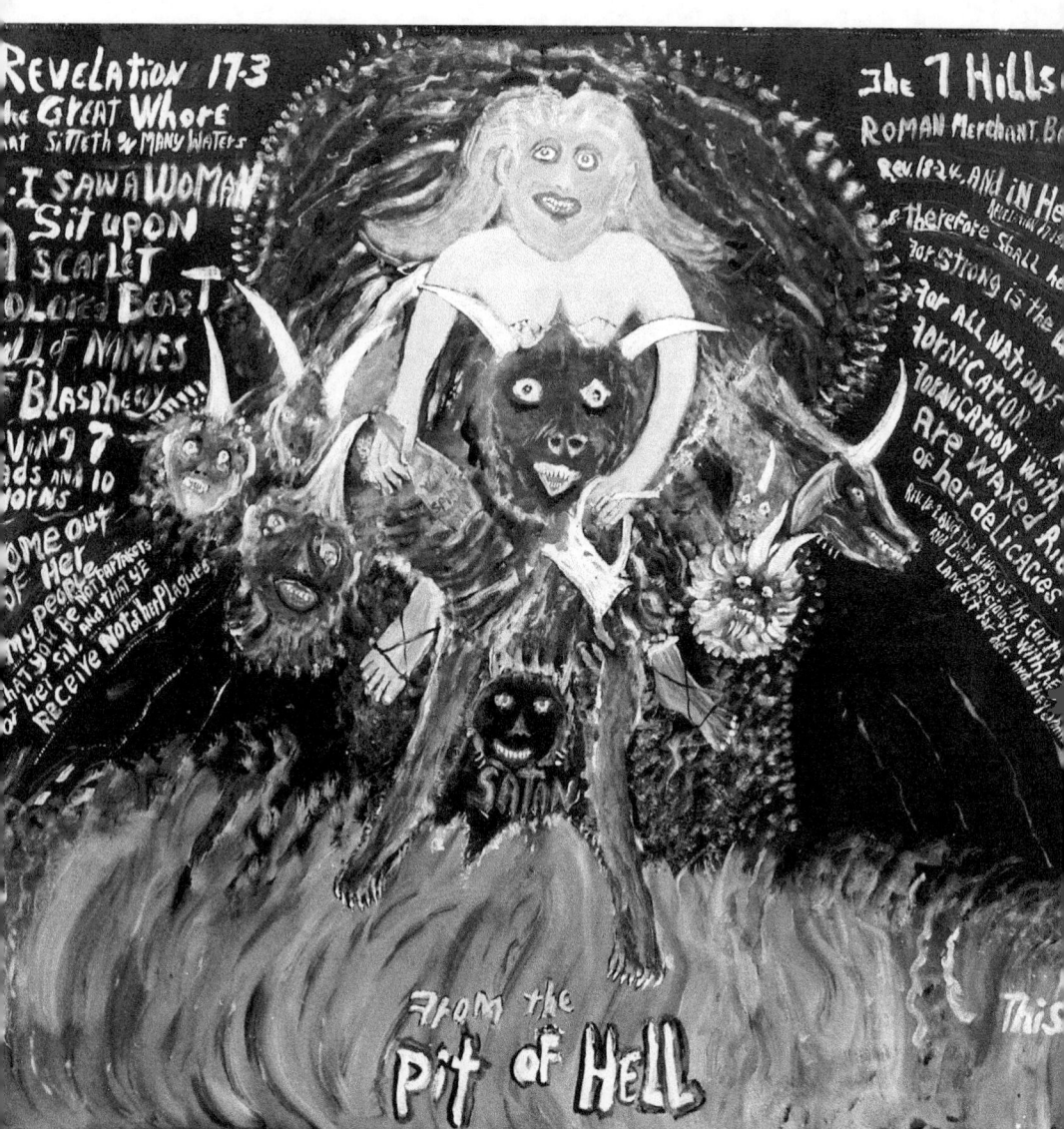

pl. 8 William Thomas Thompson, *Revelation Revealed (Detail)*
1995-96, acrylic on canvas

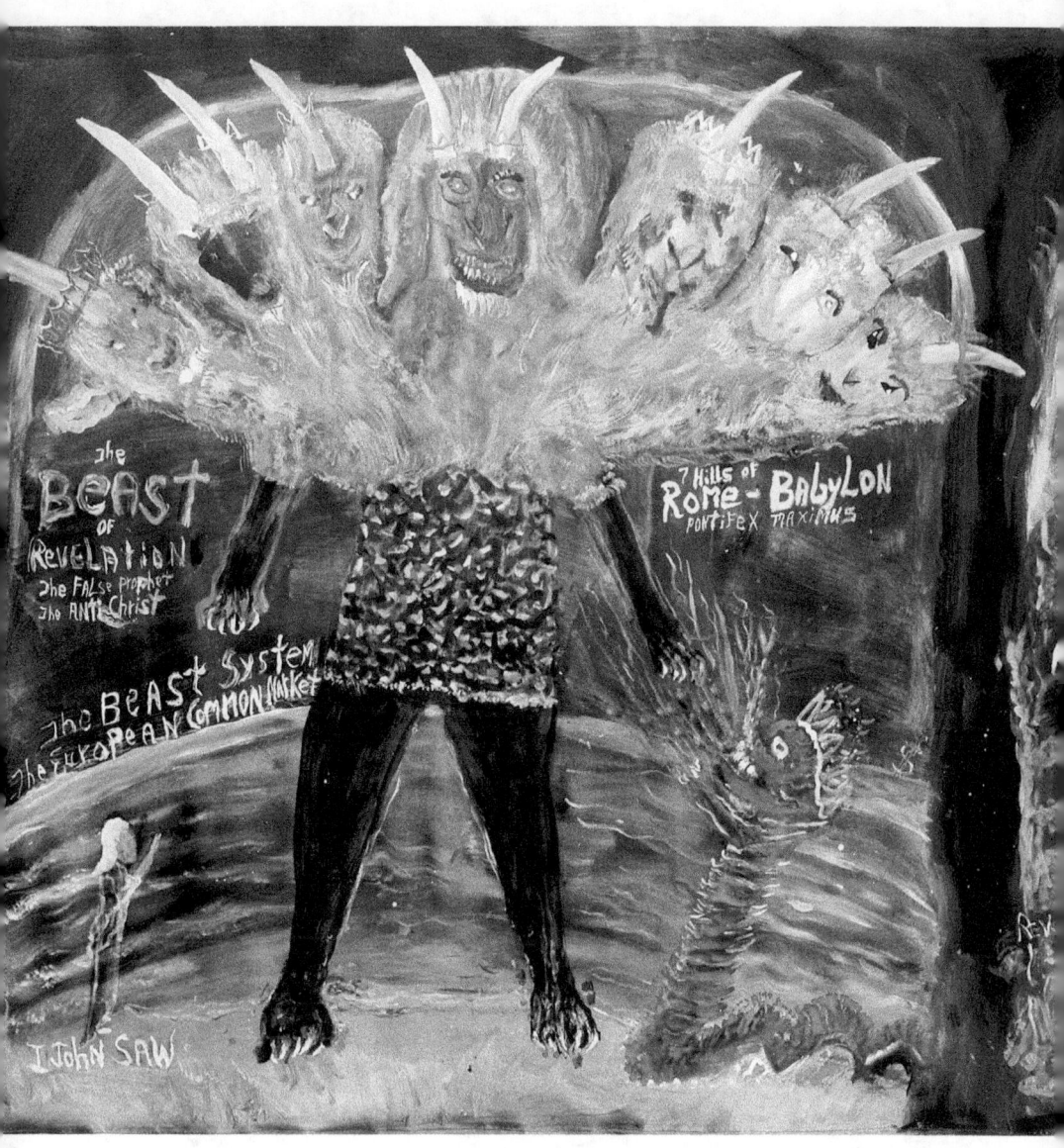

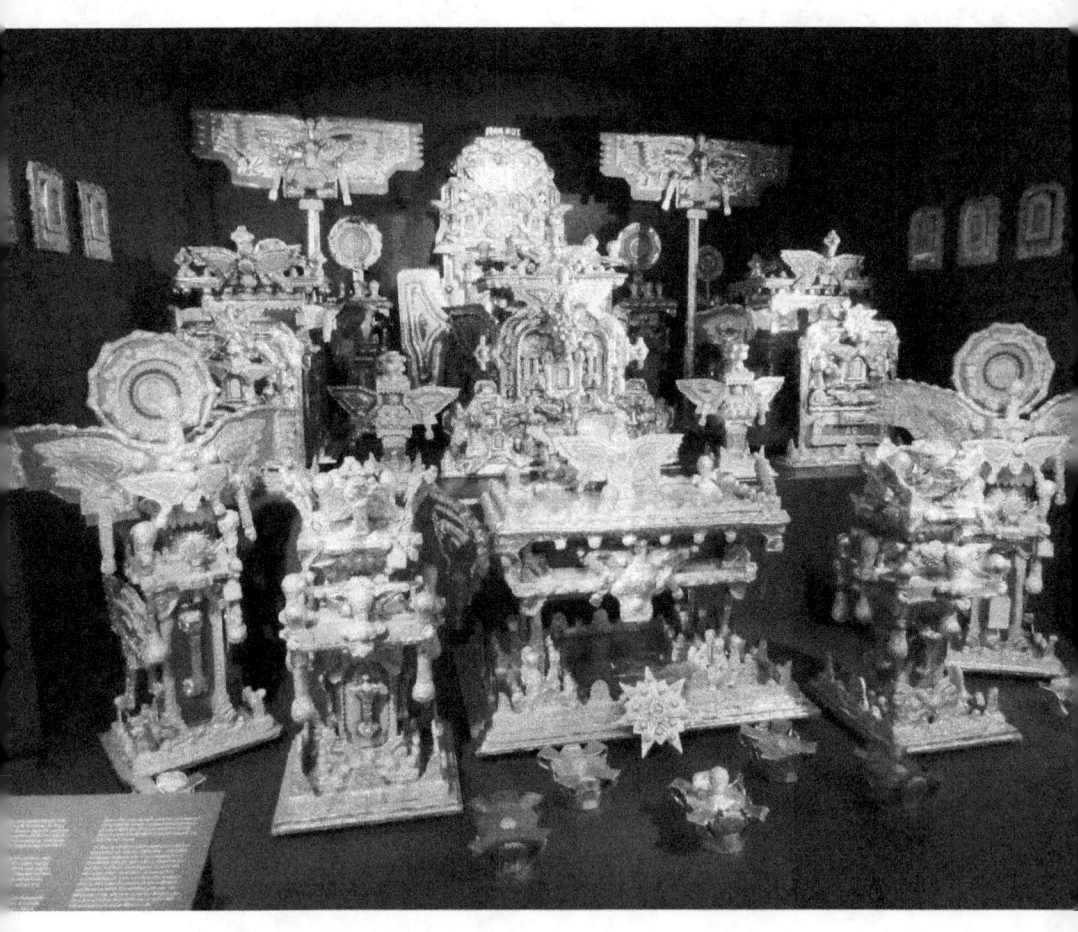

pl. 9 James Hampton, *Throne of the Third Heaven of the Nations' Millennium General Assembly*, 1950 -1964, metallic foils, paper and other mixed media, Smithsonian American Art Museum

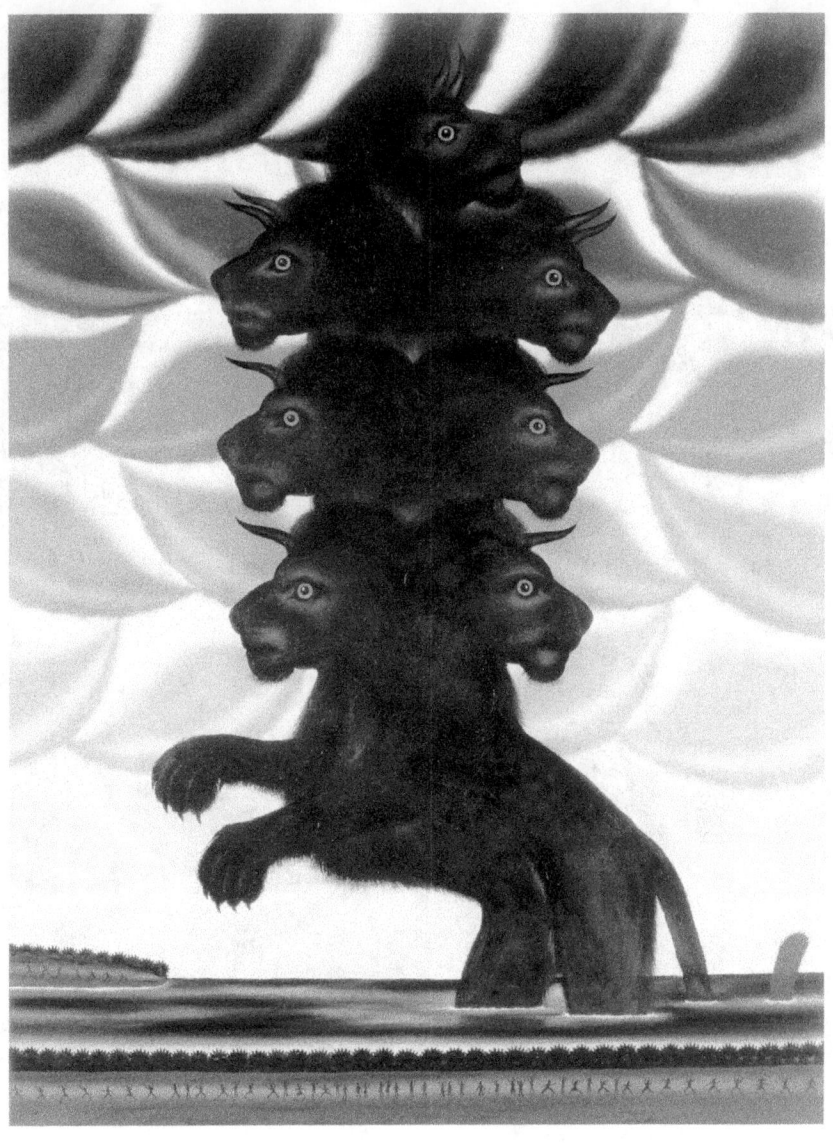

pl. 10 Roger Brown, American, *Beast Rising from the Sea*, 1983,
oil on canvas, 72 x 54 inches, School of the Art Institute of Chicago

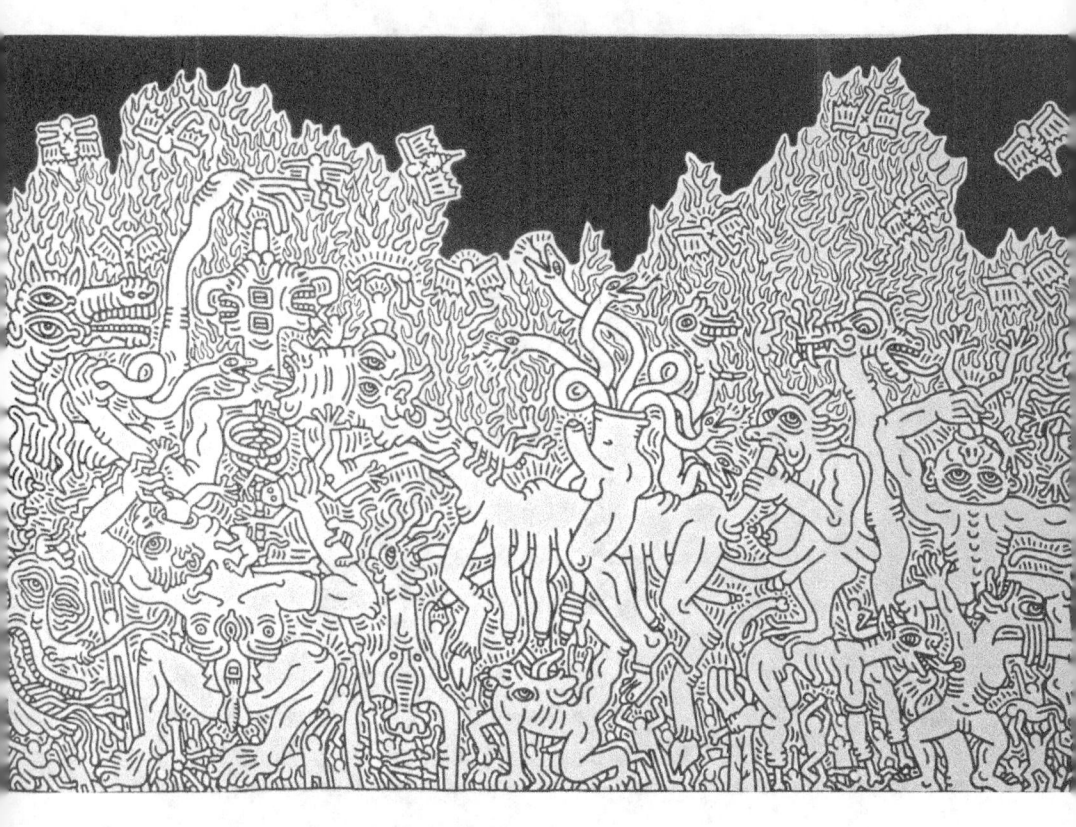

pl. 11 Keith Haring *Untitled (July 7, 1985)*,
1985, acrylic and oil.

pl. 12 Paul Pfeiffer, *Morning After the Deluge*, 2003, film still, projected video installation, 20 minutes, 12 x 16 feet

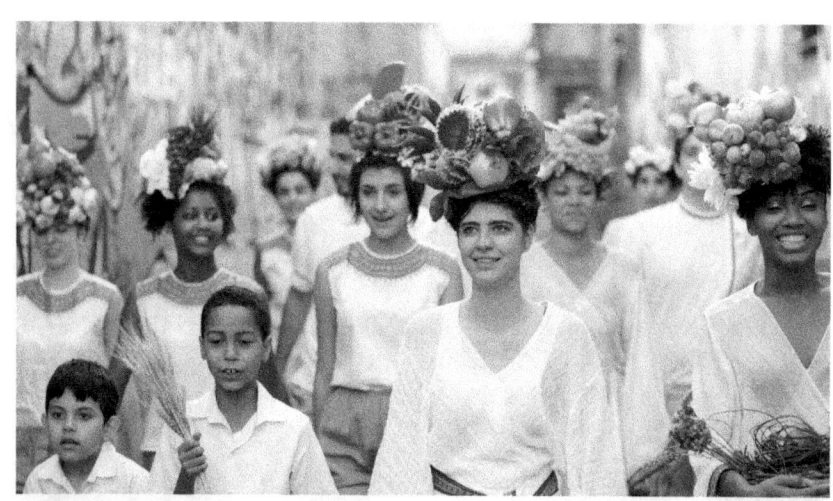

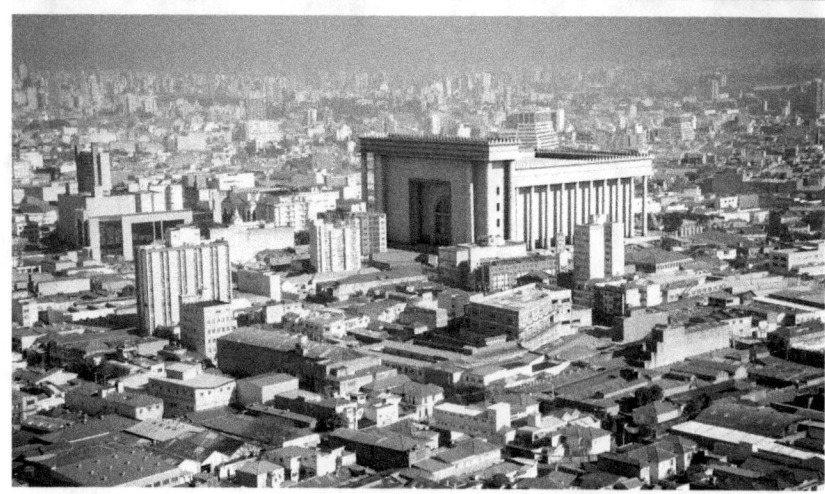

pl. 13 Yael Bartana, *Inferno*, 2013, film still,
Alexa camera transferred onto HD, 22 minutes

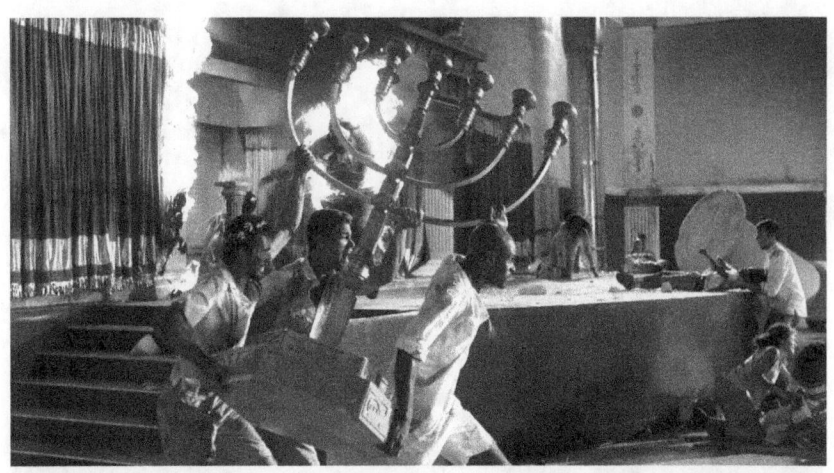

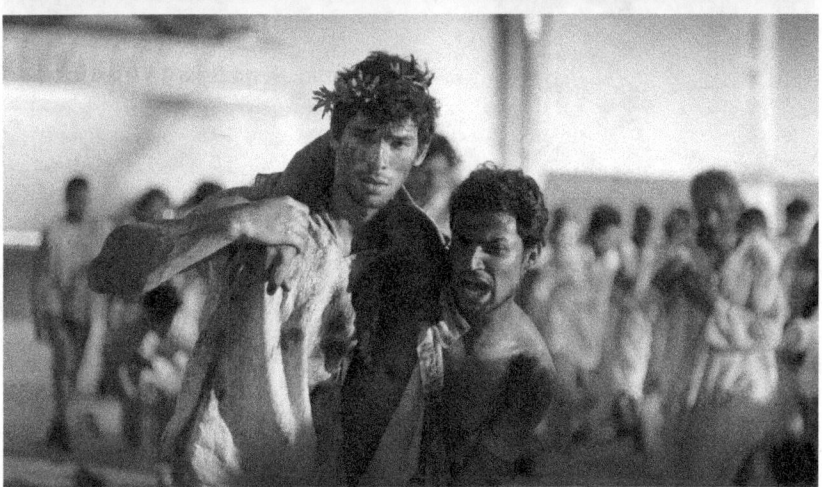

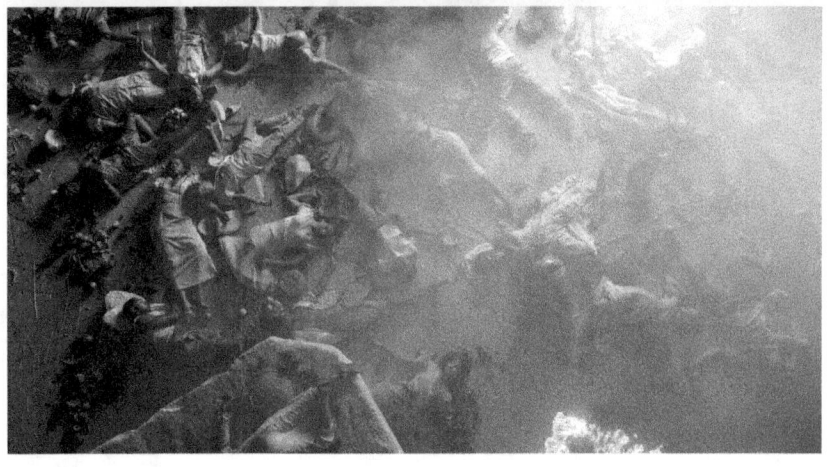

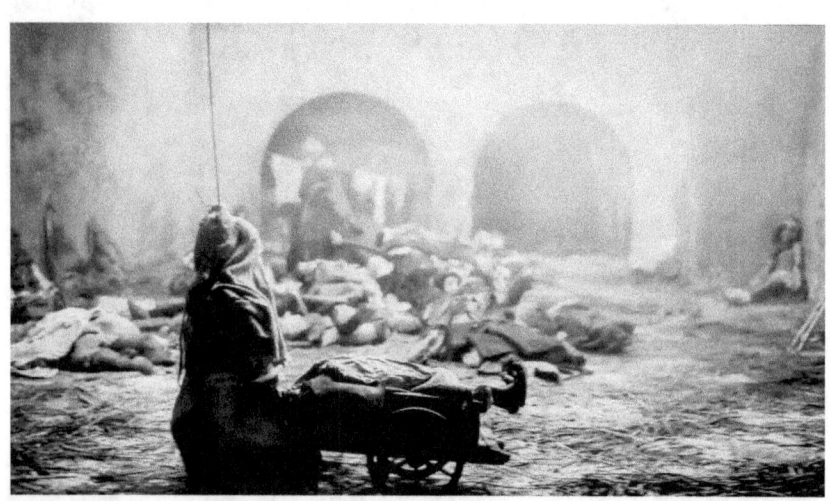

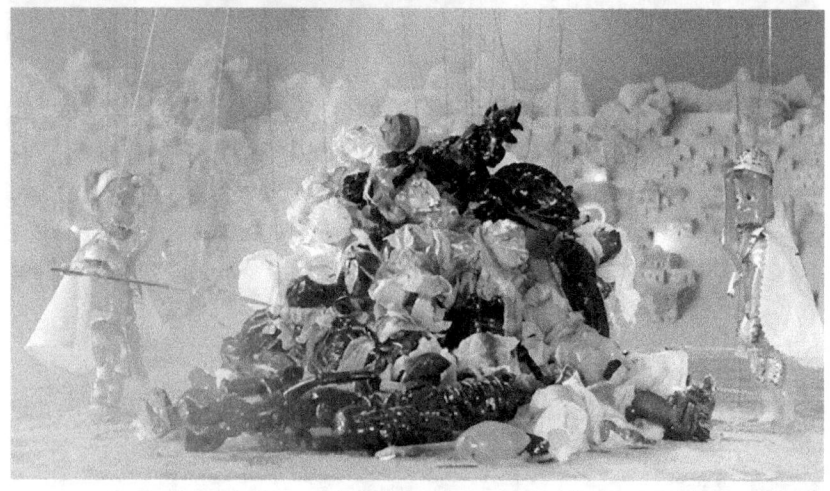

pl. 14 Wael Shawky, *Cabaret Crusades I: The Horror Show File*, 2010,
HD video, colour, sound, English Subtitles, Dimensions variable, 31:49 minutes

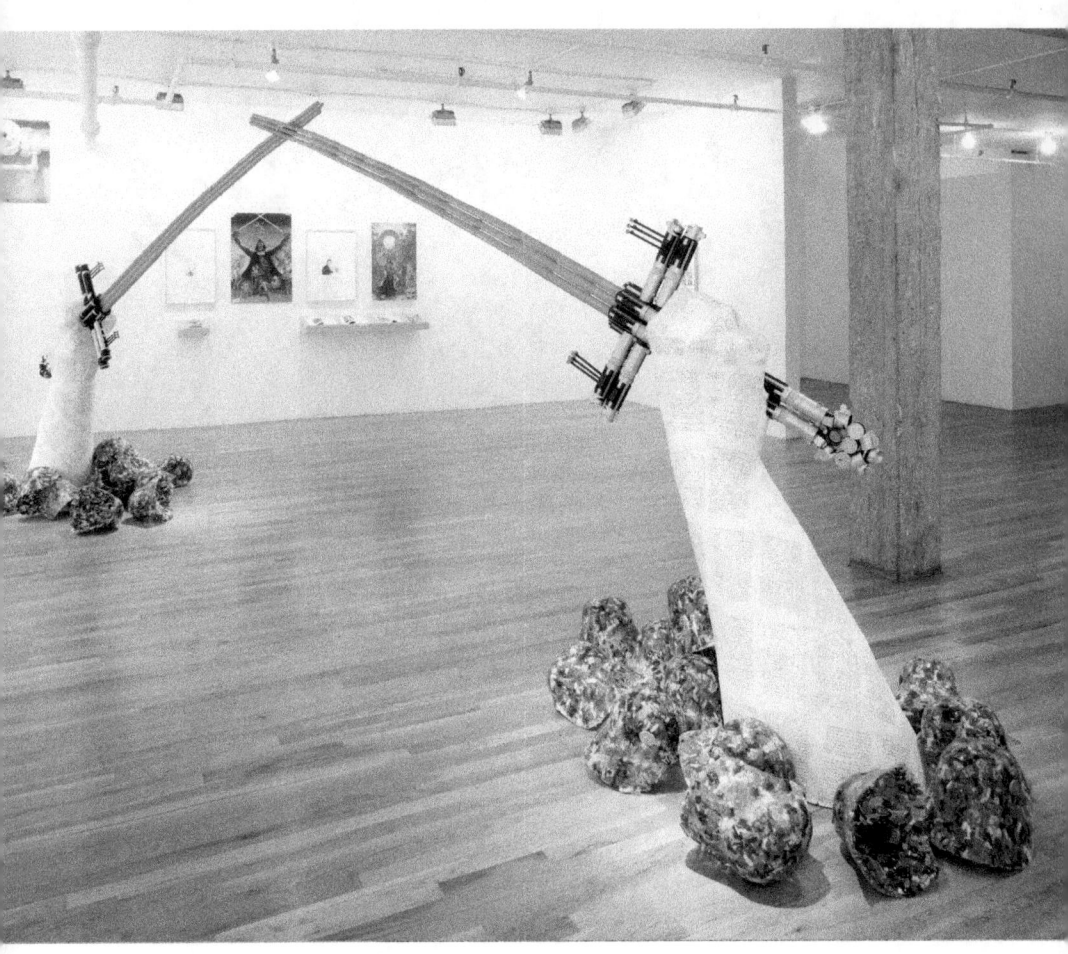

pl. 15 Michael Rakowitz, *The worst condition is to pass under a sword which is not one's own*, 2009, installation view at Lombard Freid Projects, New York

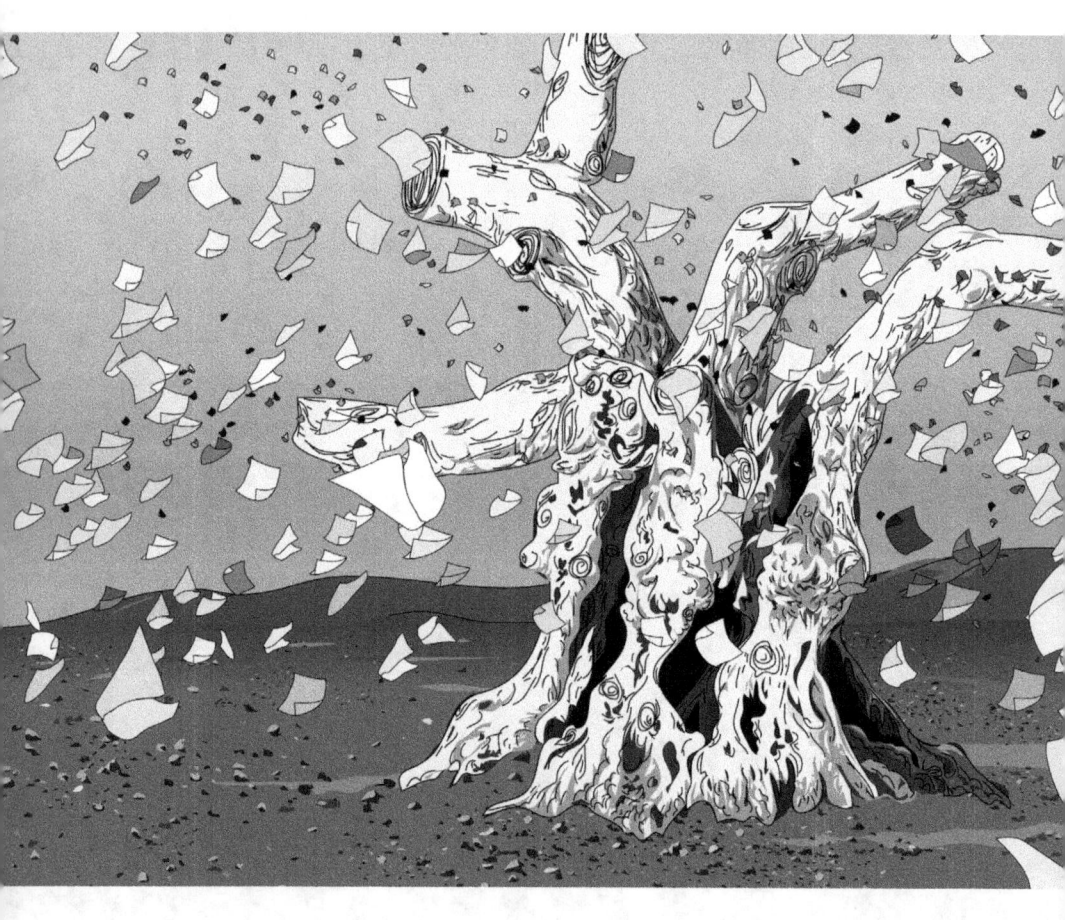

pl. 16 Paul Chan, *My birds... trash... the future*, 2004, film still,
two channel digital projection installation, 16:36 minutes

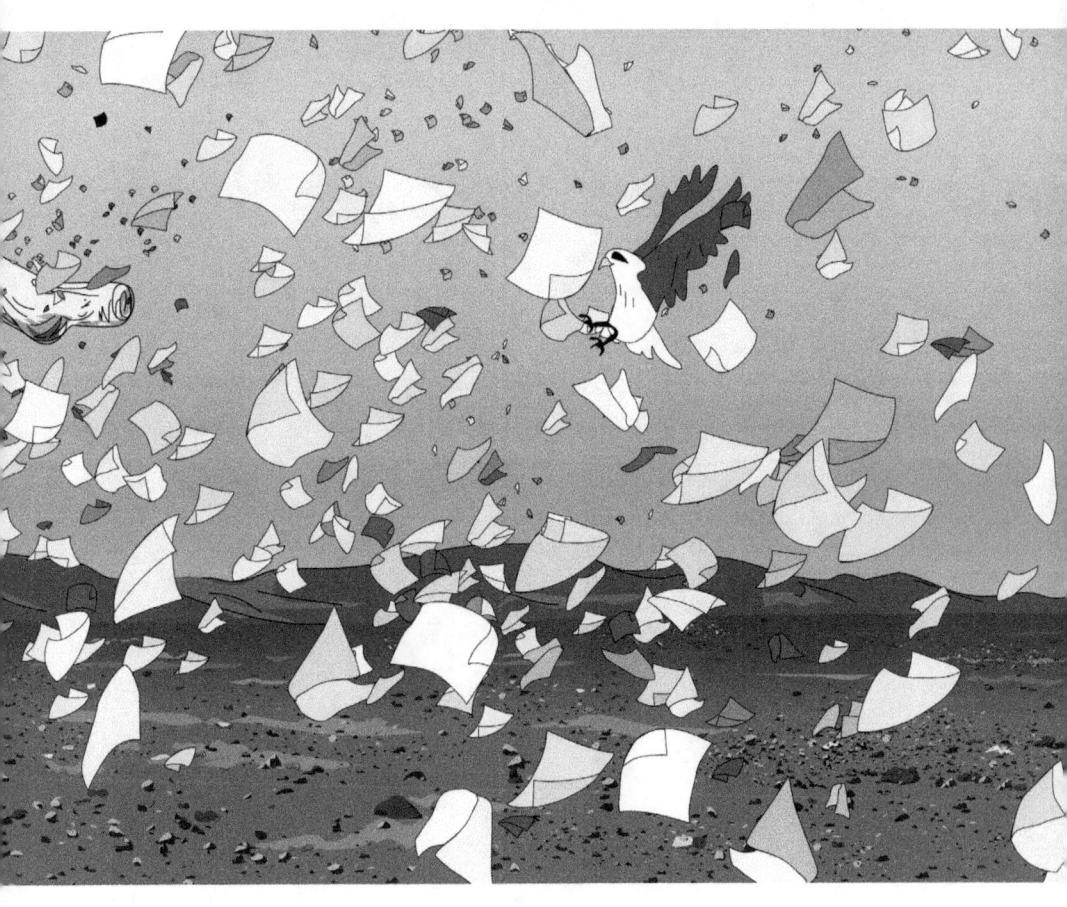

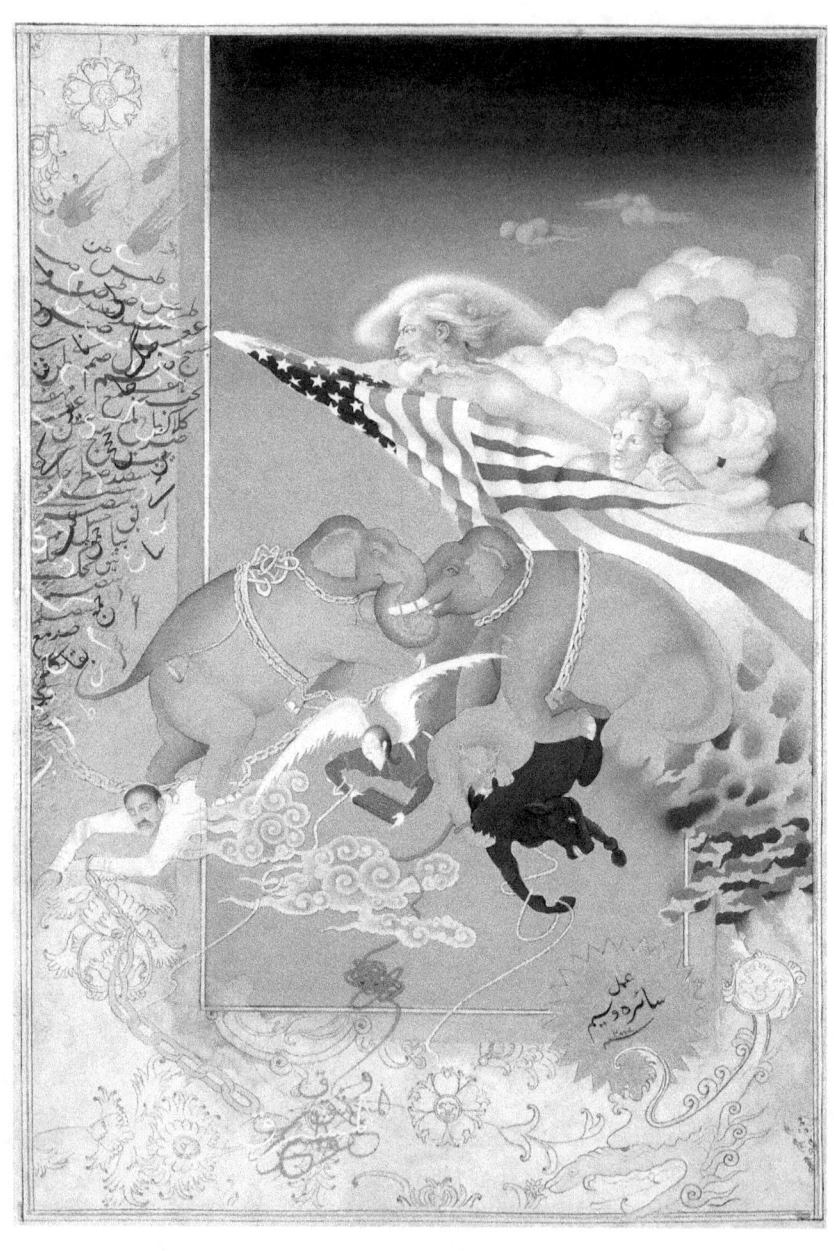

pl. 17 Saira Wasim, *Clash of Civilizations*,
2008, Gouache on wasli paper

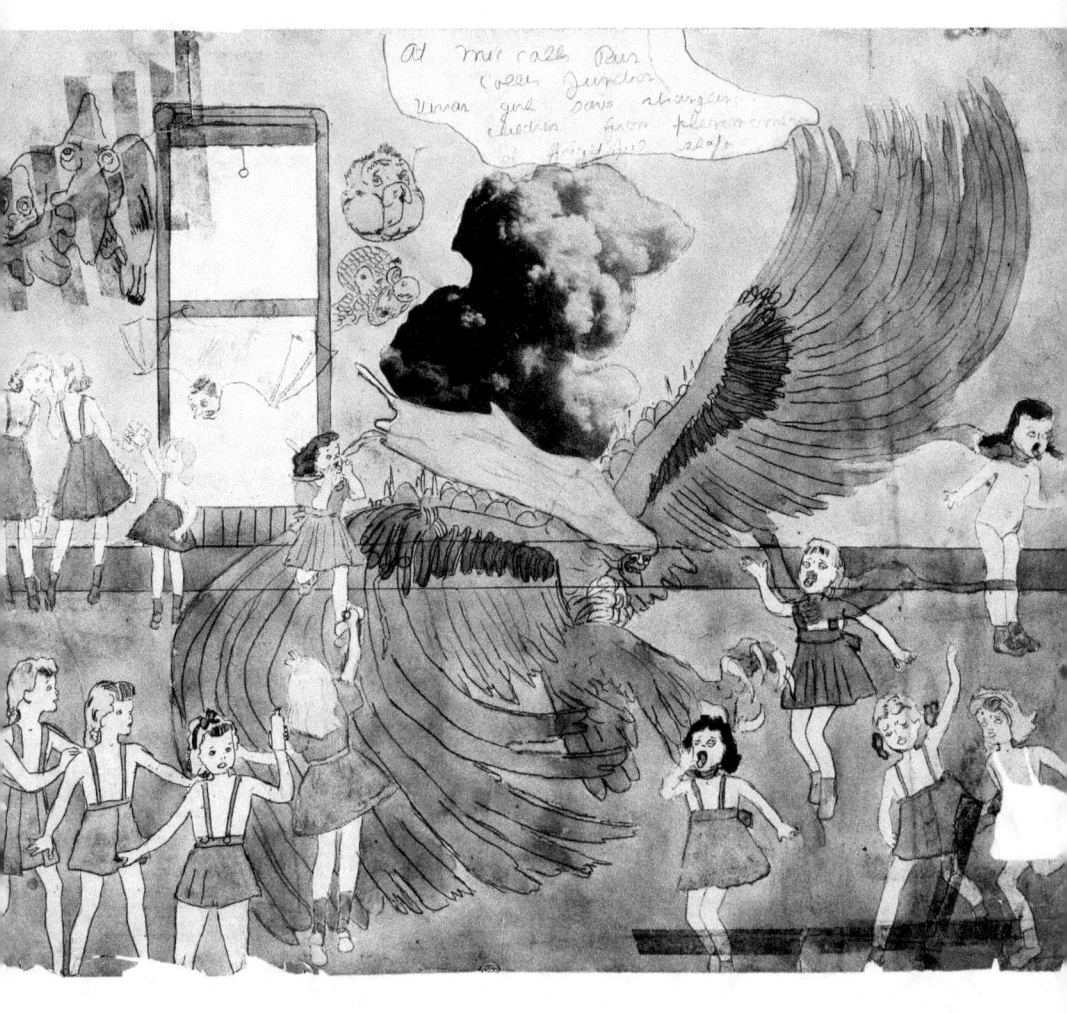

pl. 18 Henry Darger, "At McCall Run Vivian Saves Children" from
The Realms of the Unreal, n.d., work on paper, 19 x 24 inches

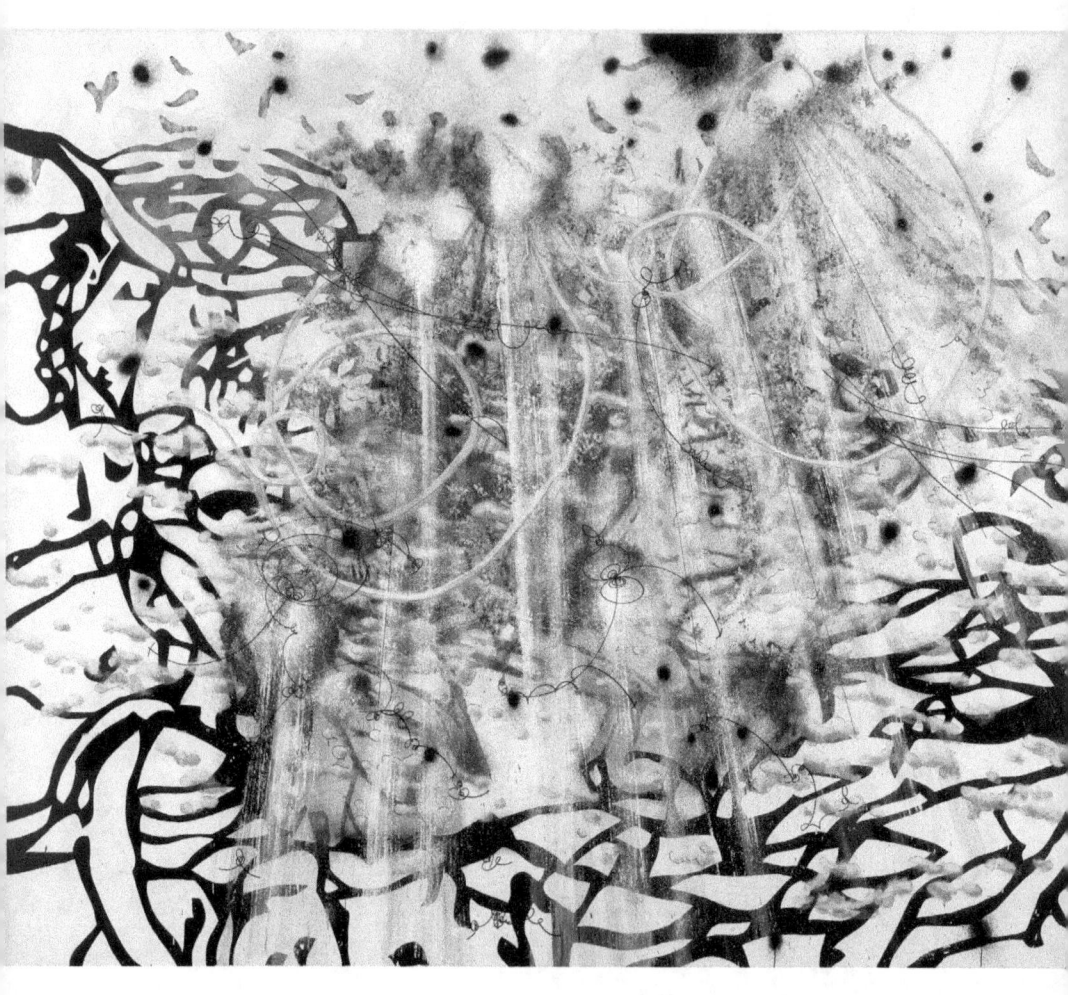

pl. 19 Matthew Ritchie, *How this Ends*,
2008, oil and marker on linen

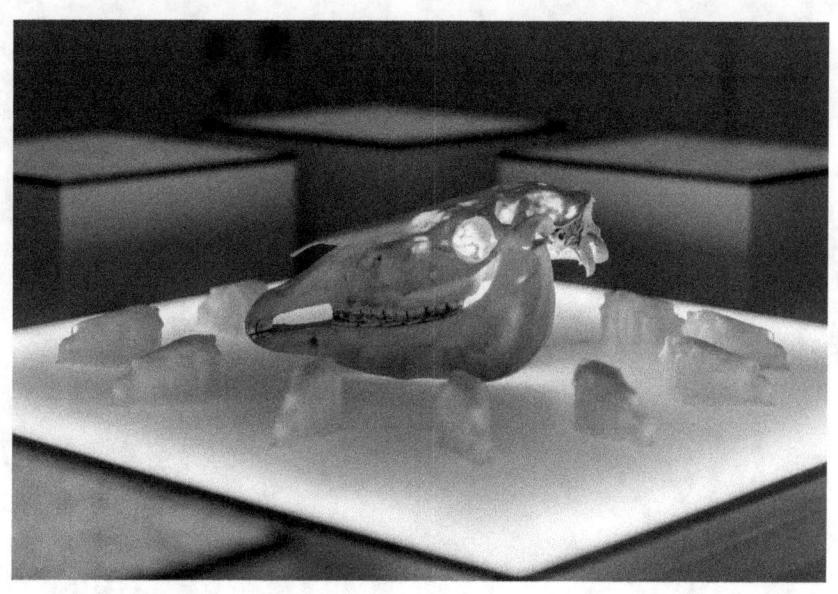

pl. 20 Michael Takeo Magruder, *The Horse as Technology*, 2014,
modular installation (with horse skull, data light boxes, 3D printer and prints,
led screen, computer, and sound system), dimensions variable

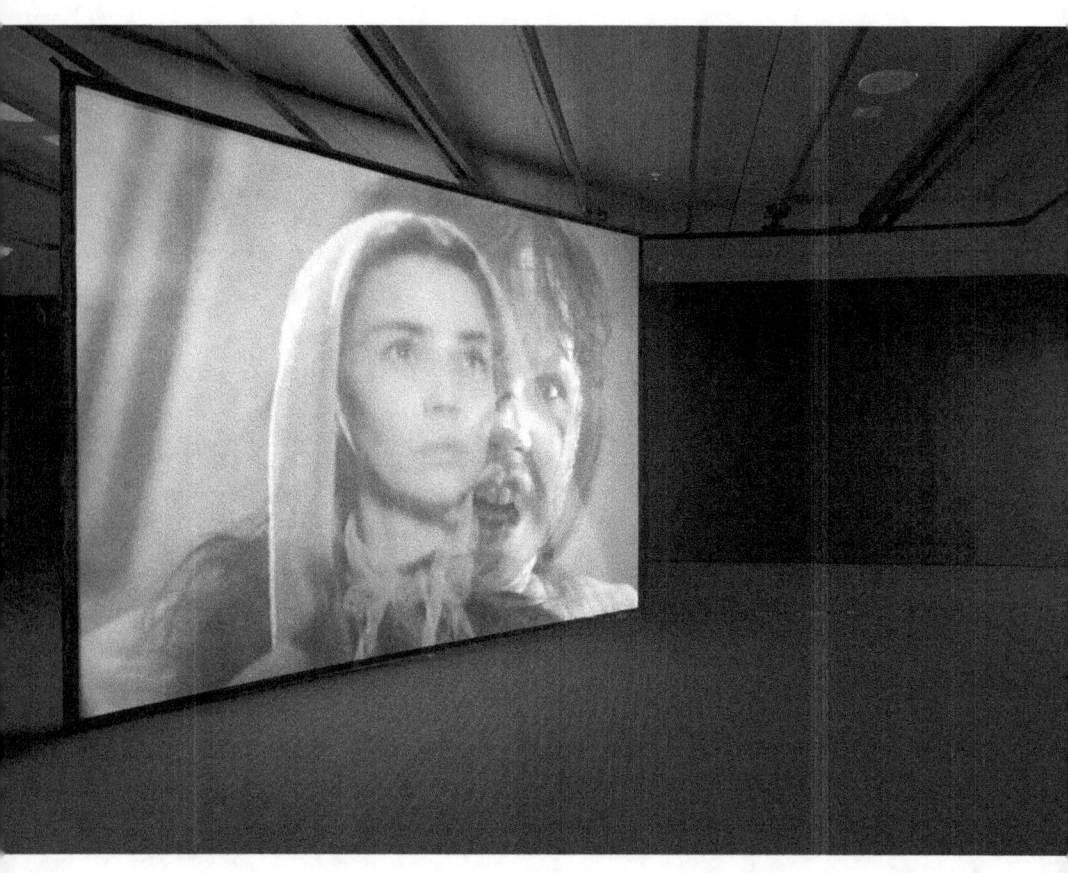

pl. 21 Douglas Gordon, *Between Darkness and Light (After William Blake)*,
1997, still, installation view of the 2006 exhibition, *Douglas Gordon:
Timeline*, The Museum of Modern Art, New York

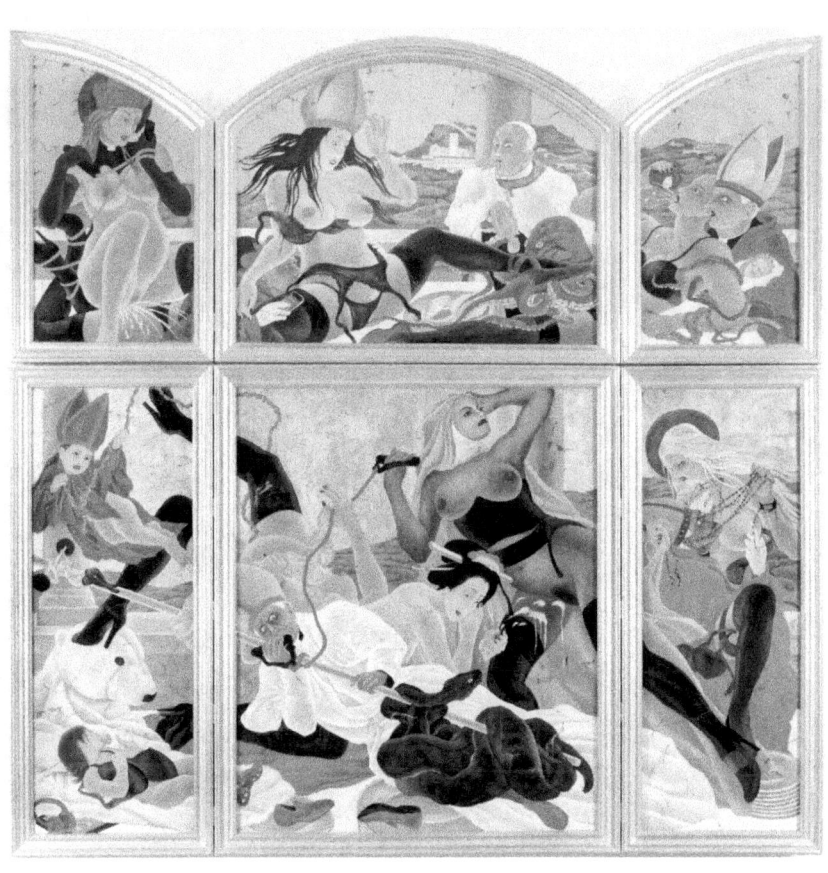

pl. 22 Masami Teraoka, *The Cloisters Last Supper/Eve and Pope's Walking Stick*, 2014, oil on panel in gold leaf double triptych frame. 123 x 120 x 3 inches

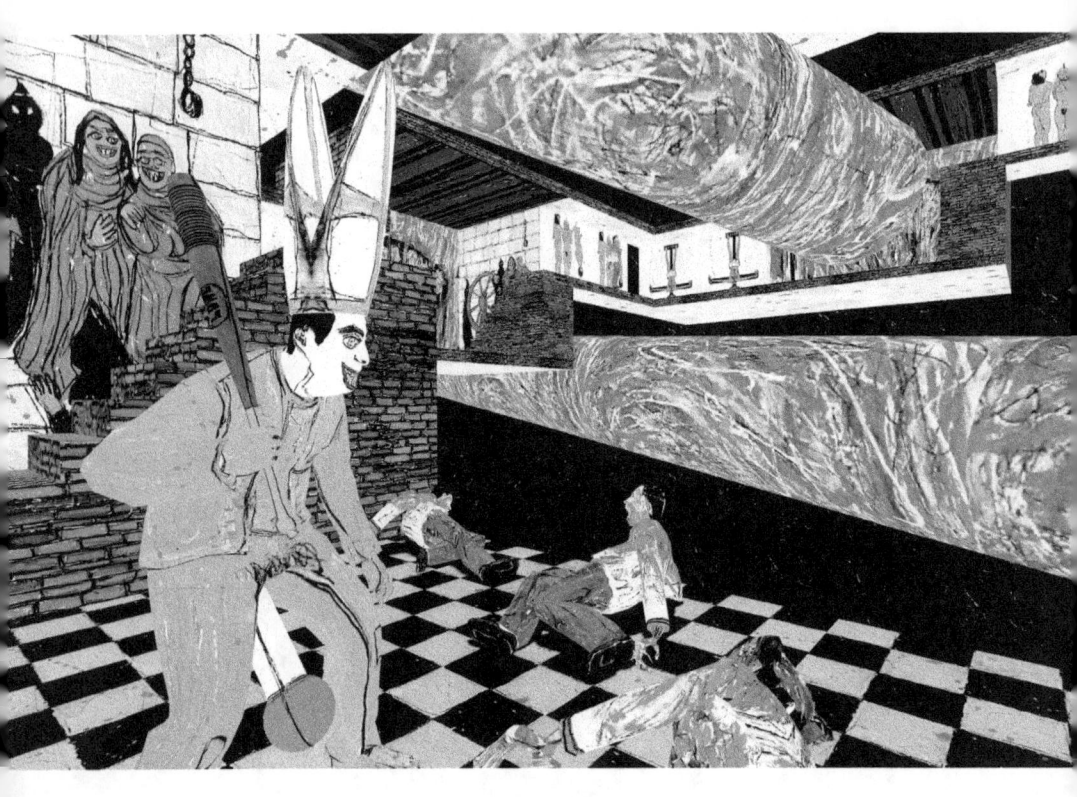

pl. 23 Federico Solmi, *The Evil Empire*, 2008, single channel video,
color, sounds, 4:13 minutes

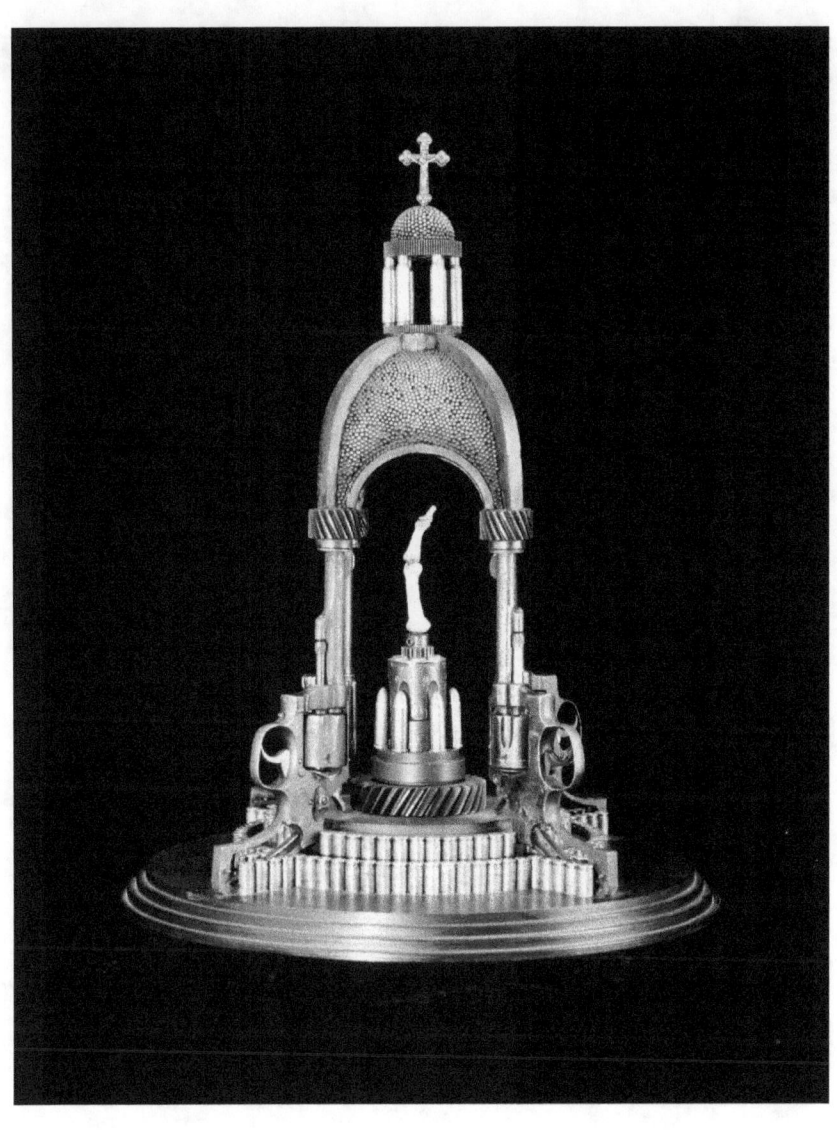

pl. 24 Al Farrow, *Trigger Finger of Santo Guerro II*, 1996, guns, gun parts, bullets, shell casings, lead shot, steel, bone, 20 x 16 x 16 inches

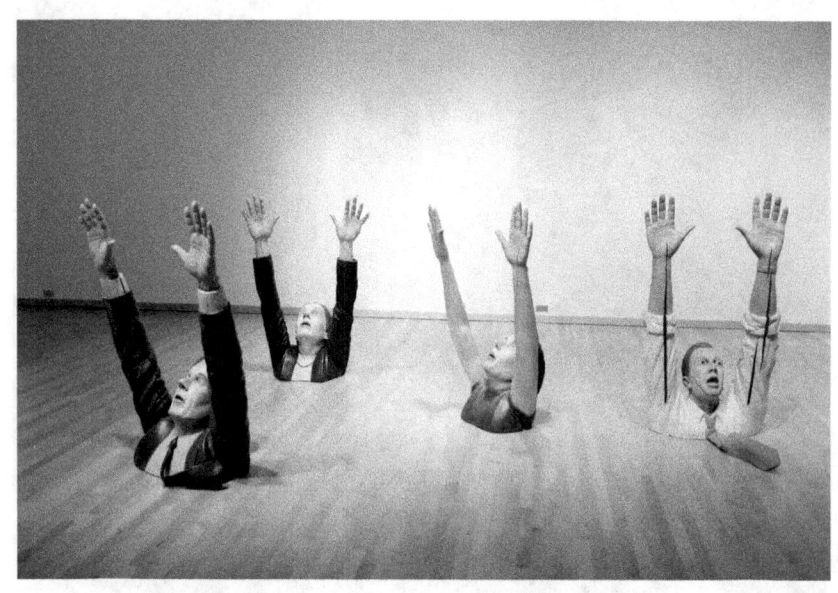

Above: pl. 25 Robert Trotman, *Chorus*, (*Martin, Kaitlin, Jane, Sinking Feeling*),
2008, wood, tempera and wax

Opposite: pl. 26 Grisha Bruskin, *Birth of a Hero*, 1988,
installation, painted bronze and aluminum

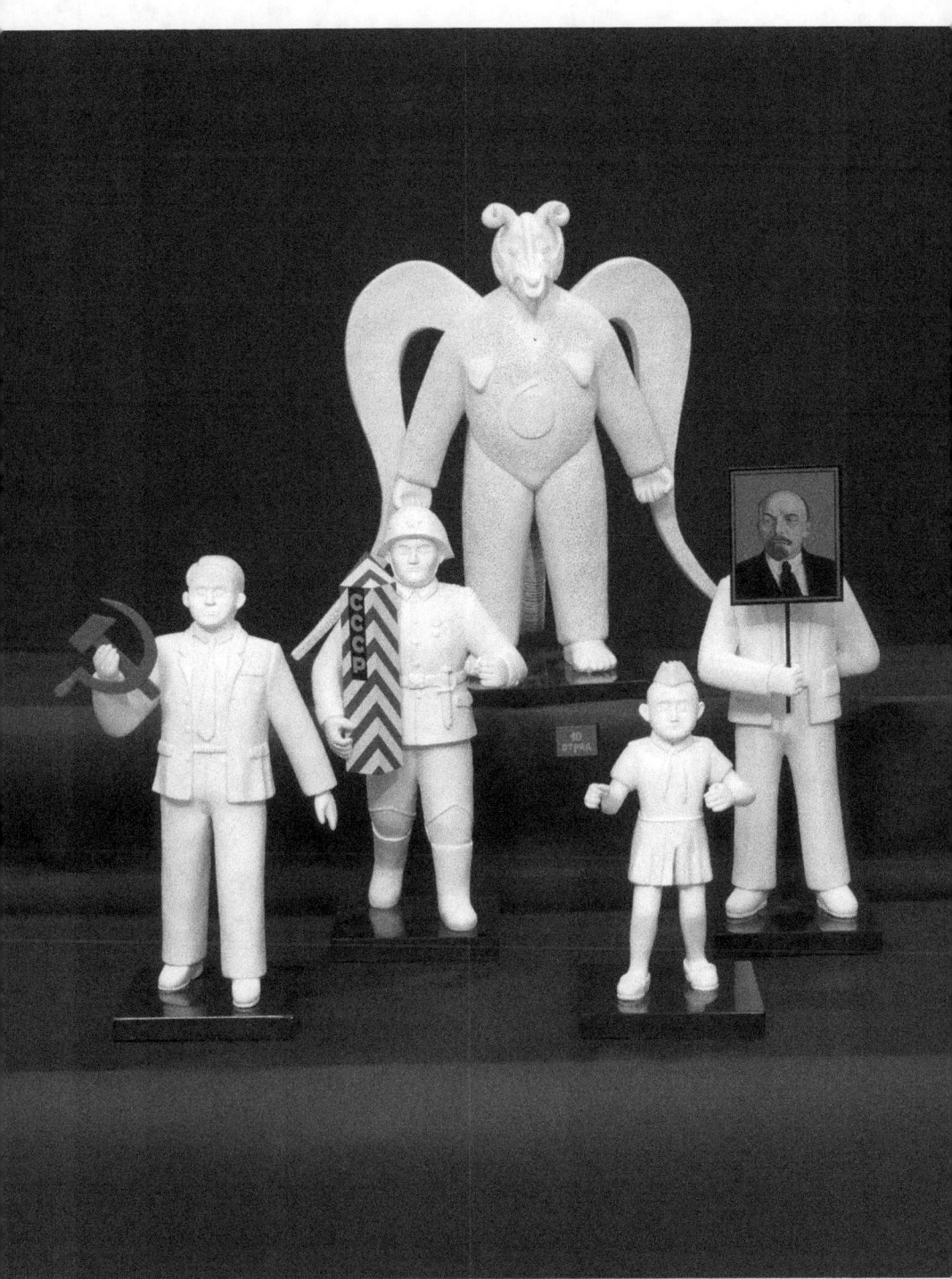

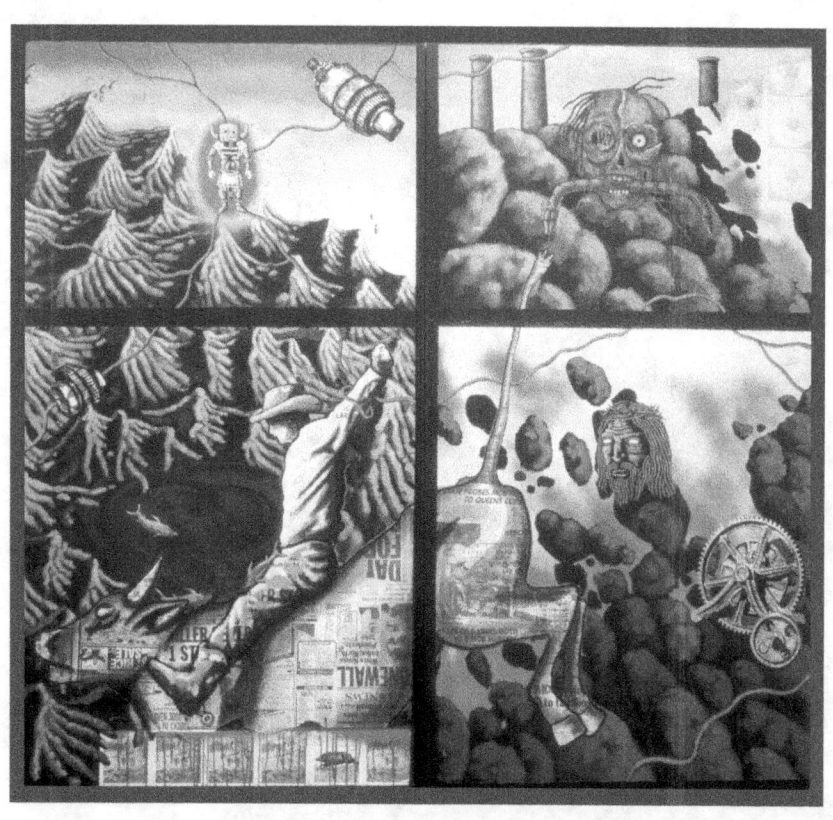

pl. 27 David Wojnarowicz, *Death of American Spirituality*,
1987, spray paint, acrylic and collage on plywood,
Two panels, 81 x 88 inches, Private collection

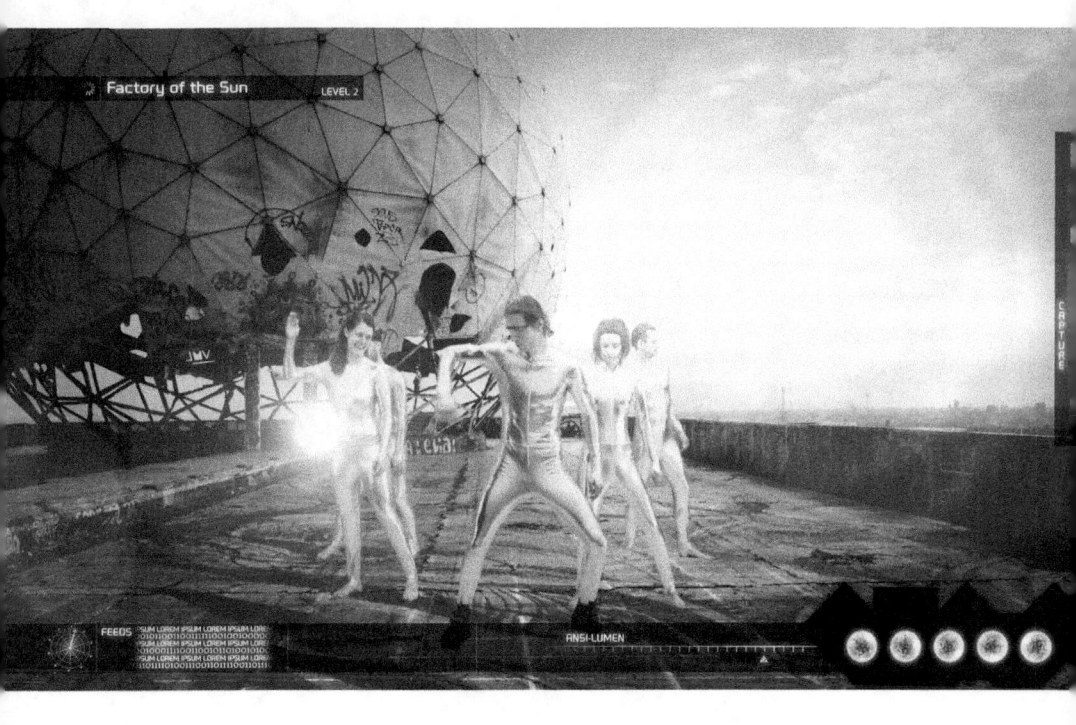

pl. 28 Hito Steyerl, *Factory of the Sun*,
2015, still, HD video, 15:52 minutes

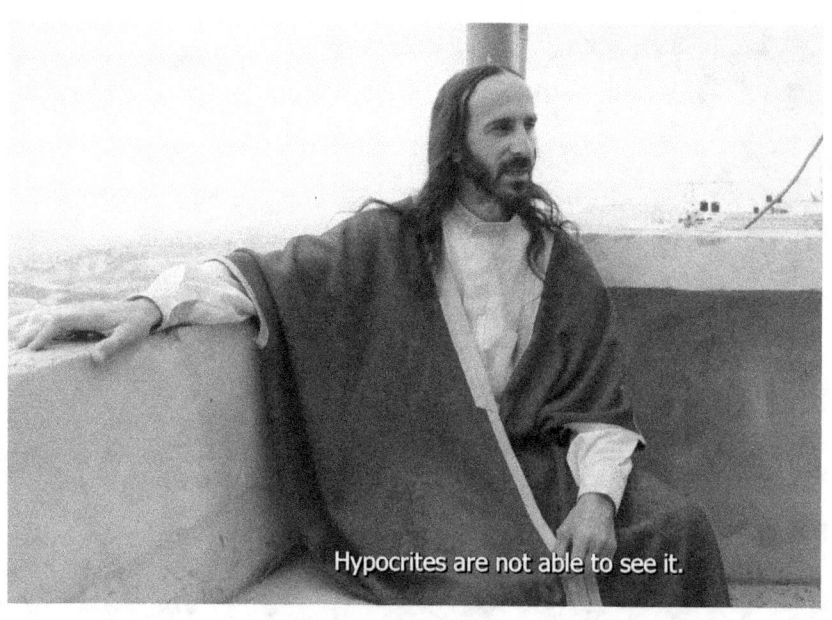

Hypocrites are not able to see it.

pl. 29 Katarzyna Kozyra, *Looking for Jesus*,
2013, still, single channel video, 70 minutes

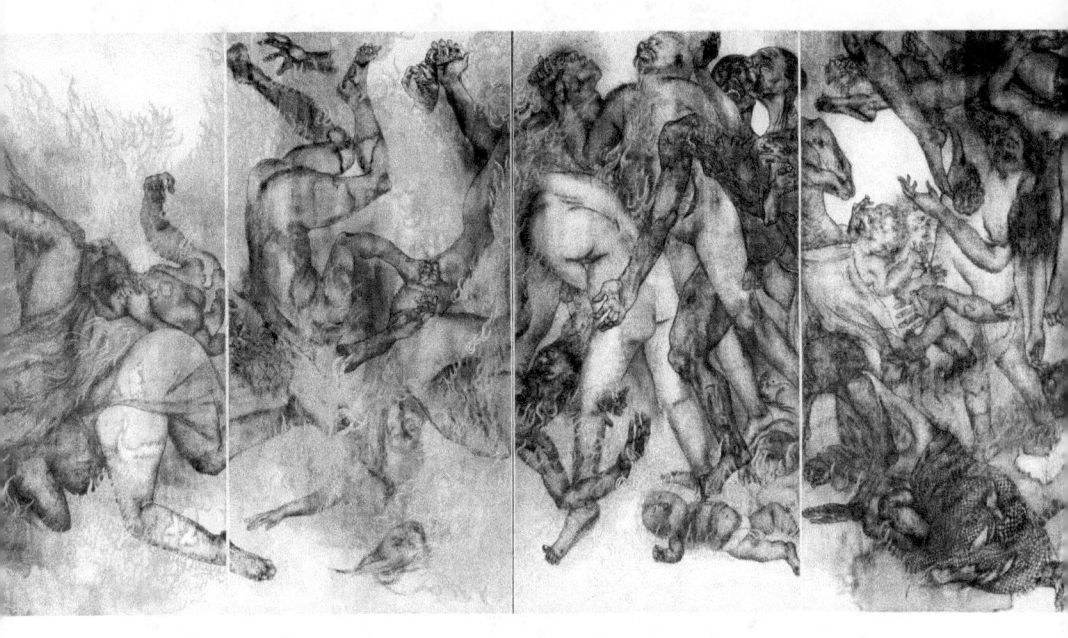

pl. 30 Iri and Toshi Maruki, *Hiroshima Panel #2: Fire*, (detail),
1950, ink, water color, chalk on paper

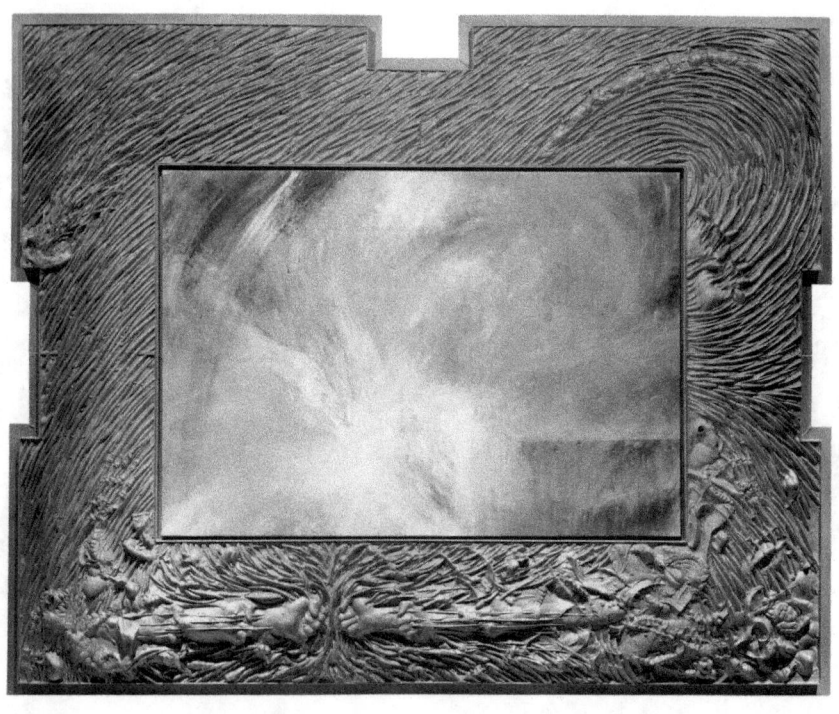

pl. 31 Robert Morris, *Untitled*, 1984,
Painted cast Hydrocal, oil on canvas

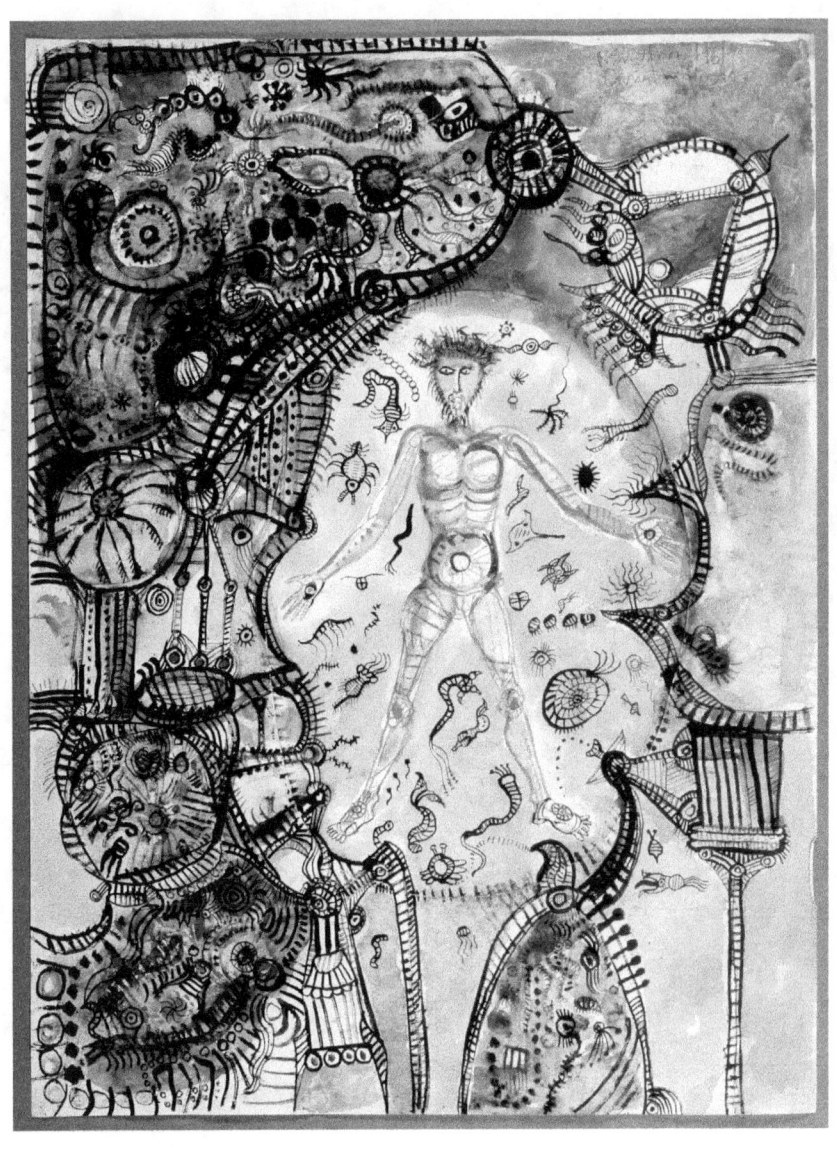

pl. 32 Robert Smithson, *Christ in Limbo*, 1961, ink, gouache on paper,
The Menil Collection, Houston

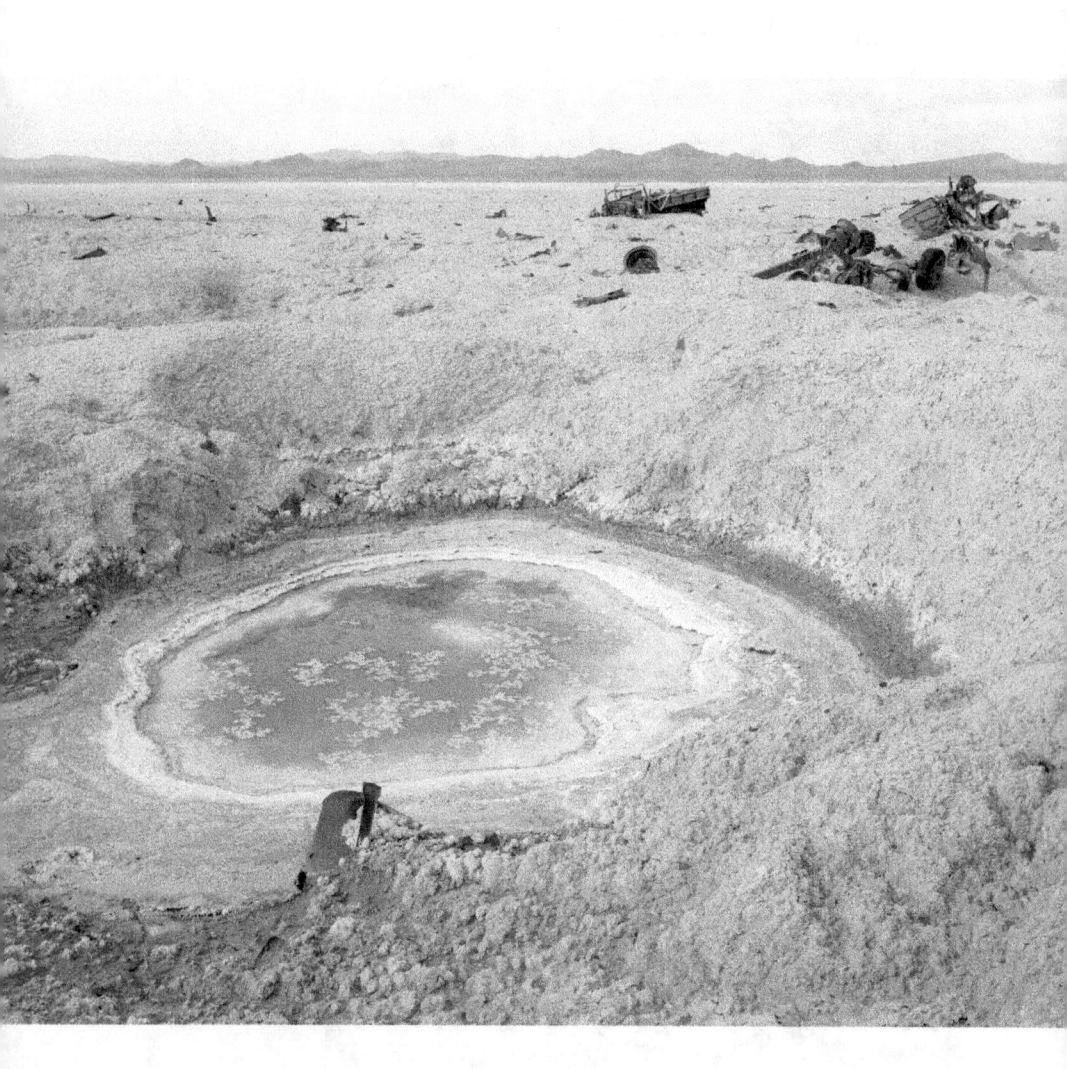

Above: pl. 33 Richard Misrach, *Bomb Crater and Destroyed Convoy*,
1986, chromogenic print, Bravo 20 Bombing Range, Nevada

Opposite: pl. 34 Werner Herzog, still, *Lessons of Darkness*,
1992, color, Super 16mm, 52 minutes

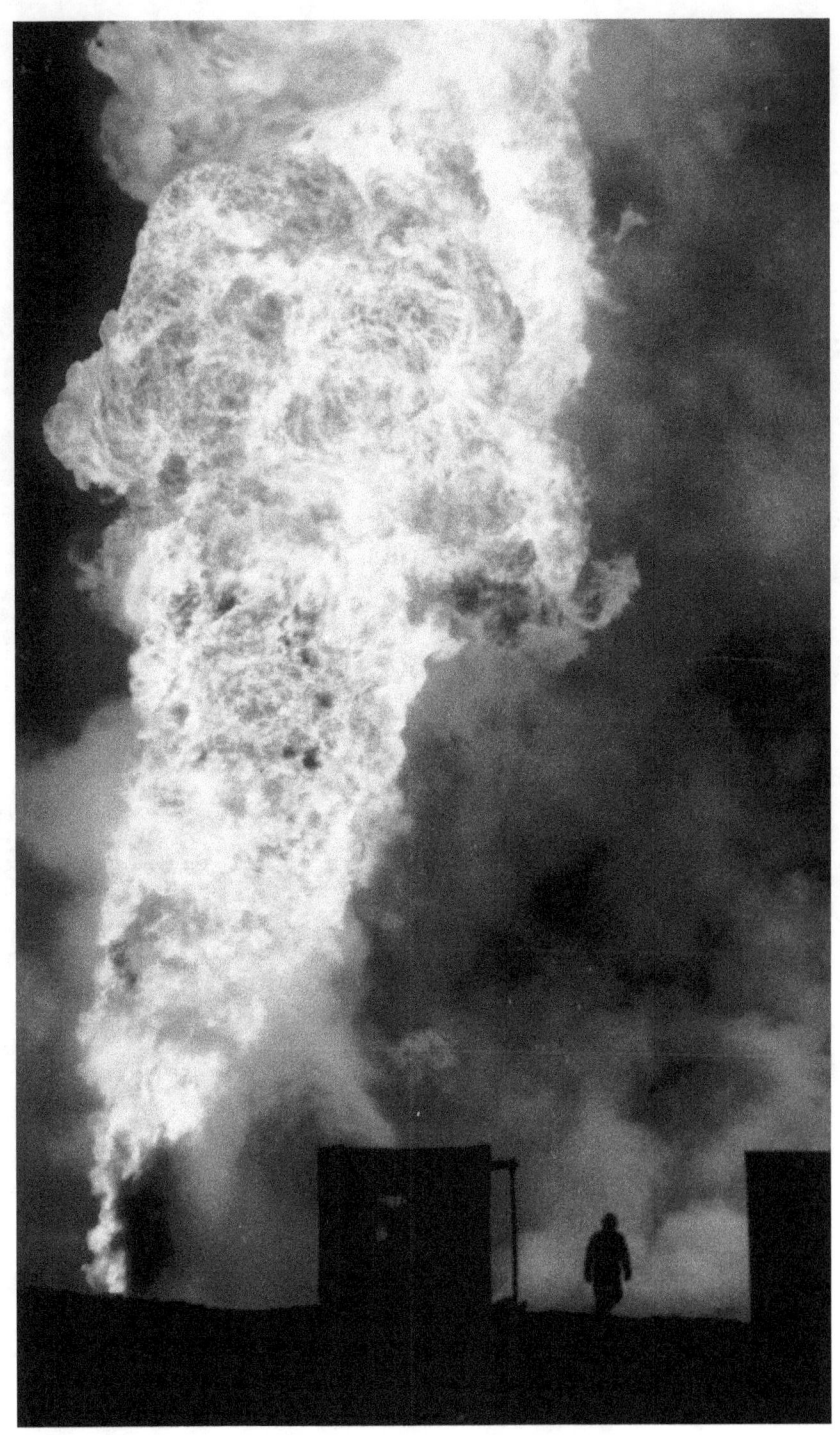

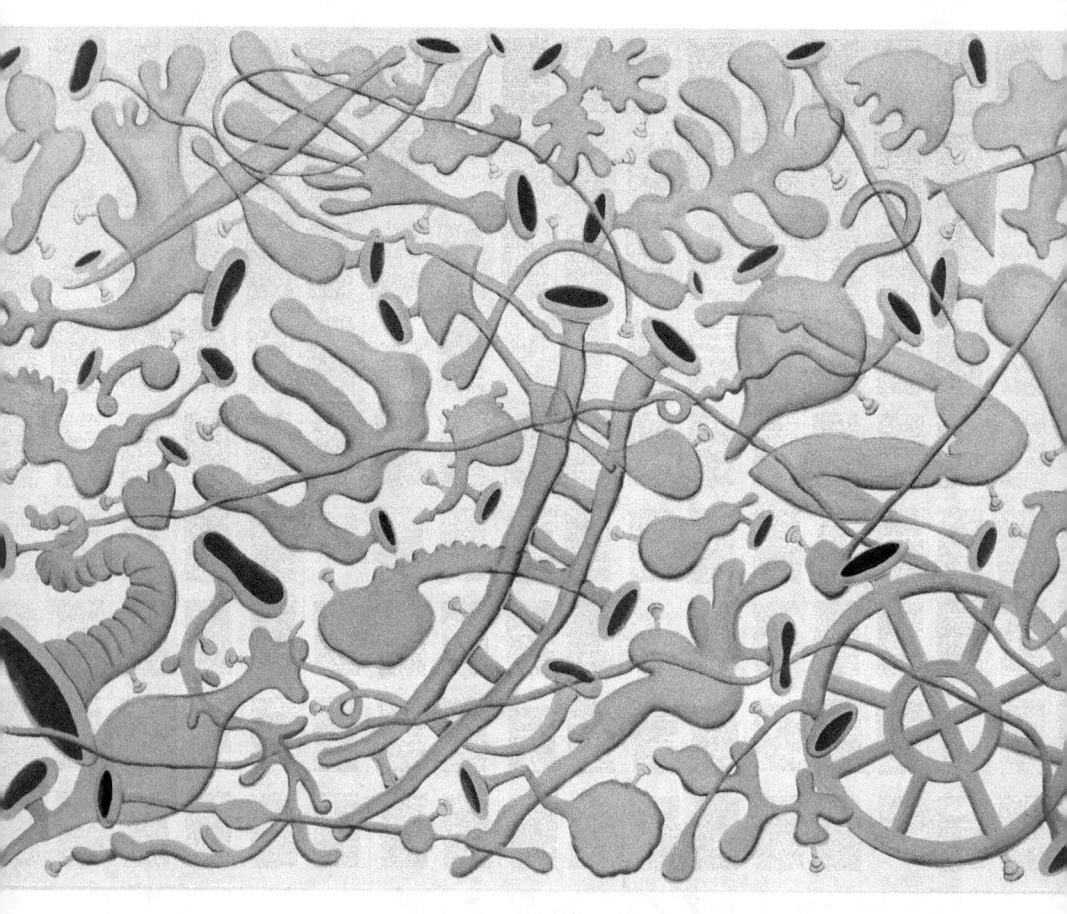

pl. 35 Tim Rollins and KOS, *Amerika the Stoker*,
1993-1994, acrylic on book pages on linen

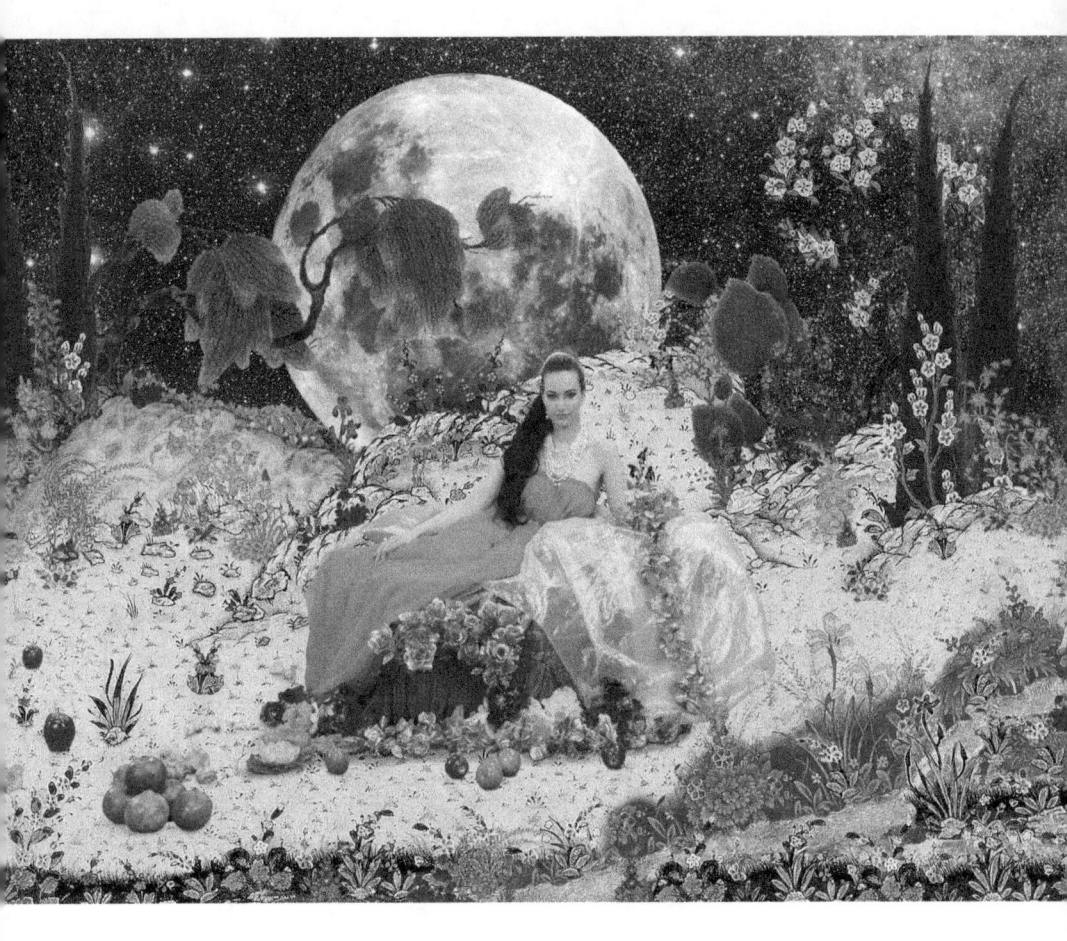

pl. 36 Shoja Azari, *The King of Black*, 2013,
HD color video with sound, 24 minutes

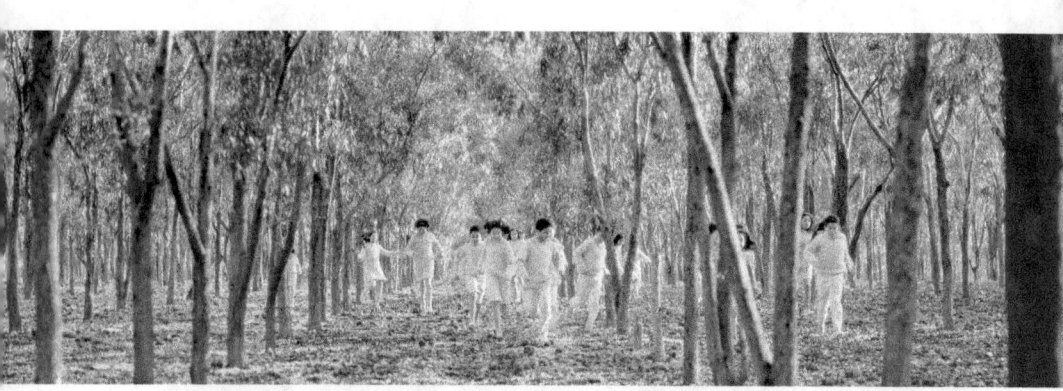

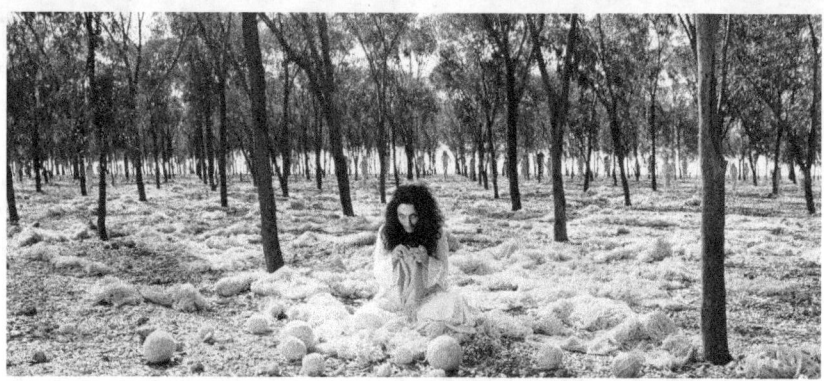

Above: pl. 37 Shirin Neshat, *Mahdokht Series*, 2004, C-print

Opposite: pl. 38 Mark Wallinger, *Angel*, 1997,
projected video installation, 7.5 minutes, ed. of 10

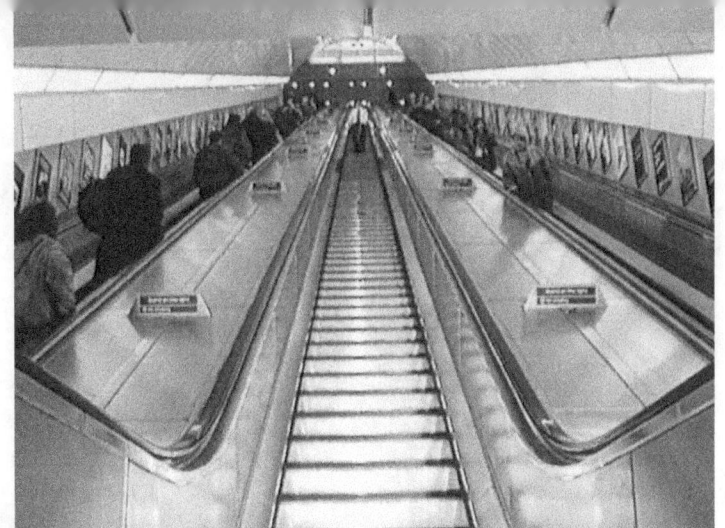

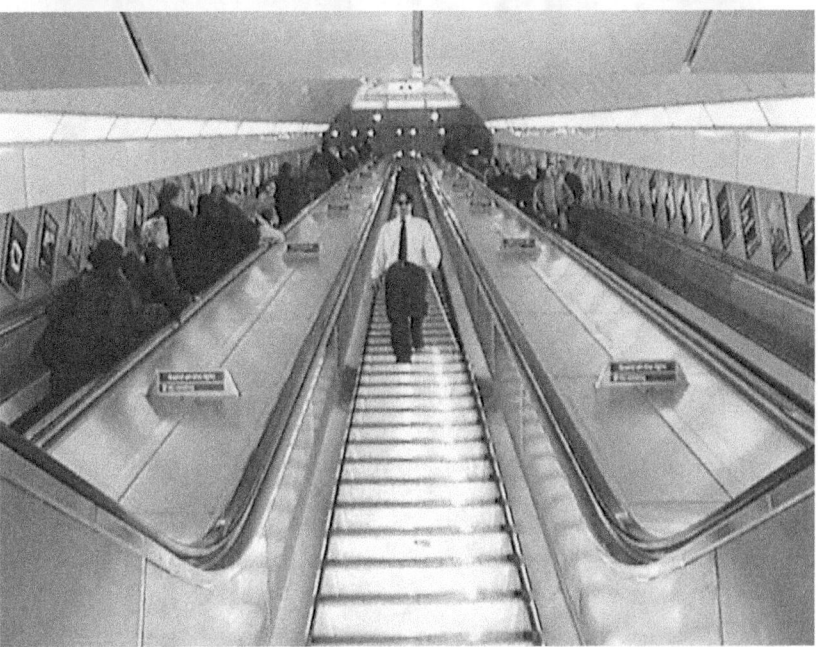

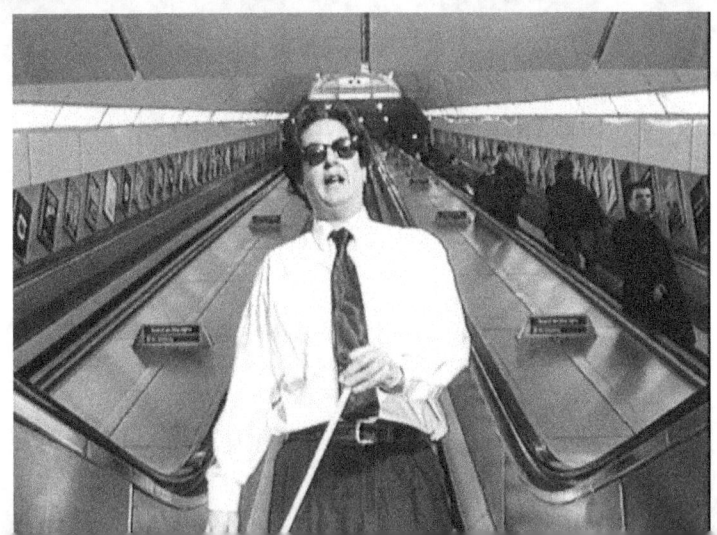

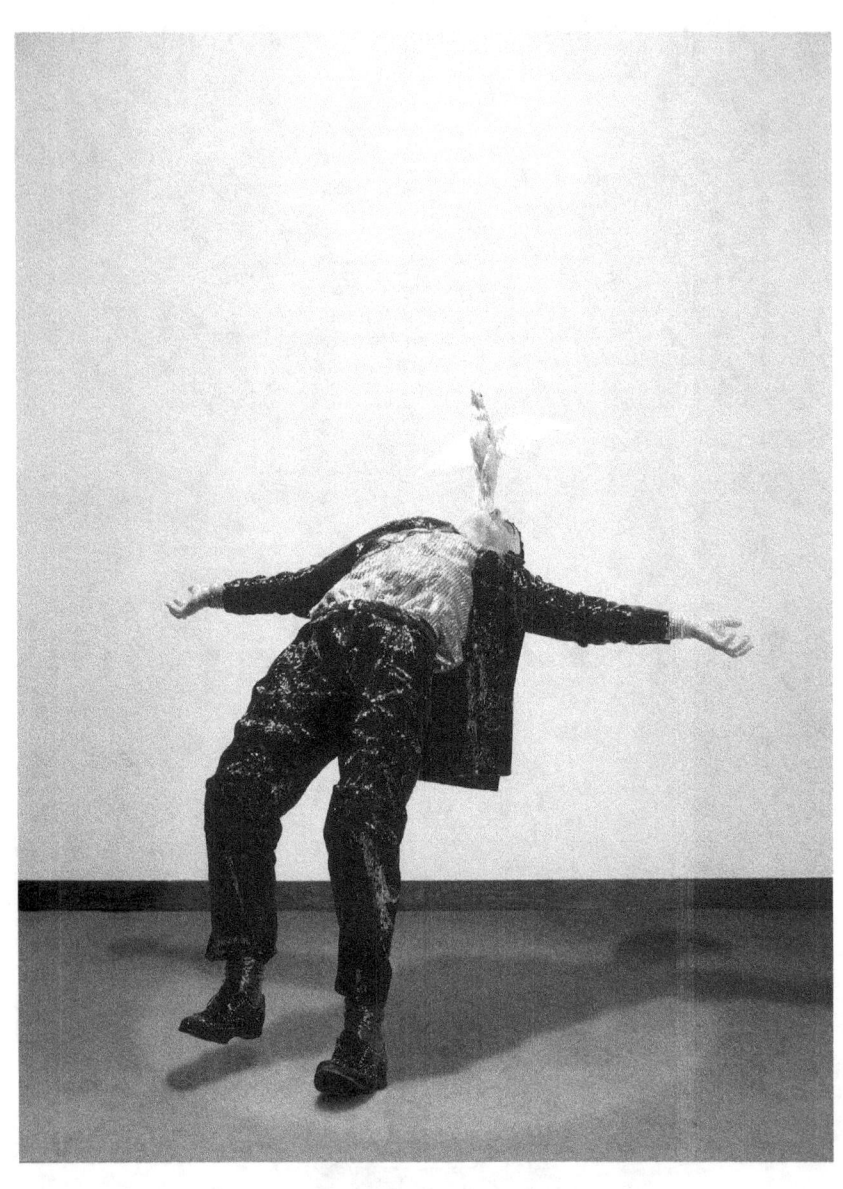

pl. 39 Liza Lou, *Man*, 2002,
glass beads on fiberglass

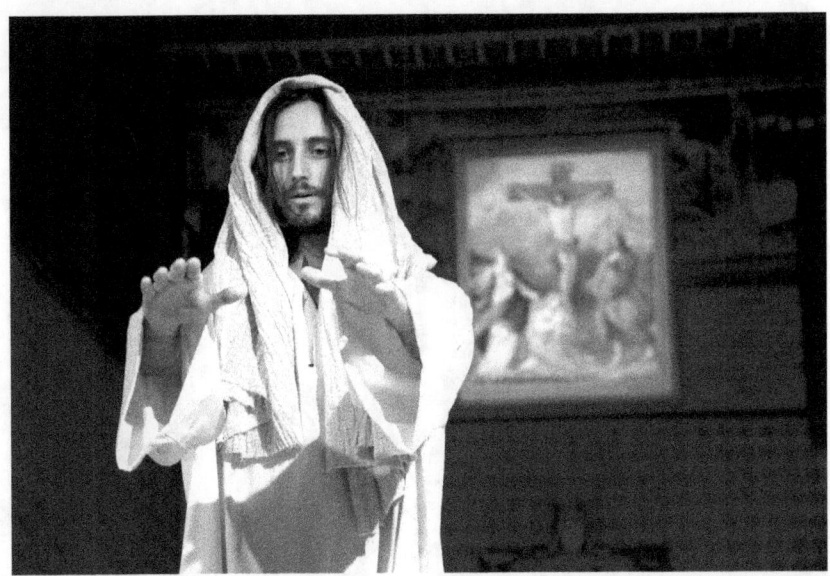

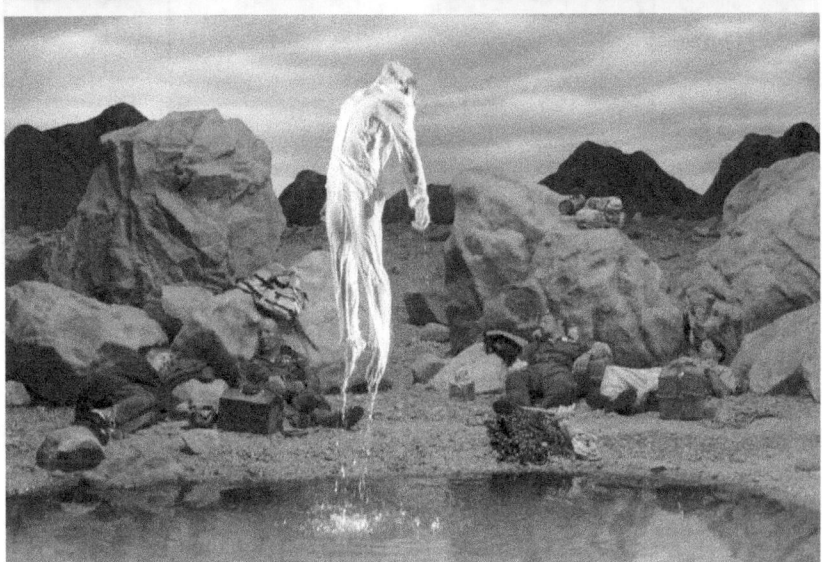

Top: pl. 40. Christian Jankowski, *Casting Jesus*,
2011, still, dual channel video projection, 60 minutes

Bottom: pl. 41 Bill Viola, *First Light*, Panel 5 of 5 panels from
Going Forth By Day, 2002 video/sound installation, 34:30 minutes

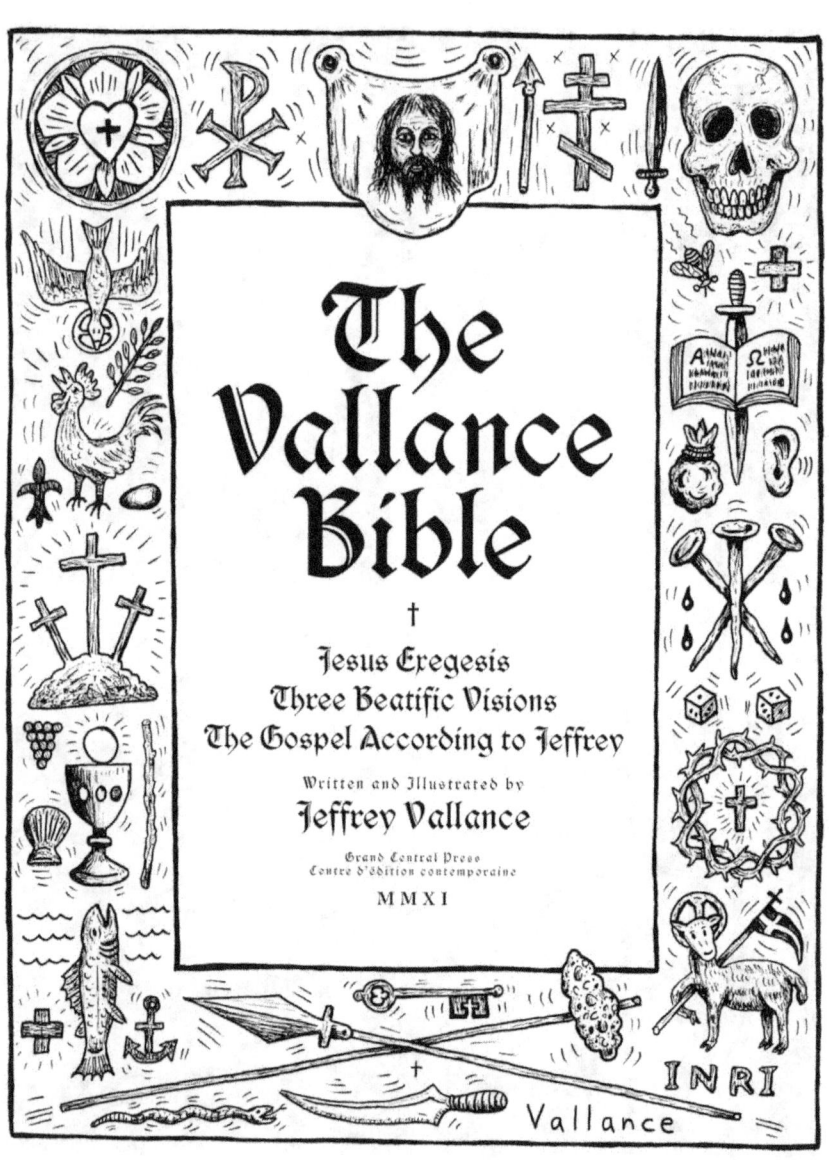

The Vallance Bible

†

Jesus Exegesis
Three Beatific Visions
The Gospel According to Jeffrey

Written and Illustrated by
Jeffrey Vallance

Grand Central Press
Centre d'édition contemporaine

MMXI

pl. 42 Jeffrey Vallance, title page to
The Vallance Bible, 2011

Endnotes

Foreword

1   John Gray, *Black Mass: Apocalyptic Religion and the Death of Utopia*, (NY: Farrar, Straus and Giroux, 2007).

Chapter 1

1   Norman Cohn, *The Pursuit of the Millennium: Revolutionary Millenarians and Mystical Anarchists of the Middle Ages*, (Oxford: Oxford University Press, 1970), p. 281.
2   Elaine Pagels, *Revelation: Visions, Prophecy, and Politics in the Book of Revelation*, (NY: Penguin, 2013).
3   Pagels, p. 47.
4   Pagels, p. 114.
5   Mary Boyce, *Zoroastrians: Their Religious Beliefs and Practices (The Library of Religious Beliefs and Practices*, (London: Routledge, 2001).
6   see *http://www.marginalia.co.uk/ journal/10apocalypse/2010_Apocalypse_ Duerer.pdf*
7   *http://www.flickr.com/photos/kintzerto- rium/2949976378/.*
8   *http://www.academia.edu/467863/Michel- angelos_Last_Judgment_The_Culmina- tion_of_Papal_Propaganda_in_the_Sis- tine_Chapel.*
9   R. H. Major, "Select Letters of Christopher Columbus with Other Original Documents Relating to His Four Voyages to the New World", Printed for the Hakluyt Society, 1870, reprinted (Charleston, SC: Nabu Press, 2012), p. 148.
10 David Bindman, "The English Apocalypse", in Frances Carey, ed., *The Apocalypse and the Shape of Things to Come*, (Toronto: University of Toronto Press, Scholarly Publishing Division, 1999), p. 212.
11 ibid., p. 211.
12 ibid., p. 228.
13 Robert C. Fuller, *Naming the Antichrist: The History of an American Obsession*, (Oxford: Oxford University Press, 1996), p. 91.
14 Walter Benjamin, *Ninth Thesis on the Philosophy of History*, reprinted in Hannah Arendt, ed., *Illuminations: Essays and Reflections*, (New York: Houghton Mifflin Harcourt, 1968).
15 Stephanie Barron, *German Expressionism, 1915-1925: The Second Generation*, (Los Angeles: Los Angeles County Museum of Art, 1988) pp. 10-37.
16 Quoted in Robert Hughes, *Rome: A Cultural, Visual, and Personal History*, (NY: Vintage, Reprint edition, 2012), p. 140.
17 George Steiner, *In Bluebeard's Castle: Some Notes Towards the Redefinition of Culture* (New Haven: Yale University Press, 1970), p. 43.
18 John Gray, "The Book that Changed My Life", *New Statesman*, Feb 5, 2009. *http:// www.newstatesman.com/books/2009/02/ norman-cohn-john-gray-world*
19 cited in Irving Sandler, *Abstract Expressionism and The American Experience: A Reevaluation*, (NY: Hardpress Editions, 2009), p. 7, and Katy Siegel, *Since '45: America and the Making of Contemporary Art*, (London: Reaktion Books, 2011).
20 ibid., p. 7.
21 Harold Rosenberg, "The American Action Painters", *Art News* 51/8, Dec. 1952, p. 22, reprinted in Harold Rosenberg, *The Tradition of the New*, (NY: DeCapo Press, 1994).
22 Quoted in Paul Schimmel, *Destroy the Picture Painting the Void 1949-1962*, (NY: Skira Rizzoli, 2012), p. 202.
23 Mark C. Taylor, *About Religion: Economies of Faith in Virtual Culture*, (Chicago: University of Chicago Press, 1999), p. 130.
24 Paul Boyer, *When Time Shall Be No More: Prophecy Belief in Modern American Culture*, (Cambridge, MA: Belknap Press, 1994), p. 175.
25 ibid.
26 *http://www.ag.org/pentecostal-evangel/ articles/conversations/4490_LaHaye.cfm*
27 Jurgen Habermas, "Notes on a post-secular society", *Sign and Sight.com*, June 18, 2008, *http://www.signandsight.com/fea- tures/1714.html*
28 Francis Fukuyama, "The End of History?" *National Interest* (Summer1989), reprinted *http://www.kropfpolisci.com/exceptional- ism.fukuyama.pdf.*
29 Mark C. Taylor, op cit. p. 132.

Chapter 2

1   Harold Bloom, *The American Religion: The Emergence of the Post Christian Nation*, (NY: Simon and Schuster, 1993), p. 37.
2   ibid.
3   ibid., p. 52.
4   ibid., p. 265.
5   ibid., p. 162.
6   ibid., p. 162.
7   "Jim Shaw in Conversation with Andy Holden", *Turps Banana*, issue 6, 2009, p. 43.
8   "Gods and Monsters", interview with Jim Shaw and Massimiliano Gioni in Natalie Bell and Dan Nadel, eds., *Jim Shaw: The End is Here*, (NY: Skira Rizzoli, 2015). p. 180.
9   Jim Shaw, "Spoiler Alert" in *Left Behind*, (Bordeaux: CAPC Musée d'Art Contemporain, 2012), p. 10.

10 ibid.

11 James Hofstadter, "The Paranoid Style in American Politics", *Harpers Magazine*, November 1964, p. 81.

12 "On the Beyond: A conversation with Mike Kelley, Jim Shaw and John C. Welchman", *Kunst und Architektur im Gespräch Art and Architecture in Discussion*, (Vienna: Springer Vienna Architecture, 2011), p. 60.

13 Carol Crown, *Sacred and Profane: Voice and Vision in Southern Self-Taught Art*, (Jackson, Miss: University Press of Mississippi, 2007).

14 Greg Bottoms, *The Colorful Apocalypse: Journeys in Outsider Art*, (Chicago: University of Chicago Press, 2007),

15 ibid.. p. 49.

16 *http://www.arthompson.com/revelation.html*

17 *http://www.lisastonearts.com/robert-roberg-street-preaching-artist.html*

18 Robert Farris Thompson, *Aesthetic of the Cool: Afro Atlantic Art & Music*, (London: Periscope, 2011).

19 Stephen Jay Gould, "James Hampton's Throne and the Dual Nature of Time", *American Art* 1:1., Spring 1987.

20 Jerry Bleem, "Devoted to Art and Truth", *Jesse Howard and Roger Brown: Now Read On*, (Kansas City: University of Missouri Kansas City Center for Creative Studies, 2005), pp. 20-27.

21 Natalie E. Phillips, "The Radiant (Christ) Child: Keith Haring and the Jesus Movement", *American Art*, Vol. 21, No.3., Fall 2007.

22 Ulrich Loock and Harald Falckenber, eds., *Raymond Pettibon: Homo Americanus*, (NY: David Zwirner Books, 2016).

23 Robert Storr, "The Language is on Fire. Spit it Out," in Ralph Rugoff, ed., *Raymond Pettibon*, (NY: Rizzoli, 2013), pp. 252-253.

24 "Doug Aitkin talks to Ed Ruscha," *Frieze*, June/July 2004, p. 102.

25 Charlene Spretnak, *The Spiritual dynamic in Modern Art: Art History Reconsidered, 1800 to the Present*, (London: Palgrave McMillan, 2014), p. 189.

Chapter 3

1 Frank Kermode, *The Sense of an Ending*, (Oxford: Oxford University Press, reissue, 2000), p. 112.

2 Andrew Delbanco, *The Death of Satan: How Americans Have Lost the Sense of Evil*, (NY: Noonday Press, 1996), p. 210.

3 Delbanco, op. cit. p. 224.

4 *http://beforeitsnews.com/prophecy/2016/03/the-book-of-revelation-and-prophecy-of-daniel-revealed-2478833.html*

5 Abby Kornfeld, "The Eternal Jerusalem", in Barbara Drake Boehm and Melanie Holcomb, eds., *Jerusalem 1000-1400: Every People Under Heaven*, (NY: Metropolitan Museum of Art, 2016), p. 271.

6 Hunt Janin. *Four Paths to Jerusalem: Jewish, Christian, Muslim, and Secular Pilgrimages, 1000 BCE to 2001 CE*. (Jefferson, North Carolina: McFarland, 2002), p. 41.

7 Eyal Danon, Benjamin Seroussi and Yael Bartana, *Yael Bartana: Inferno*, (NY: Petzel, 2015), p. 49.

8 Kermode, op. cit., p. 94.

9 Frances Fitzgerald *Way Out There in the Blue: Reagan, Star Wars and the End of the Cold War*, (NY: Simon and Schuster, 2001).

10 *http://www.thedailybeast.com/articles/2015/12/28/how-star-wars-shaped-the-u-s-military.html*

11 John Caputo, *On Religion (Thinking in Action)*, (London: Routledge, 2001), p. 78.

12 Roland Barthes, "Myth Today", *Mythologies*, Annette Lavers, trans., (NY: Hill and Wang, 1984).

13 George Baker, "An Interview with Paul Chan", *October*, No. 123. (Winter 2008) p. 214.

14 Diego Cagüeñas, "Reversed Rapture: On Salvation, Suicide, and the Spirit of Terrorism", *Public Culture* (2018) 30., p. 3.

15 *http://www.brooklynrail.org/2008/06/artseen/paul-chan*

16 Paul Chan, "The Spirit of Recession", *October*, No. 129 (Summer 2009), p. 3.

17 Nell McClister, "Paul Chan", *BOMB* 92/ Summer 2005.

18 "Interview with Saira Wasim", *Spincycle*, August 13, 2008, *http://gbytes.gsood.com/2008/08/13/interview-with-saira-wasim/*

Chapter 4

1 Quoted in Boyce, op. cit., p. 20.

2 John, Killinger, *God, The Devil, and Harry Potter: A Christian Minister's Defense of the Beloved Novels*, (NY: St. Martin's Press, 2002).

3 Kermode, op. cit., p. 39.

4 Brooke Davis Anderson, "An Artist's Studio at 851 Webster" in Klaus Biesenbach, ed., *Henry Darger*, (NY: Prestel, 2009), p. 88.

5 The word was coined for the exhibition *Dargerism: Contemporary Artists and Henry Darger*, curated by Brooke Davis Anderson at the American Folk Art Museum in New York, April 15–September 21, 2008.

6 Klaus Biesenbach, *Henry Darger*, (NY: Prestel, 2014), p. 11.

7   Michael Moon, *Darger's Resources*, (Durham, NC: Duke University Press, 2012).
8   John M. MacGregor, *Henry Darger: In the Realms of the Unreal*, (NY: Delano Greenidge Editions, 2002).
9   ibid., p. 22.
10 ibid., p. 23.
11 ibid., p. 434.
12 Quoted in Karrie Jacobs et al, *Gary Panter*, (New York: PictureBox, 2008) p. 316.
13 Gary Panter, interview with David Jacob Kramer, *The Believer*, June 2009 *http://www.believermag.com/issues/200906/?read=interview_panter*
14 ibid.
15 Matthias Wivel, "On the Mount: An Interview with Gary Panter," *The Metabunker*, Oct 23, 2012, *http://www.metabunker.dk/?p=5108*
16 ibid.
17 "Trenton Doyle Hancock & Fred Tomaselli with Dan Nadel", *The Brooklyn Rail*, May 2006, *http://www.brooklynrail.org/2006/05/art/in-conversation-trenton-doyle-hancock-fred-tomaselli-with-dan-nadel*
18 David Humphrey, "Trenton Doyle Hancock: Prayer Warrior", *Artpulse Magazine*, Vol. 5, no. 17, *http://artpulsemagazine.com/trenton-doyle-hancock-prayer-warrior*
19 *http://www.adaweb.com/influx/hardway*
20 ibid.
21 Wesley Miller, "Matthew Ritchie/ Apocalypse," *Art21* August 21 2008, *http://blog.art21.org/2008/08/21/matthew-ritchie-apocalypse/*
22 Martin Gaylord, "Playing Hide and Seek: interview with Douglas Gordon", *Modern Painters*, Winter 2002, p. 23.
23 Maureen M. Martin, *The Mighty Scot: Nation, Gender, and the Nineteenth-Century Mystique of Scottish Masculinity*, (NY: State University of New York Press, 2009), p. 84.
24 Katrina M. Brown, *Tate Modern Artists: Douglas Gordon*, (London: Tate Publishing, 2004), p. 108.
25 ibid., p. 108.
26 ibid., p. 109.
27 ibid. p. 114.
28 James Hall, "Jake and Dinos Chapman: "Collaborating with Catastrophe", Norman Rosenthal, ed., *Apocalypse: Beauty and Horror in Contemporary Art*, (London: Royal Academy of Arts, 2000), p. 218.
29 Daniel Schreiber, "Welcome to the Human Zoo: Jake and Dinos Chapman at the Kestnergesellschaft", *Deutsche Bank Artmag*, 52, http://db-artmag.com/en/52/feature/the-human-zoo-jake-dinos-chapman/
30 "Interview with Robert Rosenblum", Jake and Dinos Chapman, *Unholy Libel: Six Feet Under*, (New York: Gagosian Gallery, 1997), p. 150.
31 Terry Eagleton, *On Evil*, (New Haven: Yale University Press, 2001), p. 82.

Chapter 5

1   Kristofer Widholm, "Antichrist: An Interview with Bernard McGinn," *Cabinet*, Issue 5 *Evil*, Winter 2001/02, *http://www.cabinetmagazine.org/issues/5/widholm.php*
2   Graeme Wood, "What Isis Really Wants", *The Atlantic*, March 2015.
3   William James, *The Varieties of Religious Experience: A Study in Human Nature*, originally published (New York, London, Bombay, Calcutta and Madras: Longmans, Green and Co, 1917), facsimile republished as Ebook by Project Gutenberg, 2014, p. 337.
4   Correspondence with the author, January 26, 2014.
5   *http://federicosolmi.com/*
6   "Interview with Renato Miracco", *Federico Solmi*, (Milano, Edizione Charta, 2010), p. 60.
7   Chris Hedges, *War is a Force that Gives us Meaning*, (New York: Anchor Books, 2003), p. 158.
8   Carolyn Walker Bynum, "Material Continuity, Personal Survival and the Resurrection of the Body: A Scholastic discussion in Its Medieval and Modern Contexts", in *Fragmentation and Redemption*, (New York: Zone Books, 1992).
9   Excerpted from Walter Benjamin, *Selected Writings Vol.1*, Rodney Livingstone, trans., (Cambridge, MA: Belknap Harvard Press, 1921, 1996), pp. 288-291. Reprinted in http://brotherwisedispatch.blogspot.com/2014/03/capitalism-as-religion-by-walter.html
10 Max Weber, *The Protestant Ethic and the Spirit of Capitalism*, originally published 1905, Talcott Parsons, trans., 1930 reprinted by (London: Routledge Classics, 2001), p. 123.
11 "Bob Trotman in Conversation with Crista Cammaroto", in Mark Sloan, ed., *Business as Usual: Bob Trotman*, (Charleston, SC: Halsey Institute of Contemporary Art, 2018), p. 129.
12 Quoted in Robert Manley, "Minding Business" in Sloan, *Business as Usual*, p. 30.
13 David M. Bethea, *The Shape of Apocalypse in Modern Russian Fiction*, (Princeton: Princeton University Press, 1989), p. 154.
14 Lucy Lippard. "Out of the Safety Zone", *Art in America*, December 1990, p. 136.
15 *reprinted in http://www.historyisaweapon.com/defcon1/closetothekniveswojnarowicz.html*

16 Lippard, op.cit., p. 182.
17 Simon Penny, "The Intelligent Machine as Antichrist: A Brief History of Antropomorphism in Art & Science", *ISEA Symposium Archives*, 1990, *http://isea-archives.org/*
18 Robert Geraci, *Apocalyptic AI: Visions of Heaven in Robotics, Artificial Intelligence, and Virtual Reality*, (Oxford: Oxford University Press; 2012).
19 ibid.
20 Hito Steyerl, "In Free Fall: A Thought Experiment on Vertical Perspective", *e-flux*, Journal #24 - April 2011, *http://www.e-flux.com/journal/24/67860/in-free-fall-a-thought-experiment-on-vertical-perspective/*
21 Carl Jung, "The Tibetan Book of the Great Liberation", 1954, reprinted in *Psychology and Religion: East and West (The Collected Works of C. G. Jung, Volume 11)* 2nd ed. (Princeton: Princeton University Press, 1975), p. 488.
22 Thessalonians 2:9 and 2:10
23 Fyodor Dostoevsky, *The Diary of a Writer*, quoted in Bethea, p. 69.
24 "Katarzyna Kozyra in conversation with Joanna Ruszczyk" in *Looking for Jesus* (Lublin: Galeria Labirynt, 2014) p. 65.
25 ibid., p. 66.

Chapter 6

1 *http://www.atomicarchive.com/Movies/Movie8.shtml*
2 Bernard McGinn, *Antichrist: Two Thousand years of the Human Fascination with Evil*, (New York: Columbia University Press, 2000), p. 276.
3 Slavoj Zizek, *Living in the End Times*, (London: Verso, 2010), p. x.
4 Kenan Malik, "The God Wars in Perspective" in Maria, Hlavajova, Sven Lutticken and Jill Winder, eds., *The Return of Religion and Other Myths: A Critical Reader in Contemporary Art*, (Utrecht: Post Editions / Basis voor actuele Kunst, 2010), p. 124.
5 Susan Sontag, "The Imagination of Disaster", 1965, reprinted in Susan Sontag, *Against Interpretation, and Other Essays*, (New York: Penguin Modern Classics, 2009), p. 224.
6 Iri Maruki, *The Hiroshima Panels*, (Hiroshima: Maruki Gallery for the Hiroshima Panels Foundation, Revised edition, 1988), p. 2.
7 ibid.
8 quoted in *http://www.tate.org.uk/whats-on/tate-britain/exhibition/art-60s-was-tomorrow/art-sixties-exhibition-themes/art-sixties-7*

9 "Interview with Peter Boswell" in Joan Rothfuss, ed., *2000 BC: The Bruce Conner Story, Part 2*, (Minneapolis: Walker Art Center, 1999), p. 30.
10 ibid.
11 "American Quartet", originally published in *Art in America*, December 1981, reprinted in Robert Morris, *Continuous Project Altered Daily: the writings of Robert Morris*, (Cambridge, MA: The MIT Press, 1994), p. 245.
12 Nena Tsouti-Schillinger, *Robert Morris and Angst*, (New York: George Braziller, 2001), p. 117.
13 Edward F. Fry and Donald Burton Kuspit, *Robert Morris: Works of the Eighties*, (Los Angeles: Newport Harbor Art Museum, 1986), p. 17.
14 ibid.
15 *https://thebulletin.org/sites/default/files/Final%202017%20Clock%20Statement.pdf*
16 "Entropy Made Visible," interview with Allison Sky, *On Site #4*, 1973, reprinted in Nancy Holt, ed., *The Writings of Robert Smithson*, (New York: New York University Press, 1979), p. 190.
17 Robert Smithson, "A Tour of the Monuments of Passaic, New Jersey", *Artforum*, December 1967, reprinted in Holt, op. cit., p. 54.
18 Robert Smithson, "The Iconography of Desolation", in Eugenie Tsai, *Robert Smithson Unearthed*, (New York: Columbia University Press, 1991), p. 64.
19 See Eugenie Tsai, ed., *Robert Smithson*, (Berkeley: The Museum of Contemporary Art, Los Angeles and University of California Press, 2004), and Jennifer L. Roberts, *Mirror Travels: Robert Smithson and History*, (New Haven: Yale University Press, 2004).
20 Roberts, op. cit., p. 14.
21 Kermode, op.cit., p. 88.
22 ibid.
23 Tsai, op. cit. p. 38.
24 Robert Smithson, "The Spiral Jetty", in Gyorgy Kepes, ed., *Arts of the Environment*, 1972, reprinted in Holt, op. cit., p. 111.
25 "Art and the Political Whirlpool or the Politics of Disgust", *Artforum*, September 1970, reprinted in *Robert Smithson, the Collected Writings*, Jack Flam, ed., (Oakland: University of California Press, 1996), p. 143.
26 Interview with Melissa Harris, originally published in Issue 14 of *Aperture Photography App*. March 1992, reprinted in *Aperture Archive*, *https://aperture.org/blog/archival-interview-richard-misrach/*

27 Rebecca Solnit, "Scapeland" in Anne Wilkes Tucker, Richard Misrach and Rebecca Solnit, *Crimes and Splendors: The Desert Cantos of Richard Misrach*, (Houston: Museum of Fine Arts, Houston, 1996), p. 57.

28 see also *http://spot.hcponline.org/pages/richard_misrach_with_peter_brown_488.asp*

29 Susan Sontag and Richard Misrach, *Violent Legacies: Three Cantos*, (Reading, PA: *Aperture*, 1994), p. 88.

30 Paul Cronin and Werner Herzog, *Herzog on Herzog, Conversations with Paul Cronin*, (New York: Farrar, Straus and Giroux, 2003), p. 246.

31 Smithson, *"A Tour of the Monuments of Passaic, New Jersey"*. reprinted in Holt, op. cit.

32 Brian Dillon, "Fragments from a History of Ruin", *Cabinet*, Issue 20 Ruins Winter 2005/06, *http://www.cabinetmagazine.org/issues/20/dillon.php*

33 Frank Kermode, op.cit. p. 95.

Chapter 7

1 "The Panacea Museum", *Atlas Obscura*, *https://www.atlasobscura.com/places/the-panacea-museum-bedford-england*

2 Boyer, op.cit..

3 Matthew Avery Sutton, *American Apocalypse*, (Cambridge, MA: Harvard University Press, 2014).

4 quoted in Michelle Wallace, "Tim Rollins + KOS: The 'Amerika' Series", in Gary Garrels, ed., *Amerika: Tim Rollins + K.O.S.*, (New York: Dia Art Foundation, 1989), p. 47.

5 Patti Smith, *Woolgathering*, (New York: New Directions, 2011)

6 Ray Padgett, "The Story Behind Patti Smith's Gloria", *Cover Me Songs*, August 4, 2014 *http://www.covermesongs.com/2014/08/the-story-behind-patti-smiths-gloria.html*

7 Patti Smith, *The New Jerusalem*, (NY: Nexus Institute, 2018), p. 25.

8 ibid., p. 35.

9 ibid., p. 39.

10 Martin Herbert, *Mark Wallinger*, (London: Thames and Hudson, 2011), p.100.

11 ibid., p.116.

12 Yve-Alain Bois, Guy Brett, Margaret Iversen and Julian Stallabrass, "An Interview with Mark Wallinger", *October Magazine*, February 2008, p. 196.

13 Ethan Acres, *The Sermons of Reverend Ethan Acres*, (Los Angeles: Art Issues Press, 2001), p. 59.

14 Doug Harvey, "Rev. Ethan Acres at Patricia Faure", *Art issues*, 1997, reprinted in *http://www.dougharvey.la/doug_harvey.php?ID=279*

15 Acres, op. cit., p. 99.

16 Christian Jankowski, "The Holy Artwork Script" in Bill Arning, ed., *Christian Jankowski: Everything Fell Together*, (Des Moines: Des Moines Art Center, 2006).

17 Krishna Kumar, "Apocalypse, Millennium and Utopia Today" in Malcolm Bull, *Apocalypse Theory and the Ends of the World*, (Cambridge, MA.: Blackwell, 1995), p. 210.

Coda

1 Bill Viola and John Hanhardt, *Going Forth by Day*, (New York: Guggenheim Museum, 2003), p. 101.

2 David Ross, ed,, *Bill Viola*, (New York and Paris: Whitney Museum of American Art with Flammarion, 1997), p. 143.

3 Viola, op. cit., p. 68.

4 The John Tusa Interviews: *Bill Viola*, BBC Radio, March 13, 2002 *https://www.bbc.co.uk/programmes/p00njlsw*

5 Jeffrey Vallance, *The Vallance Bible*, (Santa Ana: Grand Central Press and Centre d'edition contemporaine, 2011).

6 ibid., p. 3.

7 ibid., p. 25.

Selected Bibliography

Acres, Ethan. *The Sermons of Reverend Ethan Acres*. Los Angeles: Art Issues Press, 2001.

Arning, Bill, ed. *Christian Jankowski: Everything Fell Together*. Des Moines: Des Moines Art Center, 2006.

Barkun, Michael. *A Culture of Conspiracy: Apocalyptic Visions in Contemporary America*. Berkeley: University of California Press, 2013.

Bell, Natalie and Nadel, Dan, eds. *Jim Shaw: The End is Here*. New York: Skira Rizzoli, 2015.

Bethea, David M. *The Shape of Apocalypse in Modern Russian Fiction*. Princeton: Princeton University Press, 1989.

Biesenbach, Klaus. *Henry Darger*. New York: Prestel, 2014.

Blair, Sheila S. and Bloom, Jonathan M. *Images of Paradise in Islamic Art*. Austin: University of Texas Press, 1991.

Bloom, Harold. *The American Religion: The Emergence of the Post Christian Nation*. New York: Simon and Schuster, 1993.

Boehm, Barbara Drake and Holcomb, Melanie, eds. *Jerusalem 1000-1400: Every People Under Heaven*. New York: Metropolitan Museum of Art, 2016.

Bottoms, Greg. *The Colorful Apocalypse: Journeys in Outsider Art*. Chicago: University of Chicago Press, 2007.

Boyce, Mary. *Zoroastrians: Their Religious Beliefs and Practices (The Library of Religious Beliefs and Practices*. London: Routledge, 2001.

Boyer, Paul. *When Time Shall Be No More: Prophecy Belief in Modern American Culture*. Cambridge, MA: Belknap Press, 1994.

Brown Katrina M. *Tate Modern Artists: Douglas Gordon*. London: Tate Publishing, 2004.

Bull, Malcolm. *Apocalypse Theory and the Ends of the World*. Cambridge, Mass.: Blackwell, 1995.

Caputo, John. *On Religion*. London: Routledge, 2001.

Carey, Frances, ed. *The Apocalypse and the Shape of Things to Come*. Toronto: University of Toronto Press, Scholarly Publishing Division, 1999.

Christianson, Eric S. and Partridge, Christopher. *Holy Terror: Understanding Religion and Violence in Popular Culture*. London: Routledge, 2014.

Cohn, Norman. *Comos Chaos, and the World to Come*. New Haven: Yale University Press, 2001.

Cohn, Norman. *The Pursuit of the Millennium: Revolutionary Millenarians and Mystical Anarchists of the Middle Ages*, Oxford: Oxford University Press; 1970.

Crown, Carol. *Sacred and Profane: Voice and Vision in Southern Self-Taught Art*. Jackson: University Press of Mississippi, 2007.

Danon, Eyal, Seroussi, Benjamin and Bartana, Yael. *Yael Bartana: Inferno*. New York: Petzel, 2015.

Delbanco, Andrew. *The Death of Satan: How Americans Have Lost the Sense of Evil*. New York: Noonday Press, 1996.

Eagleton, Terry. *On Evil*. New Haven: Yale University Press, 2001.

Fuller, Robert C. *Naming the Antichrist: The History of an American Obsession*. Oxford: Oxford University Press, 1996.

Geraci, *Robert. Apocalyptic AI: Visions of Heaven in Robotics, Artificial Intelligence, and Virtual Reality*. Oxford: Oxford University Press, 2012.

Gray, John. *Black Mass: Apocalyptic Religion and the Death of Utopia*. New York: Farrar, Straus and Giroux, 2007.

Hlavajova, Maria, Lutticken, Sven and Winder, Jill, eds. *The Return of Religion and Other Myths: A Critical Reader in Contemporary Art*. Utrecht: Post Editions / Basis voor actuele Kunst, 2010.

Holt, Nancy, ed. *The Writings of Robert Smithson*. New York: New York University Press, 1979.

Kermode, Frank. *The Sense of an Ending.* Oxford: Oxford University Press, reissue, 2000.

Loock. Ulrich and Falckenber, Harald, eds. *Raymond Pettibon: Homo Americanus.* New York: David Zwirner Books, 2016.

MacGregor, John M. *Henry Darger: In the Realms of the Unreal.* New York: Delano Greenidge Editions, 2002.

Manley, Roger. *The End is Near: Visions of Apocalypse, Millennium and Utopia.* Los Angeles: Dilettante Press, 1998.

McGinn, Bernard. *Antichrist: Two Thousand years of the Human Fascination with Evil.* New York: Columbia University Press, 2000.

O'Hear, Natasha and O'Hear, Anthony. *Picturing the Apocalypse: The Book of Revelation in the Arts over Two Millennia.* Oxford: Oxford University Press, 2017.

Pagels, Elaine. *Revelation: Visions, Prophecy, and Politics in the Book of Revelation.* New York: Penguin, 2013.

Roberts, Jennifer L. *Mirror Travels: Robert Smithson and History.* New Haven: Yale University Press, 2004.

Rosenthal, Norman. ed. *Apocalypse: Beauty and Horror in Contemporary Art.* London, Royal Academy of Arts, 2000.

Ross, David ed. *Bill Viola.* New York and Paris: Whitney Museum of American Art with Flammarion, 1997.

Rugoff, Ralph, ed. *Raymond Pettibon.* New York: Rizzoli, 2013.

Shaw, Jim. *Left Behind.* Bordeaux: CAPC Musée d'Art Contemporain, 2012.

Sloan, Mark, ed, *Business as Usual: Bob Trotman.* Charleston: Halsey Institute of Contemporary Art, 2018.

Smith, Patti. *The New Jerusalem.* New York: Nexus Institute, 2018.

Spretnak, Charlene. *The Spiritual dynamic in Modern Art: Art History Reconsidered, 1800 to the Present.* London: Palgrave McMillan, 2014.

Sutton, Matthew Avery. *American Apocalypse.* Cambridge, MA: Harvard University Press, 2014.

Taylor, Mark C. *After God: Religion and Postmodernism.* Chicago: University of Chicago Press, 2009.

Tsai, Eugenie, ed. *Robert Smithson.* Berkeley: The Museum of Contemporary Art, Los Angeles and University of California Press, 2004.

Viola, Bill and Hanhardt, John. *Going Forth by Day.* New York: Guggenheim Museum, 2003.

Wójcik, Daniel. *The End of the World as We Know It: Faith, Fatalism, and Apocalypse in America.* New York: New York University Press, 1999.

Image Credits

Cover:
frontispiece courtesy Bob Trotman and North Carolina Museum of Art

Figures:
figs. 1-6 courtesy Wikimedia Commons; fig. 7 photo credit: Gabriele Burchielli; fig. 8 courtesy Creative Commons; fig 9 © Robert Roberg; fig 10 © Raymond Pettibon, Published by Brooke Alexander Editions, New York and David Zwirner; fig. 11 © Ed Ruscha, courtesy Gagosian Gallery; fig. 12 courtesy of the artist and Jane Lombard Gallery; fig. 13 Courtesy the artist and Greene Naftali, New York; fig. 14 courtesy of the artist and Fredericks & Freiser, NY; fig 15 © Trenton Doyle Hancock, courtesy of James Cohan, NY; fig 16 courtesy Creative Commons; fig. 17 courtesy of the artist; fig 18, 19 courtesy Creative Comons; fig. 20 courtesy National Archives and Records Administration; fig. 21 courtesy Creative Commons; fig. 22 courtesy of Panacea Charitable Trust; fig. 23 photo credit: The William Blake Archive; fig 24 courtesy the artist and Lehmann Maupin, New York, Hong Kong, and Seoul; fig 25 © Reverend Ethan Acres; fig. 26 courtesy of the artist and Petzel, NY; fig. 27 courtesy of the artist.

Plates:
pls. 1-4 courtesy Wikimedia Commons; pl. 5 courtesy of Los Angeles County Museum of Art; pl. 6 photo credit Quentin Verwaerde; pl. 7 © LeeAnn Nickel, courtesy of the artist; pl. 8 courtesy of the artist; pl. 9 courtesy Wikimedia Commons; pl. 10 © The School of the Art Institute of Chicago and the Brown family; pl. 11 Keith Haring artwork © Keith Haring Foundation; pl. 12 © Paul Pfeiffer. Courtesy Paula Cooper Gallery, NY; pl. 13 courtesy of the artist and Petzel, NY; pl. 14 © Courtesy of Wael Shawky and Lisson Gallery; ARoS Aarhus Art Museum Photography: Anders Sune Berg; pl. 15 courtesy of the artist and Jane Lombard Gallery; pl. 16 courtesy the artist and Greene Naftali, NY; pl. 17 courtesy of the artist; pl. 18 Photo courtesy of the Estate of Henry Darger/Art Resource, NY, © ARS, NY, © 2019 Kiyoko Lerner/Artists Rights Society (ARS), NY; pl. 19 © Matthew Ritchie, courtesy of James Cohan, NY; pl. 20 Installation view as part of *De/coding the Apocalypse*, presented by the Cultural Institute at King's College London, Somerset House, London, UK, 2014, photo credit: Jana Chiellino, courtesy of the artist; pl. 21 Photo credit: Jonathan Muzikar, digital Image © The Museum of Modern Art/Licensed by SCALA/Art Resource, NY/Artists Rights Society (ARS), NY 2019; pl. 22 courtesy of the artist and Catharine Clark Gallery, San Francisco, CA; pl. 23 courtesy Anita Beckers Gallery, Frankfurt, Adn Gallery, Barcelona, Luis De Jesus Los Angeles, Ronald Feldman Gallery, NY; pl. 24 courtesy of the artist and Catharine Clark Gallery, San Francisco, CA; pl. 25 photo credit: Kevin Remington, courtesy of the artist; pl. 26 courtesy of the artist; pl. 27 courtesy of the Estate of David Wojnarowicz and P.P.O.W, NY; pl. 28 © 2019 Artists Rights Society (ARS), New York/SABAM, Brussels, courtesy of the artist and Andrew Kreps Gallery, NY; pl. 29 courtesy of the Katarzyna Kozyra Foundation, CCA Warsaw; pl. 30 courtesy of Maruki Museum; pl. 31 courtesy Castelli Gallery; pl. 32 © 2019 Holt/Smithson Foundation/ Licensed by VAGA at Artists Rights Society (ARS), NY courtesy James Cohan, NY; pl. 33 © Richard Misrach, courtesy Fraenkel Gallery, San Francisco, CA; pl. 34 courtesy Deutsche Kinemathek; pl. 35 photo credit: Matthew Herrmann, courtesy Studio K.O.S., Lehmann Maupin, New York, Hong Kong, and Seoul; pl. 36 ©Shoja Azari, courtesy of the artist and Leila Heller Gallery, NY; pl. 37 ©Shirin Neshat, courtesy of the artist and Gladstone Gallery, New York and Brussels; pl. 38 ©Mark Wallinger, courtesy the artist and Hauser & Wirth; pl. 39 photo credit: Mick Haggerty, courtesy the artist and Lehmann Maupin, New York, Hong Kong, and Seoul; pl. 40 courtesy of the artist and Petzel, NY; pl. 41 photo credit: Kira Perov, courtesy of the artist and James Cohen Gallery; pl. , courtesy of the artist.

Index

Acknowledgements

Doomsday Dreams has been long in the making. Many of the artists here are people I have known and whose work I have written about over many years. I want to thank them all and am most grateful to them for their brilliant work and for the assistance so many of them provided in preparing the text and images for this book. I also want to thank those whose ideas have helped me formulate the concepts presented here. In particular, I am in debt to Elaine Pagels whose *Revelations*: *Visions, Prophecy, and Politics in the Book of Revelation* made me aware of the richness and ongoing importance of apocalyptic literature. I returned again and again to Frank Kermode's *The Sense of an Ending*, always finding new insights into the pervasive influence of apocalyptic thinking on modern culture. I would also like to thank Charlene Spretnak whose *The Spiritual Dynamic in Modern Art* so cogently makes the case for the crucial influence of spirituality and religion on modern and contemporary art. And then there are the many friends and colleagues with whom I have discussed the apocalyptic imagination in art – sometimes I fear to the point of obsession. Their insights and reactions have been invaluable. They include Helaine Posner, Nancy Princenthal, Sue Scott, Lanny deVuono, Sara Lynn Henry, Debra Balken, Pam Joseph, Rob Brinker, Natasha O'Hear, Betsy Baker, Barbara Rose, Aaron Rosen, Dan Seidell and Irving and Lucy Sandler. Many thanks to Silver Hollow Press for taking on this rather eccentric project and to its incomparable book designer Aldo Sampieri. And finally of course, my deepest gratitude goes to my partner and most important supporter. Larry Litt has been with me through all my books and has once again provided an invaluable sounding board as I regaled him with tales of The End.

Biography

Eleanor Heartney has been writing about contemporary art for over thirty-five years. While broadly covering the changing art scene, she has given particular attention to the relationships between art and politics and between art and religion. Her *Postmodern Heretics: The Catholic Imagination in Contemporary Art* was the first book to explore this subject in depth and became the springboard for the current study. Her other books include *Critical Condition: American Culture at the Crossroads, Postmodernism, Defending Complexity: Art Politics and the New World Order* and *Art and Today*. Heartney is co-author of *After the Revolution: Women who Transformed Contemporary Art* and *The Reckoning: Women Artists of the New Millennium.* She is a Contributing Editor to *Art in America* and *Artpress* and a past President of AICA-USA, the American section of the International Art Critics Association. Heartney was awarded the College Art Association's Frank Jewett Mather Award for Distinction in Art Criticism in 1992 and was honored by the French government as a Chevalier dans l'Ordre des Arts et des Lettres in 2008.

www.ingramcontent.com/pod-product-compliance
Lightning Source LLC
Chambersburg PA
CBHW072132170526
45158CB00004BA/1336

* 9 7 8 0 9 9 8 9 5 6 8 0 0 *